Media Access

Books by Andrew O. Shapiro
(Written with John M. Striker)

Mastering the Draft:
A Comprehensive Guide for Solving Draft Problems

Super Tenant:
New York City Tenant Handbook — Your Legal
Rights and How to Use Them

Media Access

Your Rights to Express Your Views on Radio and Television

Andrew O. Shapiro

Little, Brown and Company

Boston   Toronto

FIRST EDITION

T 03/76

Library of Congress Cataloging in Publication Data

Shapiro, Andrew O
  Media access.

  Includes bibliographical references and index.
    1. Broadcasting — law and legislation — United States. 2. Public interest. 3. Freedom
of information — United States. 4. Right of reply — United States.
I.   Title.
KF2805.S45   343'.73'0998   75-40109
ISBN 0-316-78287-4

Design by D. Christine Benders

*Published simultaneously in Canada
by Little, Brown & Company (Canada) Limited*

PRINTED IN THE UNITED STATES OF AMERICA

For Sue and Buzz and Randy

Preface

'

This book focuses upon one key aspect of broadcasting law: namely, those rules which require a broadcaster to provide air time to concerned citizens for self-expression.

Many listeners and viewers are unaware of their rights when it comes to the possibility of appearing on radio or television. A common misconception posits absolute authority on the part of broadcasters to decide whether anyone, outside of regular announcers and performers, will ever be given the opportunity to air his views. According to this misconception, the broadcaster has a proprietary interest in the airwaves he utilizes, rather than a mere license to use them temporarily and in the public interest.

An important goal of this book is to disabuse citizens of the notion that broadcasters enjoy complete autonomy in the selection of viewpoints to be expressed over the air.

The issue of broadcaster control raises difficult legal questions. Many broadcasters, as well as some legislators and jurists, believe that the Constitution guarantees complete freedom of expression to broadcasters. That position, however, has never been part of the regulatory scheme which Congress established for broadcasting; nor has it been adopted by the United States Supreme Court.

Since this book is primarily a how-to guide, it accepts, rather than attacks or questions, the current state of the law and concentrates on explaining the meaning and mechanics of that law.

Out of the entire gamut of broadcast regulation, I have focused on those principles and procedures governing public participation in the broadcast discussion of important ideas and issues. Throughout, I have tried to answer three recurrent questions: What kinds of programming give rise to an obligation on the part of a broadcaster to share his facilities with citizens whose views may differ from his own? What manner of opportunity is a citizen entitled to when he wishes to air his views? How can he avail himself of that opportunity?

I have endeavored to translate often technical legal rules into terms which laymen can readily grasp and put to work. Whenever possible, I have illustrated important principles by relating pertinent cases decided by the Federal Communications Commission. Sometimes I have created hypothetical examples, usually involving a citizen's interaction with imaginary broadcast stations — WWW Radio or WWW-TV.

Although the book translates law for laymen, I have included a system of legal annotations, sufficient to alert attorneys to the authorities that I have relied upon.

I hope this book proves useful to four distinct audiences. First, citizens intent upon communicating their views and positions to large numbers of listeners and viewers. These concerned citizens may be acting as individuals. Or they may be acting in concert with fellow members of a civic, cultural, or social group, or other public interest organization.

Second, candidates for public office, their supporters, and advisors. Today, broadcasting is the most powerful means for informing the electorate. If the medium is to fulfill its promise, people who seek public office must understand their opportunities for air time and how to take advantage of them.

Third, students of broadcasting. In colleges and journalism schools nationwide, more and more students are preparing to embark upon careers in broadcasting or some closely related field. This book will acquaint them with an important area of the broadcaster's responsibility to the citizens he serves.

Fourth, broadcasters. This book is not intended as a guerrilla text solely for listeners and viewers. Most broadcasters recognize their responsibility to air public debate on important issues. This responsibility might be dispatched with greater care and effectiveness in many cases if broadcasters understood more clearly exactly what was expected of them by the Federal Communications Commission. To the degree this book increases that understanding, it will have made a worthwhile contribution.

Acknowledgments

I wish to express deep thanks to Bill Phillips, my editor. Several years ago he patiently and meticulously guided my first book into print. Since then he has urged me to make time in my career for continued writing. Without his encouragement, the present work might never have been undertaken.

I am indebted to Milton Gross of the Federal Communications Commission for his clear and complete answers to the many questions I asked about the agency's Fairness/Political Broadcasting Branch, over which he serves as chief administrator.

Chuck Shepherd of the National Citizens Committee for Broadcasting helped to direct my research and provided a wealth of information on citizen groups dedicated to improving the current state of broadcasting.

Frank Lloyd from the Citizens Communications Center generously took time from his demanding legal practice to give me his perspective on many key issues in communications law.

Phil Jacklin of the Committee for Open Media shared with me many of his innovative ideas, as well as his hopes, for expanding citizen participation in broadcast communications.

My research was greatly facilitated by the contribution of many other people with whom I spoke and corresponded. For the information, advice, and documentation they provided, I want to thank Ellen Agress, attorney, Citizens Communications Center; Kathy Bonk, attorney, Media Task Force, National Organization for Women; Peggy Charren, President, Action for Children's Television; Gwen Evans, Director, Public Media Center, Inc.; Josh Kane, Director, Public Information, National Broadcasting Company; Thaddeus Kowalski, attorney; James McCuller, Chairman, and Pluria Marshall, Treasurer, National Black Media Coalition; Frank Orme, Executive Vice President, National Association for Better Broadcasting; the Reverend W. James Richards, Deputy Director, Office of Communication, United Church of Christ; Marvin Segelman, Director, Public Advertising Council; Harvey Shulman, attorney, Media Access Project; Leslie Slocum, librarian, Television Information Office, National Association of Broadcasters; Dr. Leslie Spence, American Council for Better Broadcasts; R. Peter Straus, President, Straus Communications, Inc.; Tracy Westen, attorney, Director, Public Communication, Inc.; Ridley Whitaker, Executive Director, New Jersey Coalition for Fair Broadcasting.

I gained helpful background information from Ken Alvord of WNBC-TV News and Dan Grabel of NBC's News Program Service, under whom I studied at the New School for Social Research.

I owe special thanks to Margaret White from the Public Information Office of the Federal Communications Commission. She located many documents I needed and supplied them promptly and cheerfully.

As was the case with my prior books, I must once again thank Professor Julius Marke and the staff of the law library at New York University School of Law for fulfilling a wide array of research needs quickly and efficiently.

Contents

Media Access

1
Broadcasting in the Public Interest

We Interrupt This Broadcast

We frequently read newspaper articles with which we disagree. It seems to us only one side of the story is being told or, perhaps, the editorial position taken by the paper is a misguided one. If the newspaper's coverage is egregiously one-sided, we may be moved to write a letter to the editor. However, the newspaper is under no legal obligation to print the views of its readers. Under the constitutional guarantee of freedom of the press, the newspaper cannot be compelled to accommodate differing opinions in its columns.[1] Thus, if a paper is unresponsive to our suggestions and incompatible with our point of view, we may simply stop buying it. Short of the economic impact we have as subscribers, there is little way for us, so to speak, to stop the presses.

We can, however, interrupt the broadcast that pours daily from our radio and television sets. A broadcaster, unlike a newspaper publisher, is not free to present only those views that suit his personal convictions. Instead, he has a legal obligation to facilitate the expression of contrasting views held by listeners and viewers — namely, us.

We are going to explore the basic legal rules a broadcaster must follow when carrying out his obligation to the public. These rules are aimed at enlarging and diversifying debate on important issues, events, and people. For example, we will discover that

(1) the *fairness doctrine* requires a broadcaster to afford air time to opposing spokesmen, who may present their views on controversial issues;

(2) the *personal-attack rule* gives a right of reply to individuals or groups who are maligned on the air;

(3) the *political-editorial rule* gives a right of reply to candidates whose election is opposed in a station editorial; and

(4) the *equal-time rule* entitles a candidate to the same opportunities for air time enjoyed by his opponent. Our goal will be to learn how these rules operate and when we can invoke them in order to secure a broadcast outlet for our views or those of organizations we belong to. Many actual case histories will be examined in depth. Occasionally, we will consider hypothetical examples involving an imaginary station we shall call WWW.

Before proceeding to the details of a broadcaster's duty to the public, we should ask why it exists in the first place. Why does a broadcaster owe any duty at all to listeners and viewers? To answer this question we must consider the unique nature of the broadcast medium and the system of federal regulation imposed upon it.

The Need for Broadcast Regulation

Broadcasting is made possible by the transmission of signals via electromagnetic waves, known as *radio waves*. These waves radiate outward from a transmitting antenna at the speed of light. Their behavior has been compared to that of waves created when a pebble is dropped into a still pool of water. The waves travel outward in a series of alternating peaks and troughs. In broadcast terminology, a complete waveform — from the peak of one wave to the peak of the next wave — is known as a cycle; and the number of cycles generated per second is called the *frequency* of the radio wave. The full range of radio waves of all different frequencies comprises the so-called *radio spectrum*.[2]

If two stations in close enough proximity transmit on identical frequencies, the result will be *interference,* an electrical phenomenon which hinders, if not prevents, reception of broadcast signals. The problem of interference is not confined to multiple transmissions on the same frequency. Transmissions on one frequency can exert adverse electrical effects upon adjacent frequencies. Therefore, a channel of multiple frequencies is generally necessary for an individual station, even though only one frequency within the channel is actually used for transmission purposes.[3]

Largely because of the phenomenon of interference, the frequencies comprising the radio spectrum have come to be regarded as a scarce natural resource, utilization of which must be adequately controlled. Prior to 1927, when Congress enacted comprehensive broadcast regulation, there were no effective controls. Several hundred pioneer broadcasters launched radio stations in the early 1920s. In the eight-month period from July, 1926, to February 23, 1927 (when Congress finally acted), almost two hundred new stations went on the air.

"These new stations used any frequencies they desired, regardless of the interference caused to others. Existing stations changed to other frequencies and increased their power and hours of operation at will. The result was confusion and chaos. With everybody on the air, nobody could be heard."[4] Responding to the crisis, Congress passed the Radio Act of 1927, which created the Federal Radio Commission — precursor of today's Federal Communications Commission.

"The plight into which radio fell prior to 1927," explained Supreme Court Justice Felix Frankfurter in 1943,

> was attributable to certain basic facts about radio as a means of communication — its facilities are limited; they are not available to all who may wish to use them; the radio spectrum simply is not large enough to accommodate everybody. There is a fixed natural limitation upon the number

of stations that can operate without interfering with one another. Regulation of radio was therefore as vital to its development as traffic control was to the development of the automobile. In enacting the Radio Act of 1927, the first comprehensive scheme of control over radio communication, Congress acted upon the knowledge that if the potentialities of radio were not to be wasted, regulation was essential.[5]

Since the 1920s, technological advances have allowed utilization of higher and higher frequencies in the radio spectrum. While usable space in the spectrum is thus expanding, so too is the demand for frequencies. Many services other than broadcasting to the public at large must be accommodated: for example, marine and aviation navigation, military preparedness, amateur radio, and land mobile services (police, fire department). The excess in the number of people who wish to broadcast, over the number of available frequencies, is the true measure of the continuing scarcity problem.[6]

The Federal Communications Commission and the Public Interest

Congressional concern that the limited radio frequencies not be wasted is reflected in the current Federal Communications Act. It was originally passed in 1934, pursuant to Congress's power to regulate interstate and foreign commerce. One avowed purpose of the Act is to secure for all the people of the United States the maximum benefits of radio communication.[7]

To realize the vast potential of radio communication, Congress created the Federal Communications Commission (FCC) and endowed it with comprehensive powers. The FCC is an independent federal agency, which reports directly to Congress. It regulates interstate and foreign communications by radio, television, wire, cable, and satellite. The FCC's mission is to facilitate the full and orderly development of broadcast services as well as the establishment of nationwide and worldwide telephone and telegraph services. Supervising all FCC activities are seven commissioners, appointed by the President, with the approval of the Senate, to serve seven-year terms of office.[8]

Among the FCC's primary responsibilities is allocation of space in the radio spectrum. The commission designates bands of frequencies for specific communication uses. (As we have seen, many of these uses do not involve broadcasting to the public at large.) Special band widths are reserved for radio — AM and FM — and television — both VHF (very high frequency) and UHF (ultrahigh frequency). Within the appropriate band, an individual station is assigned a particular frequency on which to operate. In essence, the FCC acts as an electronic traffic cop, monitoring use of the spectrum to prevent interference.[9]

No one may operate a radio or television station without first having obtained from the FCC a license to broadcast. Congress empowered the commission to issue and renew licenses for terms not exceeding three years. The statutory standard governing grant and renewal of licenses is the "public interest, convenience and necessity" — commonly referred to as the *public interest standard.* A license will be granted or renewed if the FCC finds that the public interest would be served by such action.[10]

A licensee does not own the frequency assigned for his use; ultimate control over use of the radio spectrum is retained by the federal government. The licensee is merely accorded the temporary privilege of using the frequency for the benefit of the audience in his service area. In effect, the licensee is a *public trustee;* if he betrays his trust to present programming in the public interest, he may find his license in jeopardy at renewal time.

Generally speaking, the public interest is the stake all listeners and viewers have in the larger, more effective use of the broadcast medium. The public interest is fulfilled through the licensing process to the extent that the best practicable broadcast service is secured for each community.

> The Commission's licensing function cannot be discharged, therefore, merely by finding that there are no technological objections to the granting of a license. If the criterion of "public interest" were limited to such matters, how could the Commission choose between two applicants for the same facilities, each of whom is financially and technically qualified to operate a station?[11]

The commission must necessarily pay careful attention to the nature of the program service to be provided by each broadcaster.

Under the broad public interest standard, the FCC's powers are truly expansive. They are not, however, unlimited. The commission cannot interfere with a broadcaster's programming decisions to the extent of denying him freedom of expression. The First Amendment prohibits government abridgement of freedom of speech or press. Broadcasters are part of the press, and their communication of ideas over radio and television is clearly a form of expression entitled to constitutional protection.[12] Mindful of the Constitution's restraint upon government, Congress specifically withheld all powers of censorship from the FCC: "Nothing in this Act shall be understood or construed to give the Commission the power of censorship over the radio communications of signals transmitted by any . . . station, and no regulation or condition shall be promulgated or fixed by the Commission which shall interfere with the right of free speech by means of radio communication."[13] According to the Supreme Court, Congress clearly intended "to permit private broadcasting to develop with the widest journalistic freedom consistent with its public obligations. Only when the interests of the public are found to outweigh the private journalistic interests of the broadcasters will government power be asserted within the framework of the Act."[14]

Thus, the regulatory system enacted by Congress casts broadcasters in a difficult dual role: on the one hand, broadcasters are licensed by government to serve the public interest; on the other hand, broadcasters are entitled to function as journalistic free agents.

> The tensions inherent in such a regulatory structure emerge more clearly when we compare a private newspaper with a broadcast licensee. The power of a privately owned newspaper to advance its own political, social, and economic views is bounded by only two factors: first, the acceptance of a sufficient number of readers — and hence advertisers — to assure financial success; and, second, the journalistic integrity of its editors and publishers. A broadcast licensee has a large measure of journalistic freedom but not as large as that exercised by a newspaper. A licensee

must balance what it might prefer to do as a private entrepreneur with what it is required to do as a "public trustee."[15]

The FCC, for its part, must guard the public interest while at the same time preserving the First Amendment values written into the Act. Clearly, administration of the Act is a delicate task, "calling for flexibility and the capacity to adjust and readjust the regulatory mechanism to meet changing problems and needs."[16]

The Right of Viewers and Listeners

The First Amendment shields broadcasters from government censorship as we have already seen. However, broadcasters are not the only ones who may invoke the Constitution in regard to radio and television communications. We, the public, as listeners and viewers, have a definite interest in broadcasting, which the First Amendment also protects. In essence, we are entitled to hear diverse points of view on important issues, without censorship by the government *or by broadcasters*. The United States Supreme Court has sanctioned an unusual balancing of interests — both ours and those of the broadcasters — in order to fulfill the overall aims of the First Amendment. It is worth our while to consider the court's reasoning, since it validates the FCC rules we will be studying shortly.

To begin with, the court holds that freedom of speech does not include the right to broadcast without first obtaining a license from the FCC. Ordinarily, government licensing would be intolerable — for example, if it were used to determine who could publish a newspaper. But broadcasting, as we know, is subject to physical restrictions imposed by the radio spectrum. Not everyone who wishes to broadcast can do so.

> Where there are substantially more individuals who want to broadcast than there are frequencies to allocate, it is idle to posit an unabridgeable First Amendment right to broadcast comparable to the right of every individual to speak, write, or publish. If 100 persons want broadcast licenses but there are only 10 frequencies to allocate, all of them may

have the same "right" to a license; but if there is to be any effective communication by radio, only a few can be licensed and the rest must be barred from the airwaves.[17]

Thus, government licensing, far from violating the First Amendment, actually implements it: "It would be strange if the First Amendment, aimed at protecting and furthering communications, prevented the Government from making radio communication possible by requiring licenses to broadcast and by limiting the number of licenses so as not to overcrowd the spectrum."[18]

Once a license is granted, what is the licensee's status under the First Amendment? Does the licensee enjoy an absolute right to present his own views to the exclusion of those of his less privileged fellow citizens; or is he obliged, to some extent, to honor the First Amendment interests of those citizens who are necessarily denied the opportunity to operate a broadcast station? These questions were answered by the Supreme Court in its landmark 1969 decision, *Red Lion Broadcasting Company, Inc. v. FCC.*[19]

The *Red Lion* case involved constitutional challenges leveled by broadcasters against the fairness doctrine, the personal-attack rule, and the political-editorial rule. In *Red Lion,* broadcasters claimed their freedom of speech and press was being abridged by the FCC's enforcement of these three rules. Justice Byron White summarized the broadcasters' position:

> Their contention is that the First Amendment protects their desire to use their allotted frequencies continuously to broadcast whatever they choose, and to exclude whomever they choose from ever using that frequency. No man may be prevented from saying or publishing what he thinks, or from refusing in his speech or other utterances to give equal weight to the views of his opponents. This right, they say, applies equally to broadcasters.

The Supreme Court rejected this argument and upheld the constitutionality of the challenged rules.

The fairness doctrine, personal-attack, and political-editorial rules are all aimed at facilitating what Justice White called "enforced sharing of a scarce resource." Such enforced sharing at the direction of the FCC is a much less drastic approach than the one Congress might have enacted.

> Rather than confer frequency monopolies on a relatively small number of licensees, in a Nation of 200,000,000, the Government could surely have decreed that each frequency should be shared among all or some of those who wish to use it, each [user] being assigned a portion of the broadcast day or the broadcast week. The [rules] at issue here do not go so far. They assert that under specified circumstances, a licensee must offer to make available a reasonable amount of broadcast time to those who have a view different from that which has already been expressed on his station.

Does enforced time sharing violate a broadcaster's rights under the First Amendment? No, said Justice White. A broadcaster has no constitutional right to monopolize a scarce resource, use of which has been denied to other citizens by the government.

> There is nothing in the First Amendment which prevents the Government from requiring a licensee to share his frequency with others and to conduct himself as a proxy or fiduciary with obligations to present those views and voices which are representative of his community and which would otherwise, by necessity, be barred from the airwaves.

As far as the First Amendment is concerned, licensees stand no better than citizens to whom licenses are refused.

"It is the right of the viewers and listeners," Justice White emphasized, "not the right of the broadcasters, which is paramount. . . . It is the right of the public to receive suitable access to social, political, esthetic, moral, and other ideas and experiences which is crucial here. That right may not constitutionally be abridged either by Congress or the FCC." Thus, the individual right to free speech of any broadcaster is neither the sole, nor the paramount, First Amendment interest in broadcasting. Instead, the paramount interest is *the public's collective right* to have broadcasting function consistently with the goals of the First Amendment.

What are these goals? In *Red Lion,* Justice White summarized them: "It is the purpose of the First Amendment to preserve an uninhibited marketplace of ideas in which truth will ultimately prevail. . . ." Dedication to this principle of free trade in ideas underlies more than a half-century of First Amendment theory. Preserving an uninhibited marketplace of ideas does more than protect the individual's right to express himself freely; it also safeguards *the public's right to be informed.* A well-informed public is essential in a democratic society, where the people are responsible for conducting their own affairs and maintaining the vitality of their institutions. That is why we have "a profound national commitment to the principle that debate on public issues should be uninhibited, robust, and wide-open."[20] Our constitutional guarantee of freedom of speech and press "rests on the assumption that the widest possible dissemination of information from diverse and antagonistic sources is essential to the welfare of the public"; indeed, in the Supreme Court's words, "a free press is a condition of a free society."[21]

Justice White concluded that the fairness doctrine, personal-attack, and political-editorial rules promoted First Amendment goals. These three rules increase the flow and diversity of broadcast communications and, hence, raise the audience's level of awareness. Without the affirmative push provided by the FCC's rules, the airwaves might be monopolized by narrowly dictated points of view. "Station owners and a few networks would have unfettered power to make time available only to the highest bidders, to communicate only their views on public issues, people and candidates, and to permit on the air only those with whom they agreed." Such a private monopoly upon the dissemination of information would be inconsistent with the First Amendment. "There is no sanctuary in the First Amendment," warned Justice White, "for unlimited private censorship operating in a medium not open to all."

Justice White's use of the phrase "private censorship" underlines the limitations upon the First Amendment rights of a broadcaster. What the broadcaster might choose to regard as his exercise of freedom of speech and press can, in the circumstances described by Justice White, be an act of censorship inimical to the First

Amendment. This principle sounds alien to our traditional notions about freedom of expression. We usually think of free speech only in terms of a restraint upon government — not upon private individuals; on its face, the First Amendment prohibits the *government* from abridging freedom of speech or press. However, *Red Lion* establishes an unusual hierarchy of First Amendment interests in broadcasting. At the apex is the public's collective right to have broadcasting function as a free marketplace of ideas — not a closed monopoly. That right cannot be abridged either by the government *or by private broadcasters.*

To Oversee without Censoring

From our examination of the Federal Communications Act and the Supreme Court's reasoning in *Red Lion,* we can see how delicately balanced the system of broadcast regulation is. There exists, so to speak, a "broadcast constituency": broadcasters form one part; the public, the other. Each part has an important interest in broadcasting protected by the First Amendment. It is up to the FCC to strike a proper balance between these often competing interests — maintaining the values of private broadcast journalism while, at the same time, enforcing standards of public accountability.[22]

In essence, the FCC must oversee without censoring.[23] As overseer the commission is charged with protecting and advancing the public interest. Licensees cannot be allowed to monopolize their frequencies to the exclusion of representative views and voices from the community. Such misuse of a radio frequency constitutes private censorship and violates the trust imposed upon licensees under the Federal Communications Act. Equally violative of the Act, however, is unauthorized intrusion by the FCC upon the journalistic freedom of broadcasters. "Congress appears to have concluded . . . that of these two choices — private or official censorship — Government censorship would be the most pervasive, the most self-serving, and the most difficult to restrain and hence the one most to be avoided."[24]

To oversee without censoring, the FCC "walks a tightrope between saying too much and saying too little."[25] It usually attempts to resolve this dilemma by imposing only general affirmative obligations upon broadcasters; the manner in which specific content is given to these broad duties lies within the broadcaster's journalistic discretion. We will learn, for instance, that the FCC's fairness doctrine imposes two affirmative obligations upon broadcasters: coverage of public issues must be adequate and it must fairly reflect conflicting points of view. Given these overall obligations, broadcasters may exercise discretion as to which issues will be discussed by whom and when.

As long as a broadcaster exercises his discretion reasonably and in good faith, his journalistic judgments are inviolate. To the extent that he acts arbitrarily, however, the public interest is transgressed.

> Licensee discretion is but a means to a greater end, and not an end in and of itself, and only insofar as it is exercised in genuine conformity with the paramount right of the listening and viewing public to be informed on the competing viewpoints on public issues can such discretion be considered an adequate means of maintaining and enhancing First Amendment interests in the broadcast medium.[26]

It is in overseeing the reasonableness of specific judgments by broadcasters that the FCC must strike the most delicate balance between public and private interests.

2

Broadcast Journalism and the Public Interest

General Principles

Reporting news of current events and issues is a basic aspect of programming in the public interest. This nation relies increasingly upon broadcasting, especially television, as its primary source of news and information. It is precisely because of the contribution radio and television can make toward informing the public, that the FCC has allocated so much spectrum space to broadcasting.[1] Broadcasters are expected to "devote a reasonable percentage of their broadcast time to the presentation of news and programs devoted to the consideration and discussion of public issues of interest in the community served by the particular station."[2]

The level of public enlightenment gained from broadcast news depends in large part upon the quality of the reporting. To the extent that reporting is fair and objective, listeners and viewers will have a sound basis for judgments they must make on public issues. If, however, a broadcaster suppresses or distorts the news, the public interest is harmed in at least two ways. First, a misinformed citizenry is obviously ill prepared to participate effectively in the democratic process: "Rigging or slanting the news is a most heinous act against the public interest," the FCC has warned; "indeed, there is no act more harmful to the public's ability to handle its affairs."³

Second, no true debate on public issues can be conducted if it rests upon a distorted presentation of the underlying facts.

> The basis for any fair consideration of public issues, and particularly those of a controversial nature, is the presentation of news and information concerning the basic facts of the controversy in as complete and impartial a manner as possible. A licensee would be abusing his position as a public trustee of these important means of mass communication were he to withhold from expression over his facilities relevant news or facts concerning a controversy or to slant or distort the presentation of such news. No discussion of the issues involved in any controversy can be fair or in the public interest where such discussion must take place in a climate of false or misleading information concerning the basic facts of the controversy.⁴

Discussion of controversial issues is, as we shall see later, the goal of the FCC's fairness doctrine. The whole point of that doctrine would be undermined if opposing spokesmen on any given issue relied upon distorted information.

The FCC's dilemma in regard to news distortion is how to insure honest reporting without, at the same time, intervening in the processes of broadcast journalism. On the one hand, the commission is sensitive to broadcast journalism's right to freedom of the press and mindful of the prohibition against government censorship: "The general rule is that we do not sit to review the broadcaster's news judgment, the quality of his news and public affairs reporting, or his taste."⁵

Ordinarily, therefore, the commission will decline to act upon complaints of news distortion. "For example," the commission explained in 1969,

> the complaint is frequently received that "Commentator X has given a biased account or analysis of a news event" or that the true facts of the news event are different from those

presented. . . . In a democracy, dependent upon the
fundamental rights of free speech and press, no Government
agency can authenticate the news, or should try to do so.
Such an attempt would cast the chill of omnipresent government censorship over the newsmen's independence in news
judgment. Were this the case a newsman might decide to
"play it safe," and not broadcast for fear he might later be
held up to censure. This Commission is thus not the national
arbiter of the "truth" of a news event. It cannot properly
investigate to determine whether an account or analysis of a
news commentator is "biased" or "true."[6]

Despite such oft-repeated disavowals of censorship, the commission has still acted to discourage journalistic excesses deemed
inimical to the public interest. "Broadcasting is the press, and
something more," the commission has rationalized, "the 'more' being the requirement, because of the system of Federal licensing
which excludes all others from use of the frequency, that the
broadcast operation be consistent with the public interest. . . ."[7]
In its attempt to oversee broadcast news practices without engaging in censorship, the commission has assiduously avoided issuance of specific "do's" and "don't's"; such a list would involve the
commission directly in editorial decisions about specific program
content. To avoid this dangerous intrusion upon the electronic
press, the commission has followed its usual exhortatory approach:
it enunciates general licensee responsibilities considered conducive
to a well-informed public. Then it calls upon licensees to exercise
their discretion in carrying out these affirmative obligations.[8]

Basically, a licensee is responsible for maintaining the integrity
of his news operations. He must adopt a definite policy requiring
honesty from his news staff. Members of the staff should be clearly
informed of the licensee's standards for journalistic integrity, and
reasonable precautions must be taken by the licensee to insure that
these standards are actually observed. When any substantial complaint of news distortion is received by the licensee, he must investigate the incident thoroughly and conscientiously. If any
wrongdoing on the part of staff members is discovered, the licensee must take whatever action is deemed appropriate: for example, disciplining the person who committed the infraction, or

adopting preventive measures for the future. Serious questions will be raised about a broadcaster's fitness to retain his license if he attempts to cover up wrongdoing rather than deal with it.[9]

Ordinarily, the FCC does not intervene in disputes over whether the truth has been twisted on news programs. Complaints of any substance will be referred to the broadcaster for his investigation and, if necessary, remedial action. The commission is apt to launch its own investigation only if it receives so-called *extrinsic evidence* of deliberate news distortion. The extrinsic evidence rule requires something more than mere disagreement over the truth of a news report. Given only unsubstantiated charges of news distortion, the commission will not weigh conflicting versions of the "real story" and attempt to establish the truth. For example, the commission will not intervene if a politician contends he has been misquoted, or an eyewitness complains about misleading coverage of an event he observed.[10]

Extrinsic evidence usually consists of "testimony, in writing or otherwise, from 'insiders' or persons who have direct personal knowledge of an intentional attempt to falsify the news."[11] For example, a newsman might divulge a memorandum from station management ordering news personnel to discriminate in their coverage of certain events, causes, politicians, or private interests. Or the subject of some news story might claim that he was offered a bribe by a newsman to say or do something on the air. Confronted with such extrinsic evidence of deliberate distortion, the FCC would investigate.[12]

As a result of its inquiry, the commission will decide whether to take any action. In general, the commission will not question a broadcaster's fitness to retain his license if, despite some incident of news distortion, he has been diligent in maintaining the overall integrity of his news operations. The isolated lapse of a news employee, acting on his own, without the knowledge of his superiors, will not be a serious enough affront to the public interest to jeopardize the broadcaster's license. However, a pattern of repeated acts of news distortion by employees may raise serious questions as to whether the broadcaster is adequately supervising his personnel.

The gravest consequences would arise were there extrinsic evidence that the broadcaster himself had instructed his employees to distort the news. "Such slanting of the news amounts to a fraud upon the public and is patently inconsistent with the licensee's obligations to operate his facilities in the public interest. It calls for a full hearing to determine the facts and thus whether the licensee is qualified to hold the broadcasting permit."[13]

With the threat of this ultimate sanction — loss of license — lurking in the background, if only in the distant background, the FCC is hard put to tread lightly whenever it so much as inquires about a licensee's news operations. The inhibitory effect of such an inquiry upon broadcast journalism is often undeniable. Several years ago, the commission inquired of ABC, CBS, and NBC regarding their television coverage of the 1968 Democratic National Convention.[14] The commission had received a number of complaints charging the networks with slanting the news through their selectivity in covering only certain events and spokesmen. Both CBS and NBC protested that the very fact of the commission's formal inquiry would cast a chill over broadcast journalists. "Few spectres can be more frightening to a person concerned with the vitality of a free press," NBC wrote to the FCC, "than the vision of a television cameraman turning his camera to one aspect of a public event rather than another because of concern that a governmental agency might want him to do so, or fear of Government sanction if he did not." All three networks, however, dutifully responded to the commission's inquiry. Until some licensee challenges the FCC's authority to probe into broadcast news operations, the commission will, no doubt, continue its precarious tightrope act in an attempt to balance the public interest with the rights of broadcasters.

We will now focus upon four categories of news distortion, which have been the subject of serious complaints to the FCC: slanting the news through selectivity in the stories — or aspects of stories — to be covered; inaccuracy in reporting the facts of a story; misrepresentation through editing techniques applied to film and tape; and staging news stories. The general principles discussed thus far apply to each of these categories.

News Coverage

The selection of which events to cover as "news" is the responsibility of the broadcaster. He must be free to act as an independent journalist, allocating coverage according to his estimate of the relative newsworthiness of events. Different broadcasters may, of course, make different news appraisals — even about the same event; the fact that one station affords more coverage than another to any given event does not necessarily impugn the judgment of either station. The FCC will not substitute its sense of news values for those of the broadcast journalist; it will act only if it has extrinsic evidence that a news event was deliberately suppressed for the purpose of misrepresentation.[15]

In 1972 the commission received a complaint about inadequate news coverage by radio station KID (Idaho Falls, Idaho).[16] Kenneth Cooper wrote that KID reported daily upon United States involvement in the Vietnam War. He admitted the coverage was both extensive and balanced in terms of the FCC's fairness doctrine. However, Cooper complained that the "other side" of the conflict — namely, Russian and Chinese participation — had not been adequately exposed to KID listeners. Cooper argued that KID should be required to present the other side so that he could function as a well-informed citizen.

The commission refused to direct KID to present the particular news coverage Cooper wished to hear.

> Were the Commission to adopt the position here urged upon it, it would upon complaint be compelled to review the coverage by more than 8,000 broadcasting stations of every news event cited by complainants; to determine whether the coverage of the event accorded with the notions of each complainant, and, if not, whether the licensee was "at fault."
> . . . Any attempt to evaluate such complaints as to "what should have been broadcast" as against, or in addition to, what had been broadcast would place this agency in the role of national arbiter of the news; in fact, dictator of which news items should be broadcast. Since there are only so many hours in the broadcast day and most listeners seem to

desire other programming in addition to news (e.g., music, drama), it obviously is impossible for each licensee to present as much news about every event as every member of the public might desire. Thus, licensees and networks must exercise their journalistic judgment on what news is of greatest significance and interest to the public generally.

Broadcast coverage of political campaigns is often a source of controversy. Candidates rarely feel they receive enough exposure over radio and television, and this dissatisfaction sometimes manifests itself in complaints about news suppression. Here, too, the FCC will generally not interfere with reasonable judgments over the news value inherent in a given campaign or candidate.[17] It is possible, however, that excessive coverage of one candidate may run afoul of the fairness doctrine; the issue of who should be elected is generally regarded as a controversial one, which must be treated in a balanced manner under the fairness doctrine (see pages 162–168).

Once a broadcaster has chosen a particular event to report on, the selectivity with which he covers that event is entitled to the same journalistic leeway as his original choice. Following the 1968 Democratic National Convention in Chicago, the FCC received hundreds of complaints from television viewers, who objected to unfair news coverage by ABC, CBS, and NBC.[18] Some viewers felt the networks devoted too much time to floor coverage while slighting official proceedings at the podium. According to one complaint, the networks actually "attempted to influence the course of the proceedings, spreading rumors — especially concerning the possibility of a Kennedy draft — stirring controversy where none existed, and giving priority to the views of dissident or dissatisfied delegates." Viewers also claimed to detect a network bias favoring spokesmen opposed to the Johnson administration's conduct of the Vietnam War. Nor were viewers any more pleased with the coverage outside the convention hall, where protest demonstrations and eventual riots surged through the streets of Chicago. There were complaints that television reports were one-sided: they failed to show the provocative acts of the demonstrators or reveal their violent intentions; instead, the pictures that were presented reflected unfairly upon the seeming brutality of the Chicago police.

In response to an FCC inquiry, the networks defended their news coverage. They pointed out that many of the complaints were simply mistaken; coverage of "the other side" of various events had, in fact, been presented. Sometimes, however, rounded coverage was prevented for technical reasons related to the nature of electronic news-gathering. For example, ABC pointed out that its mobile remote unit in the streets of Chicago could respond only to events already taking place. That limitation, combined with restrictions upon setting up cameras imposed by the city of Chicago, precluded coverage of certain events leading up to the outbreak of violence.

NBC vigorously denied it had misrepresented convention proceedings through its selective coverage. NBC interviews regarding a possible Kennedy draft reflected actual interest and activity within the convention. Reports of delegates dissatisfied with the conduct of the convention and the behavior of the Chicago police simply reflected the fact that such discontent existed among the delegates. NBC also pointed out that selection of a presidential nominee involves more than merely speeches at the podium, and, therefore, it had presented supplementary coverage from the floor and from outside the auditorium.

After its inquiry, the FCC concluded it was barred from attempting any determination of whether the convention coverage had been unfair in the sense of not presenting the "truth." Were the commission to embark upon such a determination, it would rapidly be drawn into the editorial process.

The question of whether a news medium has been fair in covering a news event would turn on an evaluation of such matters as what occurred, what facts did the news medium have in its possession, what other facts should it reasonably have obtained, what did it actually report, etc. For example, on the issue whether the networks "fairly" depicted the demonstrators' provocation which led to the police reaction, the Commission would be required to seek to ascertain first the "truth" of the situation — what actually occurred; next what facts and film footage the networks possessed on the matter; what other facts and film footage they "fairly" and reasonably should have obtained; and finally in light of the foregoing, whether the reports actually presented were fair.

Such inquiries into methods of news-gathering, even though conducted in the soothing name of "fairness," would have been entirely inappropriate for a government licensing agency.

> This is not because such actual fairness is not important, but rather because its determination by a Government agency is inconsistent with our concept of a free press. The Government would then be determining what is the "truth" in each news situation — what actually occurred and whether the licensee deviated too substantially from that "truth." We do not sit as a review body of the "truth" concerning news events.

Therefore, the commission declined to take any further action on the complaints against the three networks.

A broadcaster's selection of subjects for news coverage is frequently prompted by publicity requests from outside sources. Individuals and groups in both private and public life commonly ply broadcasters with suggestions for coverage of an event or viewpoint. Sometimes proposals are offered by government officials. The FCC sees nothing inherently wrong with such outside pressure, but broadcasters are expected to respond to it according to the dictates of their independent journalistic judgment.[19]

In certain circumstances, when a broadcaster is receptive to outside news sources, he is obliged to identify them for the benefit of the listening or viewing audience. This requirement applies to political programs or any program involving the discussion of controversial public issues. Such programs may at times include various tapes, films, scripts, or other material supplied by outside sources as an inducement to air the program. If so, the broadcaster must announce that the materials being used were supplied by the source in question.[20] The public should not be misled into believing the source of the material was the broadcaster's own news crew.[21] As the commission has said, "Listeners are entitled to know by whom they are being persuaded."[22]

For example, some candidates for public office are no longer content merely to alert the media to their campaign plans and then hope a news crew will show up to tape or film. Instead, the candidate's activities are recorded by his own staff, and the resulting film or audio tape is delivered to the news departments of local radio and television stations. The broadcasters must then determine whether the material supplied should be aired as "news."

In 1972 the FCC noted this growing phenomenon and found nothing objectionable about it, so long as the public is not misled about the source of the "news."

> Increasingly, candidates have been supplying radio and television broadcasters with audio recordings and film excerpts produced by the candidates, e.g., depicting their campaign efforts that day or containing statements of their position on current issues. Obviously, these excerpts are designed to show the candidate in the best light and, if presented on a newscast, have the added advantage of increased impact or credibility over a paid political presentation. We do not hold that the station cannot exercise its good faith news judgment as to whether and to what extent it wishes to present these tape or film excerpts. If it believes that they are newsworthy, it can appropriately use them in newscasts. But the public should be informed that the tape or film was supplied by the candidate as an inducement to the broadcasting of it.[23]

In other words, the broadcaster is free to use "canned" news stories in the form of film or tape releases, but he must announce to the audience the identity of his supplier. If the tape or film was edited by the broadcaster, he may add some suitable phrase, such as "edited by the WWW news department."

The FCC's disclosure requirements do not cover a broadcaster's use of printed press releases. Such materials are routinely supplied to broadcasters by government, business, and civic organizations; candidates frequently furnish advance copies of speeches or mimeographed position papers on various issues. A broadcaster may read from or comment upon these releases as he chooses. No announcement need be made identifying the source of the broadcaster's story.[24]

News Accuracy

The FCC has said that "in this democracy, no Government agency can authenticate the news, or should try to do so."[25] The commission is chary of entering disputes in which the true facts of an event are claimed to differ from those reported by the broadcaster. Before the commission will investigate, it must be presented with more than a mere disagreement over accuracy. There must be extrinsic evidence of a deliberate attempt to deceive the public.

On May 21, 1968, CBS presented a documentary entitled "Hunger in America."[26] In the opening minutes, an unusually small baby was shown receiving emergency medical treatment. The narrator commented: "Hunger is easy to recognize when it looks like this. This baby is dying of starvation. He was an American. Now he is dead." In fact, the baby was not dying of starvation, but rather complications caused by premature birth.

How did CBS's erroneous report come about? The dying-baby sequence had been captured quite unexpectedly while the CBS film crew was shooting background footage in the nursery of a San Antonio hospital. Since the crew had not intended to concentrate on any particular infant, it made no inquiries about individual case histories. Suddenly one of the cameramen noticed a baby had stopped breathing. The resident physician was summoned. He resuscitated the baby under the watchful eye of the CBS camera. (The baby in this sequence was the one shown in the documentary.) On the next day the baby died — of prematurity, not malnutrition.

Why did CBS mistakenly conclude that the unidentified baby was dying of malnutrition? "We relied for our information," explained Richard Salant, president of CBS News, "on statements given to our newsmen by the hospital official through whom they dealt principally in their visit to the hospital." Vera Burke, the hospital's head of social services, had informed Martin Carr, producer of "Hunger in America," about the high incidence of premature births due to malnutrition in the mothers. According to Carr,

Burke had also told him that the baby in the CBS sequence died as a result of maternal malnutrition. Burke, however, denied ever having stated that any particular infant was dying or had died from malnutrition.

"From the foregoing," observed the FCC,

> it is apparent that in view of the statements made by Mrs. Burke . . . at the least, CBS had reasonable basis for assuming a very high prevalence of malnutrition in the nursery and pediatric wards. The issue thus comes down to whether, regardless of the statements that the wards were filled with babies suffering from malnutrition, CBS nevertheless engaged in sloppy journalism or was recklessly indifferent to the truth in not ascertaining the cause of death of the . . . baby [in question].

The commission decided it could not even attempt to resolve this issue. Any resolution would have necessarily required a choice of whom to believe — Martin Carr or Vera Burke — as to whether or not the dead baby had been specifically identified as a victim of malnutrition.

> Here there is a conflict, with the memory of the CBS witnesses differing from that of the hospital personnel. In these circumstances, it is, we believe, inappropriate to hold an evidentiary hearing and upon that basis (i.e., credibility or demeanor judgments), make findings as to the truth of the situation. The truth would always remain a matter open to some question. . . .

The commission declined to investigate any further; it had been presented only with a dispute over the truth, rather than any extrinsic evidence of deliberate deception.

Charges of misquotation are a common source of debate over news accuracy. Someone quoted on a newscast complains that he actually said something quite different. In such a situation, the FCC feels it cannot appropriately enter the "quagmire of investigating the credibility of the newsman and the interviewed party" to ascertain the true quotation. The commission does not regard the complaint of the allegedly misquoted person as extrinsic evidence of distortion.[27]

Nor, for that matter, is a complaint about highly probing interview tactics extrinsic evidence of an intent to slant the news. During the 1969 mayoralty race in Omaha, WOW-TV newsman Tom Murray attended a press conference at which Albert J. Treutler announced his candidacy. After the other newsmen had left, Murray obtained a private interview with the candidate. Murray did not use the occasion to discuss politics, as a transcript of WOW-TV's evening newscast reveals.

> ANNOUNCER: Mr. Treutler is also the owner of the Ade Book Company, which sells parodies and travesties by direct mail by advertising in men's magazines such as *Man's Story*.
> WOW newsman Tom Murray asked him about the firm.
>
> MURRAY: Sir, could you describe what . . . what the Ade Book Company is?
>
> TREUTLER: I'd rather not cover that, Tom.
>
> MURRAY: Well, are you the owner of the Ade Book Company?
>
> TREUTLER: Yes.
>
> MURRAY: What kinds of books are involved and what do you do with this company?
>
> TREUTLER: They're strictly, ah, cartoons, comics, gags.
>
> MURRAY: How are they sold?
>
> TREUTLER: By direct mail.
>
> MURRAY: Now, there have been some charges that these are obscene books.
>
> TREUTLER: There is absolutely no truth in that. There is absolutely nothing in any piece of literature that is turned out of this office that is even slightly off-color, that a five-year-old could not read.
>
> MURRAY: Are they advertised as a come-on, as an obscene come-on?
>
> TREUTLER: No, they are advertised as, ah, parodies, travesties, ah, satires.
>
> MURRAY: [supplying voiceover while the book "Marital Love" is seen on camera] One of the books which Treutler gave me is entitled "Marital Love," subtitled "12 Modern Positions." The book consists of cartoons showing the hen-

> pecked husband doing housework and such while his wife
> relaxes. As advertised in "Man's Story," the book is called
> "Parody of Marital Love, 12 Modern Positions." The average
> twentieth century woman demands more. Here for the first
> time fully illustrated the way modern man keeps her happy.
> Shipped in plain wrapper.[28]

Treutler petitioned the FCC to deny renewal of WOW-TV's
license. One ground for denial, Treutler argued, was WOW-TV's
interview of him, which had been slanted to convey the illusion
that he peddled obscene literature. The FCC declined to act upon
Treutler's complaint; it lacked any extrinsic evidence of distortion.
"When we refer to cases involving extrinsic evidence," the commission explained,

> we do not mean the type of situation presented in this case
> where, as the facts show, the petitioner merely claims that
> the licensee's newsmen "proceeded to interrogate him about
> his personal and private business, a subject [he claims] in
> no way [was] relevant to his potential 'official conduct or
> ability' to serve in public office."[29]

The FCC has exhibited a willingness to allow broadcast journalists considerable leeway when they rely upon authoritative information which turns out to be inaccurate. Consider the controversy
caused by a 1961 CBS documentary, entitled "Biography of a
Bookie Joint."[30] The program, narrated by Walter Cronkite, investigated illegal gambling operations in Boston. During the program, Massachusetts State Representative Harrison Chadwick was
shown remarking: "I would like to distinguish between a whole-
sale condemnation of legislators, and the fact that relatively few
are actively involved in any of the illegal operations of the booking
business."

On December 6, 1961, an irate speaker of the Massachusetts
House of Representatives, John F. Thompson, complained to the
FCC about Chadwick's "unwarranted and unjustified" attack upon
the House. According to Speaker Thompson, Chadwick's suggestion that House members were engaged in illegal gambling was
totally unsubstantiated: "It seems quite clear to me . . . that the

Columbia Broadcasting System perpetrated a great injustice upon the Massachusetts legislature by the widespread national broadcast of unsupported general allegations which were completely false and fraudulent."

The commission was unreceptive to these charges. Even if Representative Chadwick's remarks were groundless, still there was no evidence that CBS had any *actual* knowledge of their falsity. Thus there was no indication of any deliberate deception of the public. Should CBS, nevertheless, have acquired such knowledge as a result of its journalistic investigation? In providing a negative response to this more difficult question, the FCC reasoned that broadcasters must be permitted great latitude in the production of documentaries.

> It cannot be expected that a licensee will, in every instance, independently examine the basis for the comments of each participant in the program, particularly where a participant is a person holding a high elective office and possessing experience reasonably qualifying him to be considered an expert on the subject under discussion. . . . It is reasonable to assume that Representative Chadwick, as a member of the Massachusetts House of Representatives and a former member of the Massachusetts Crime Commission, could reasonably have been regarded by CBS as possessing the experience to qualify him as an expert on the subject under discussion.

Therefore, the commission declined to investigate the matter any further.

News Editing

When it comes to the editing of broadcast news, the FCC shares the attitude recently expressed by Chief Justice Warren Burger: "For better or for worse, editing is what editors are for. . . ."[31] Unless there is extrinsic evidence of distortion, the commission does not intend to supervise the cutting and splicing of tape or film that results in an electronic news story.

During the 1973 mayoralty campaign in New York City, a debate featuring all the candidates for the Democratic nomination was planned for May 13 on WNBC-TV's "Sunday" show.[32] On May 12 a WNBC-TV reporter interviewed Abraham Beame — the leading contender for the nomination. Beame was asked whether he intended to participate in the debate. He replied that although he was at all times ready to debate the issues with his opponents, he objected to the format proposed for the "Sunday" show, because only one-and-a-half-minute responses to questions would be allowed. What's more, Beame contended, he did not want to appear on the program unless WNBC-TV first granted a pending request he had made for equal time. When the reporter pressed for a "yes" or "no" answer, Beame finally responded that he would not participate in the debate.

During its 6 P.M. newscast on May 12, WNBC-TV broadcast only the tail end of the interview in which Beame had given his negative reply; omitted were his reasons as well as his assurance that he was prepared to debate the issues in the campaign. The film clip selected by WNBC-TV was followed by another clip showing Congressman Herman Badillo, one of Beame's rivals for the Democratic nomination. Badillo was seen criticizing Beame's refusal to debate the issues.

Not surprisingly, Beame's campaign committee was distressed by what they saw on the news. They felt their man had adequately justified his reluctance to participate in the "Sunday" show. However, this justification wound up on the cutting-room floor. What emerged was an unadorned "no" answer, instantly juxtaposed with a partisan critique of that answer. The committee complained to the FCC that WNBC-TV had intentionally distorted the truth; the Beame interview, as edited for broadcast, unfairly implied the candidate was unwilling to debate during the campaign. However, the FCC detected no extrinsic evidence of deliberate distortion. The commission was, therefore, not prepared to embark upon any review of the station's editing techniques.

Perhaps the most serious dispute over broadcast editing was touched off by the Emmy-winning CBS documentary "The Selling of the Pentagon," first shown on February 23, 1971.[33] The program investigated the ways in which the Department of Defense lavished a $30 million public relations budget on massive combat demonstrations, touring displays of military hardware, lectures by a troupe of "traveling colonels," and many doctrinaire political films made by movie stars like John Wayne and Jack Webb. Because of its critical attitude toward the high-powered salesmanship of the defense establishment, the program provoked many viewers, including, among the more influential, former Vice President Spiro Agnew and Congressman Edward Hébert, then chairman of the House Armed Services Committee.

Critics of "The Selling of the Pentagon" were particularly incensed over what they considered deceptive editing techniques by CBS News. Two sequences in the program stirred the most furor. The first was a film clip of a speech delivered in Peoria by a Colonel MacNeil, one of the so-called traveling colonels. MacNeil warned that if South Vietnam fell to the Communists, Cambodia, Laos, and Thailand would be directly threatened. To the viewer, Colonel MacNeil seemed to be expressing his personal affirmation of the "domino theory" in Southeast Asia. However, what CBS did not make clear, and what was not apparent from MacNeil's address, was the fact that MacNeil was actually *quoting* views expressed by Laotian Prime Minister Souvanna Phouma. (It should be noted that the colonel actually did return to the "domino theory" later in his remarks and personally affirmed it. As Richard Salant, president of CBS News, observed, it was "difficult to tell where Souvanna Phouma left off and the Colonel started.")

The second disputed sequence was an interview with Assistant Secretary of Defense Daniel Henkin by CBS correspondent Roger Mudd. In the actual interview, one exchange between Mudd and Henkin went as follows:

> MUDD: What about your public displays of military equipment at state fairs and shopping centers? What purpose does that serve?
>
> HENKIN: Well, I think it serves the purpose of informing the public about their armed forces. It also has the ancillary benefit, I would hope, of stimulating interest in recruiting as we move or try to move to zero draft calls and increased

reliance on volunteers for our armed forces. I think it is very important that the American youth have an opportunity to learn about the armed forces.

After editing, only the first sentence of Henkin's original answer remained intact; the last two sentences were cut. In their place, CBS had transposed part of an answer Henkin had given in response to an entirely different question, dealing with the availability of military speakers. Thus, CBS viewers saw Henkin respond to Mudd's original question this way:

> HENKIN: Well, I think it serves the purpose of informing the public about their armed forces. *I believe the American public has the right to request information about the armed forces, to have speakers come before them, to ask questions, and to understand the need for our armed forces, why we ask for the funds that we do ask for, how we spend these funds, what we are doing about such problems as drugs — and we do have a drug problem in the armed forces, what we are doing about the racial problem — and we do have a racial problem. I think the public has a valid right to ask us these questions.* [Emphasis added.]

Another exchange in the actual Mudd-Henkin interview went:

> MUDD: Well, is that the sort of information about the drug problem you have and the racial problem you have and the budget problems you have — is that the sort of information that gets passed out at state fairs by sergeants who are standing next to rockets?
> HENKIN: No, I didn't — wouldn't limit that to sergeants standing next to any kind of exhibits. I knew — I thought we were discussing speeches and all.

However, the edited version of Henkin's answer was broadcast as follows:

> HENKIN: No, I wouldn't limit that to sergeants standing next to any kind of exhibits. *Now, there are those who contend that this is propaganda. I do not agree with this.* [Emphasis added.]

Where did Henkin's allusion to propaganda come from? It had been lifted from an earlier stage in the interview, when Henkin was disputing charges that the Pentagon's talk of a growing Soviet military threat was only propaganda to increase the size of our military budget.

On March 9, 1971, Congressman Harley Staggers, chairman of the House Committee on Interstate and Foreign Commerce, complained to the FCC. He inquired what action the commission would take in light of evidence that CBS had misrepresented the truth through devious editing techniques. The commission responded that it would take no action at all.

> Lacking extrinsic evidence or documents that on their face reflect deliberate distortion, we believe that this government licensing agency cannot properly intervene. It would be unwise and probably impossible for the Commission to lay down some precise line of factual accuracy — dependent always on journalistic judgment — across which broadcasters must not stray. . . . It would involve the Commission deeply and improperly in the journalistic functions of broadcasters.
>
> This function necessarily involves selection and editorial judgment. And, in the absence of evidence, documentary or otherwise, that a licensee has engaged in deliberate distortion, for the Commission to review this editing process would be to enter an impenetrable thicket. On every single question of judgment, and each complaint that might be registered, the Commission would have to decide whether the editing had involved deliberate distortion. Although we can conceive of situations where the documentary evidence of deliberate distortion would be sufficiently strong to require an inquiry — e.g., where a "yes" answer to one question was used to replace a "no" answer to an entirely different question — we believe that such a situation is not presented here.

While the FCC declined to intervene, it did not conceal its own doubts regarding the journalistic propriety of CBS's editing techniques: "It seems to us that CBS has failed to address the question raised as to splicing answers to a variety of questions as a way of creating a new 'answer' to a single question. The very use of a

'Question and Answer' format would seem to encourage the viewer to believe that a particular answer follows directly from the question preceding." What the commission suggested by way of positive action was self-criticism and self-control on the part of all broadcast journalists.

News Staging

The FCC has never formulated a detailed policy restricting news staging. Indeed, the practice known as "news staging" has yet to be fully defined by the commission. Perhaps the closest approximation we have to a formal definition is the FCC's recent observation that news staging involves "a purportedly significant 'event' which did not in fact occur but rather is 'acted out' at the behest of news personnel."³⁴ This definition, while admittedly general, reveals the two key aspects of serious news staging: first, the staged event has apparent significance; the greater that significance is made to appear, the graver the fraud perpetrated upon a believing public. Second, the event lacks spontaneity and authenticity; it has literally been "produced and directed" by the broadcast journalist.

Some instances of news staging are, in the FCC's estimation, clear-cut: "For example, the licensee's newsmen should not, upon arriving late at a riot, ask one of the rioters to throw another brick through a store window for its cameras. . . . If the window is already broken, it is staging a news event — one which did not in fact occur but rather is acted out at the request of the news personnel."³⁵ In fairness to the public, the broadcaster could present such a film only if it were accompanied by full disclosure of the surrounding circumstances.

At the opposite extreme from clear-cut staging lies what the FCC has referred to as the "pseudo-event." This term embraces certain routine formalities and relatively inconsequential activities, which journalists regularly treat as "news." In a strict sense, these pseudo-events might be characterized as "staged." For example, in a televised press conference, the participants wear makeup, occupy assigned positions, and adhere to a traditional format. At many ceremonial events, dignitaries and public officials are asked by newsmen to smile again or, perhaps, repeat handshakes. Such journalistic conventions do not disturb the FCC. Broadcasters are permitted to indulge in minor visual and aural amenities, which animate a news narrative without deceiving the public about matters of any significance.

The FCC is well aware that the very presence of lights, cameras, and microphones may exert undeniable pressures upon the development of a news event. People will react to the prospect of being covered by the media; they will tend to move, act, and speak with the limits and capabilities of the broadcast equipment in mind. The resulting news event is not considered a product of news staging. According to the FCC, "The judgment when to turn off the lights and send the cameras away is . . . not one subject to review by this Commission. We do not sit to decide: 'Here the licensee exercised good journalistic judgment in staying'; or 'Here it should have left.' "[36]

Between clear-cut staging on the one hand and innocuous pseudo-events on the other lies a gray area "where difficult decisions must be made by the broadcast journalist, keeping in mind the desire to portray the matter as graphically as possible and at the same time preserving fully the bedrock upon which the entire industry rests, namely, the integrity of the news and related programming operations."[37] The FCC has suggested, for example, that inducing a politician to repeat — for the benefit of broadcast microphones or cameras — part of an already delivered speech falls into the gray area between obvious staging and the routine coverage of pseudo-events.[38] The commission does not regard the gray area as one in which it can intervene and review a broadcaster's judgments.[39]

In controversies over alleged news staging, the FCC is chiefly concerned with the potential for serious deception of the public: "The real criterion with respect to staging is whether the public is deceived about a matter of significance. We believe that by asking himself this question, a licensee can make a determination as to what to film or record, how to edit it, and how to present it properly to the public."[40] The public is not considered totally susceptible to every degree of staging — no matter how innocuous. Instead, the public is viewed as possessing enough sophistication to insulate itself from the potentially deceptive effect of some journalistic devices.

For example, on November 1 and 2, 1967, the local news program of WBBM-TV (Chicago) carried a two-part series, entitled "Pot Party at a University."[41] A group of students from Northwestern University were filmed smoking marijuana in a campus apartment. The party had been arranged by the students for the benefit of the television cameras at the behest of a WBBM-TV newsman. Despite this direct influence by the newsman, the televised story did not strike the FCC as an instance of clear-cut staging.

> We are not involved here with a news event which did not in fact occur but rather was acted out at the behest of the news personnel. WBBM-TV set out to show a pot party involving Northwestern University students at the Northwestern campus — to point up the pervasiveness of this kind of drug violation at colleges. The party depicted did involve marihuana smoked by Northwestern students (and a teacher and two college dropouts, so identified) who did smoke marihuana at a campus rooming house apartment . . . where other pot parties had been previously held. In a sense, then, the party was authentic — it was not staged by actors or nonstudents who did not smoke marihuana or who were pretending to smoke marihuana at some station studio.

The intimation here is that clear-cut staging would have occurred had WBBM-TV hired actors to portray students or persuaded students to simulate pot smoking or produced the entire party on a television set designed to look like a campus apartment.

The commission went on to note that the public was not naïve enough to have been fooled about the essential nature of the pot party.

> . . . The public obviously was aware that the party was being held with the television camera a major factor. It knew that the camera was there, and had to have an effect

on the participants. It could hear [the newsman] asking questions of the students. In all respects, lighting, placing, questions, etc., there had to be the usual cooperative aspects of any such televised event. In short, the public thus knew fully that this was a televised pot party — an inherently different event from a private, nontelevised pot-smoking gathering.

In other words, the public was not led to believe that the camera was surreptitiously filming the event, for example, through a two-way mirror. Instead, the public could readily take into account the impact that cameras, lights, and newsmen might have upon the spontaneity of gestures and remarks.

Had WBBM-TV gone no further in its pot-party story, the FCC probably would not have found any serious deception of the public. However, WBBM-TV did go further and, in so doing, raised a novel aspect of news staging. Prior to the second installment of "Pot Party at a University," Northwestern University had charged the station with staging the party for its news cameras. This charge was reported at the beginning of the second installment and followed by WBBM's categorical denial. "We were invited," WBBM assured its viewers, "to film the party for use within our news broadcast."

According to the commission, this announcement created a false impression: namely, that WBBM had been invited to attend a pot party that was scheduled to be held and would have been held even if the cameras were not present. However, the commission found the contrary to be true: the WBBM newsman had induced the holding of the party. Without his inducement, the students in question would not have gathered to smoke marijuana at the time and place where WBBM set up its cameras to film.

In sum . . . while the pot party was authentic in many respects and thus cannot be deemed a flagrantly staged event or outright fraud on the public, it would appear that it was misleading in that the public was given the impression that WBBM-TV had been invited to film a student pot gathering which was in any event being held, whereas, in fact, its agent had induced the holding of the party.

The implication seems to be that WBBM-TV, through its misleading disclaimer, exceeded the level of sophistication that could reasonably be expected from the public. Viewers were supposedly astute enough to detect "the usual cooperative aspects" that would be predictable in a televised pot party; but they were at a loss to gauge the full extent of this cooperation between newsman and subject because of WBBM's disclaimer. Presumably, the degree of cooperation would be greater — or, at least, significantly different — in a pot party that WBBM had induced for its own coverage, as distinguished from a party to which the station had been invited as an outside observer. In order to be able to judge the true significance of the pot party, the public deserved to know WBBM's exact relationship to the party; at an absolute minimum, the public was entitled not to be misled about that relationship.

There was another, even more serious, consequence arising from WBBM's inducement to hold the pot party. A broadcaster must not induce the commission of a crime — here, the use of marijuana. Inducement of the commission of a crime is entirely inconsistent with the broadcaster's duty to serve the public interest. "Simply stated, the licensee has to be law-abiding. . . ."

Does the prohibition against inducing a crime mean that broadcast newsmen are barred from investigative journalism in situations where a crime is unfolding? The FCC said no.

> Print journalism has long engaged in such investigative exposures. It has been commended, not condemned, for these efforts to hold a mirror before the public. Broadcast journalism is no less entitled under the first amendment to show through such investigative journalism that substantial segments of society are flouting a particular law, thereby raising hard questions concerning what should be done in such situations.

Therefore, WBBM-TV could have legitimately televised a pot party to illustrate widespread drug violations on college campuses. However, the pot party would have to have been one which was being held regardless of whether WBBM-TV was there to cover it — that is, a party to which the station's newsmen were truly invited, rather than one they had induced.

3
Political Broadcasts

Introduction

Programs devoted to political candidates and election issues comprise an important element of broadcast service in the public interest. Radio and television must help to inform the electorate if our political process is to function effectively. "That process is the bedrock of the Republic," said the FCC in 1972, "and broadcasting is clearly the acknowledged leading medium for communicating political ideas."[1]

What standard is a broadcaster supposed to follow in deciding which political broadcasts to carry? The answer depends to a large extent upon who will be making the broadcast: a candidate for federal office, a candidate for state or local office, or a political party spokesman.

Candidates for Federal Office

Candidates for federal office are entitled to *reasonable access* to air time.[2] Congress enacted this requirement in 1972 as part of the

Federal Election Campaign Act. The purpose of the legislation was "to ensure candidates for Federal elective office adequate opportunity to present and discuss their candidacies and hence provide the voters with information necessary for the responsible exercise of their franchise."[3]

In order to invoke the reasonable-access requirement, a person must be a legally qualified candidate for either nomination or election to a federal office (that is, United States President, Vice President, senator, representative, and resident commissioner or delegate to Congress). The term "legally qualified candidate" is extensively defined in connection with the equal-time rule, and that definition applies in the present context as well.[4] The reasonable-access requirement applies to both commercial and noncommercial radio and television stations. It covers cable television systems that have facilities for originating their own programming (via so-called origination cablecasts).[5]

Congress set no definite standards for measuring how much air time fulfills the goal of reasonable access. The FCC follows a policy of allowing broadcasters considerable discretion in determining the amount and scheduling of time to be afforded federal candidates.

> Congress clearly did not intend, to take the extreme case, that during the closing days of a campaign stations should be required to accommodate requests for political time to the exclusion of all or most other types of programing or advertising. Important as an informed electorate is in our society, there are other elements in the public interest standard, and the public is entitled to other kinds of programing than political.[6]

What the commission looks for when reviewing a broadcaster's judgments is a reasonable good-faith effort "to accommodate both the right of Federal candidates to fully inform the voters of their candidacies and the interest of the public in programming other than political broadcasts."[7]

In general, a broadcaster can satisfy the reasonable-access requirement either by giving reasonable amounts of free time to federal candidates or by allowing them to purchase reasonable amounts of time. The broadcaster does not have to do both — that is, give free time and sell time as well.[8]

Federal candidates are entitled to buy or receive program-length periods of time — instead of just spot time (for example, sixty-second announcements). During Nevada's 1972 primaries, Walter Baring was running for the Democratic nomination to the state's at-large congressional seat.[9] He sought to purchase five-minute segments for political broadcasts over KLAS-TV (Las Vegas). The station responded that, as a matter of general policy, periods exceeding sixty seconds in length were available for political broadcasts only between the hours of 1:30 A.M. and 6 A.M. Baring complained to the FCC.

The commission concluded that KLAS-TV's policy limited virtually all effective political broadcasting to sixty-second spot announcements.

> A policy of refusing to sell time for campaign messages exceeding sixty seconds in length, except between the hours of 1:30 A.M. and 6:00 A.M., necessarily limits . . . candidates to one-minute spot announcements in the time periods during which a significant audience would be listening or viewing and allows them to more fully present and discuss their candidacies only during the hours when the vast majority of the potential voting audience is asleep.

By allowing candidates, in effect, only sixty-second segments in which to explain their views to the vast majority of voters, KLAS-TV had not fulfilled its obligation to afford reasonable access.

The commission noted the absence of any "countervailing circumstances," which might have justified KLAS-TV's policy. For instance, the station had not provided any free program time to federal candidates. Nor was there such a "multiplicity of candidates" that filling requests like Baring's would have seriously disrupted the station's overall scheduling. (In the Nevada primary, there were only eight candidates.) Had there been some countervailing circumstances, KLAS-TV's restrictive policy might not have been considered unreasonable.

The KLAS-TV case establishes the right of a federal candidate — in the absence of any countervailing circumstances — to purchase or otherwise receive program-length periods of air time. If countervailing circumstances do exist, then time for spot announcements should be made available. Some of this time — whether for spots or program-length presentations — must fall within desirable periods of the broadcast day. A broadcaster cannot pursue a rigid policy of refusing to sell or give time during peak audience periods (that is, "prime time" on television, "drive time" on radio). Such a blanket refusal would be inconsistent with the congressional purpose of affording federal candidates greater access to mass audiences.[10]

In 1974 the commission upheld the refusal of a group of broadcasters to honor a federal candidate's request for several consecutive hours of program time.[11] Peter Flaherty, the mayor of Pittsburgh, was the 1974 Democratic candidate for United States senator from Pennsylvania. In July, 1974, he asked fifteen Pennsylvania television stations to sell him time for a statewide telethon on behalf of his candidacy. The telethon was to run for four and a half hours, from 10 P.M. Saturday, September 28, to 3 A.M. on Sunday, September 29. (A half-hour would be relinquished from this time block at 11 P.M. for evening newscasts.) Five of the stations were willing to grant Flaherty's request. The other ten, however, offered more limited programming periods: some agreed to a half-hour, for instance; others, an hour.

Flaherty complained to the FCC that the ten stations had violated his right to reasonable access. The commission disagreed. It pointed out that "reasonable access" was not an absolute term, but one which broadcasters have considerable leeway in administering.

> While [we have] recognized the right of access by Federal candidates to prime time program-length time, on either a free or paid basis, we have refrained from prescribing any precise formula for measuring licensee performance in honoring that right so as not to interfere unnecessarily with licensee scheduling and program discretion. Thus, although we recognized a right of access to prime time programming,

we declined to recognize any right, by a Federal candidate, to program time of any particular or minimum duration. Nor did we recognize any right, by a Federal candidate, to have his programming or announcements given any particular placement — in terms of a specific date and/or specific time — during prime time, or during any other portion of the broadcast day. . . . To have adopted a different position, we believe would have made the task of scheduling programs by licensees very difficult. . . .

The commission refused to substitute its judgment for that of the ten Pennsylvania broadcasters.

The facts presently before us indicate that each of the licensees . . . stood ready to provide Mr. Flaherty with access to prime time programming, notwithstanding the fact that each of them failed to honor fully his request for a 4½-hour block of time on a specified date at a specified time. Furthermore, the amount of program time which each station was willing to afford the complainant in prime time was not so insignificant as to warrant our conclusion that any particular licensee had been unreasonable in its actions.

Clearly, there were countervailing circumstances, which helped to justify the broadcasters' decisions.

In general, the FCC will not interfere with the scheduling of political programs and spot announcements under the reasonable-access requirement. Placement and scheduling are regarded as judgmental areas in which broadcasters should exercise sound journalistic discretion.

To head off any possible misunderstandings or confrontations, federal candidates should meet with broadcasters early in the campaign. The FCC encourages candidate-broadcaster negotiations and cooperation:

We are aware of the fact that a myriad of situations can arise that will present difficult problems. One conceivable method of trying to act reasonably and in good faith might be for licensees, prior to an election campaign for Federal offices, to meet with candidates in an effort to work out the problem of reasonable access for them on their stations. Such conferences might cover, among other things . . . the amount of time that the station proposes to sell or give candidates, the amount and type of its other programming . . . and the amount of time it proposes to sell commercial advertisers.[12]

The FCC will consider individual complaints from candidates who believe a broadcaster is not acting reasonably or negotiating in good faith.

A final word about reasonable access is in order: Reasonable access is not the same thing as equal time. If a federal candidate buys or receives air time under the reasonable-access requirement, his "use" of the station will trigger the equal-time rule.[13] As a result, his opponent will be entitled to equal time, and equal time ought to be requested — not reasonable access. The equal-time rule not only provides the proper legal remedy, but it also tends to produce results in an automatic manner, while the reasonable-access requirement leaves more room for licensee discretion. Invoking the reasonable-access requirement is useful in gaining air time in situations where the equal-time rule has not yet been triggered.

Candidates for State and Local Office

Candidates for state and local office do not enjoy a right of access similar to that accorded federal office-seekers. A broadcaster has wide discretion in deciding how much time, if any, to provide individual candidates. In general, a broadcaster must plan his political coverage to meet the needs and interests of his community.

It is . . . the licensee's responsibility to make a good faith judgment as to what those needs are and how they can be best met, and specifically whether any particular political race warrants coverage in view of other contests and other pertinent programming considerations. . . . It would . . . be inconsistent with the public interest if the station, irrespective of the needs and interests of its community . . . , refused to give time to a political contest because of a general policy of never making its facilities available for political broadcasts. . . .[14]

Thus, the broadcaster must make individual determinations regarding particular races. Before allocating air time to any given race, or declining to do so, the broadcaster must decide what is the degree of public interest in this particular race. He cannot simply adopt a blanket policy, which arbitrarily ignores important differences between races.[15]

If a broadcaster decides a particular race is of limited importance, he can decline to give or sell time to candidates in that race. For example, a station might present programs on and sell time to candidates in major statewide races (for example, governor, attorney general) but afford no program time and only minimal news coverage to candidates for minor local offices (for example, district judgeships). Unless it could be proven that the broadcaster's assessment was unreasonable, the FCC would not question it.[16]

Another factor that may legitimately enter into the broadcaster's determination is the effect of political broadcasts on the rest of the program schedule. This factor will increase in importance if there are a large number of races within the broadcaster's service area. The broadcaster may not be able to accommodate requests for air time from candidates in every race without seriously disrupting his overall programming.[17] Not the least of the broadcaster's concerns in scheduling political broadcasts is planning ahead so as to have enough leeway to accommodate later requests for equal time for opposing candidates.

Assuming a broadcaster decides to sell time for political broadcasts, he has wide control over the variety and placement of the segments he will sell. He may, for instance, limit the period of the broadcast day during which he will sell time for political commercials (for example, from 6 to 10 P.M.); he may sell only short spot announcements (sixty seconds or less); or he may reject spots altogether (on the ground they do little to enlighten the voters) and accept only program-length presentations (for example, five minutes, a half-hour). Any one of these decisions might be entirely legitimate, so long as the broadcaster acts reasonably and in good faith.[18]

During a 1972 primary in Wisconsin, WITI-TV (Milwaukee) pursued a policy of selling candidates only spot announcements or half-hour segments during prime-time evening hours.[19] One candidate complained to the FCC that WITI-TV would not allow him to purchase a fifteen-minute segment during prime time. The commission rejected this complaint and upheld the station's policy.

> Neither the Communications Act nor the Commission's rules contain any provision requiring a licensee to sell specific periods of time for political broadcasts. . . .
> To adopt a different position would, we believe, make extremely difficult the task of scheduling programs. Here, the licensee has notified the various candidates of its policy to sell either 30-minute periods or spot announcements in prime time. Other candidates have purchased 30 minutes of time in conformity with this policy. Should the licensee now be required to cancel regular 30-minute programs in order to afford a particular candidate only 5, 10, 15, or 20 minutes within such periods, all other candidates would be entitled to the same treatment [under the equal-time rule], and might very well avail themselves of it with the result that the night-time programming of the station would . . . be fractionalized.
> We recognize that television prime time is normally divided into program periods of not less than 30 minutes in length, and we do not believe that the licensee's policy of refusing to sell prime time in shorter segments — with the alternative of buying spot announcements — is unreasonable in the circumstances of this case.
> In view of the licensee's offer of both half-hour programs and spot announcements to all candidates and its coverage of the campaign in its news broadcasts and other programming such as [a ninety-minute prime-time] documentary, it does not appear that the licensee has failed to comply with . . . its public interest responsibilities concerning political broadcasts. . . .

Political Parties

In general, a broadcaster is not obliged to give or sell air time to a political party. The FCC has ruled that a party has no right to air time in order to express its views on public issues. Instead, the broadcaster can exercise his journalistic discretion in determining whether and when party spokesmen should present their positions to the public.[20]

In certain circumstances, however, a political party may be entitled to air time. In 1970 the FCC ruled that broadcasters could not arbitrarily refuse air time to major political parties wishing to solicit funds from the public: "political parties are an integral part of our democratic process and . . . it serves the public interest to promote the widest possible support by citizens of the party of their choice."[21] A broadcaster has considerable discretion in deciding how these fund solicitations should be presented. He may sell time to the party or give it free of charge. The time may be in the form of spot announcements (for example, thirty or sixty seconds) or program-length periods (five minutes, a half-hour). All such matters of length and scheduling are largely up to the broadcaster, as long as he acts reasonably and in good faith. It would be arbitrary, for instance, if a broadcaster adopted a policy of allowing fund solicitations only during election periods, "since the need for the widest possible financial support for political parties is not confined to such periods. . . ."[22]

A political party may also gain a right to air time under the FCC's *political party doctrine*. This doctrine loosely parallels the equal-time rule and complements its operation. As we shall see, the equal-time rule applies only to candidates, not political parties: a candidate must appear in person before the rule will be triggered. If, instead, a campaign message is broadcast by one of the candidate's spokesmen or supporters — for example, the chairman of his political party, a public official elected from his party, or his campaign manager — the equal-time rule will not be triggered. An opposing candidate will have no right to equal time despite the obvious impact of the partisan campaign broadcast. In order to offset such an imbalance caused by the limited scope of the equal-time rule, the commission developed its political party doctrine.

The doctrine was formally enunciated in the FCC's 1970 *Zapple* decision.[23] In essence, the doctrine holds that:

(1) when, during a political campaign for elective public office,
(2) a broadcaster sells air time

(3) to a candidate's spokesmen or supporters,

(4) who use that time to discuss issues in the campaign, urge the candidate's election, criticize the candidate's opponent, or criticize positions taken on campaign issues by the candidate's opponent,

(5) then the spokesmen or supporters of the candidate's opponent

(6) are entitled to purchase comparable air time for a reply broadcast.

Notice that the doctrine does not require free reply time if the original broadcast was paid for. "When spokesmen or supporters of candidate A have purchased time," the commission reasoned in *Zapple,*

> it is our view that it would be inappropriate to require licensees to in effect subsidize the campaign of an opposing candidate by providing candidate B's spokesmen or supporters with free time (e.g., the chairman of the national committee of a major political party purchases time to urge the election of his candidate, and his counterpart then requests free time for a program on behalf of his candidate).

All *Zapple* says is that candidate B's supporters must be sold comparable time if they wish to buy it. Free reply time is available only when the original time was given without charge.[24]

Under *Zapple,* political parties are entitled to "comparable" opportunities for air time to present their views during a campaign.

> If the DNC [Democratic National Committee] were sold time for a number of spots, it is difficult to conceive on what basis the licensee could then refuse to sell comparable time to the RNC [Republican National Committee]. Or, if during a campaign the latter were given a half-hour of free time to advance its cause, could a licensee fairly reject a subsequent request of the DNC that it be given a comparable opportunity? Clearly, these examples deal with exaggerated, hypothetical situations that would never arise. No licensee would try to act in such an arbitrary fashion.[25]

Presumably, a comparable opportunity would be roughly the same as the original one in terms of total amount of time, scheduling, and frequency of repetition.[26]

For all practical purposes, the political party doctrine operates only during campaign periods. By its very nature, the doctrine is triggered when candidates and campaign issues are discussed. However, the doctrine might be extended to certain non–campaign period broadcasts.[27] Suppose a political party broadcasts a fund-solicitation program following a particularly expensive campaign. Such solicitations are subject to the political party doctrine, so the major opposing party would be entitled to a comparable opportunity to solicit funds.[28]

The political party doctrine is not triggered by discussions broadcast during news programs — that is, newscasts, news interviews, documentaries, and on-the-spot news coverage. (These programming categories are the same ones exempted from coverage under the equal-time rule.) Suppose during a gubernatorial race, the state's Republican Party chairman is interviewed on a regular newscast. He praises the accomplishments of the incumbent Republican governor, who is running for reelection, and criticizes the Democratic challenger's lack of experience. Supporters of the challenger will not acquire any rights to air time under the political party doctrine, because the chairman's remarks were made during an exempt newscast. (The station would, however, be obliged to afford balanced overall news coverage to the gubernatorial race under the general fairness doctrine.)[29]

Not all parties can take advantage of the political party doctrine. The FCC has indicated the doctrine is intended to facilitate responses by the major political parties. So-called fringe parties are excluded. They have no automatic right to the opportunities assured major parties. Instead, a broadcaster is called upon to make a reasonable good-faith judgment regarding the significance of a fringe party within the station's service area. If he decides there is sufficient public interest in hearing the fringe party's views, he can afford it reply time — although not necessarily comparable to the opportunity given a major political party.[30]

4
Equal Time for Political Candidates

General Principles

The equal-time rule covers broadcast appearances made by candidates for public office. Outside this narrow range of programming in which a candidate is either seen or heard, the rule has no effect. All radio and television stations — commercial and noncommercial — must abide by the equal-time rule. It also applies to candidate appearances that originate at and are carried over cable television systems (that is, so-called origination cablecasts).[1]

The equal-time rule is actually a complex of different rules, all of which operate under the rubric of equal time. Ironically, the widely used catchphrase "equal time" does not appear in the Federal Communications Act or the FCC's regulations. Legally speaking, "equal time" is a misnomer. What the law actually promises candidates is not "equal time" but "equal opportunities." In section 315 of the Federal Communications Act, Congress declared: "If any licensee shall permit any person who is a legally qualified candidate for any public office to use a broadcasting station, he shall afford equal opportunities to all other such candidates for that office in the use of such broadcasting station."[2] This legal formula is the heart of the so-called equal-time rule. Before we examine the rule and its corollaries, some general observations are in order.

Notice the broad scope of the rule. It applies to candidates for any public office. The office may be on a municipal, county, state, or national level, but there must be, at a minimum, some public office for which the candidate is running. If there is none, the candidate will fall outside the scope of the rule. For instance, the position of delegate to a national political convention is not a public office. Thus, a candidate running for a place on a slate of delegates is not covered by the equal-time rule.[3]

The rule extends to candidates in general elections, as well as special elections, primaries, and nominations by recognized parties. Not every political selection process qualifies as an election under the equal-time rule. In 1968 when Spiro T. Agnew resigned as governor of Maryland to become Vice President of the United States, the Maryland General Assembly had to elect his successor. During the course of this so-called election, one gubernatorial hopeful requested equal time from Baltimore's WBAL-TV. The FCC ruled that according to Maryland law the impending legislative action was not an election; therefore, the equal-time rule had no application.[4]

The equal-time rule remains legally inoperative until it is triggered by a candidate's "use" of a broadcasting station. Without such a use, the broadcaster has no equal-time obligations; he is not required to seek out candidates and give them air time or offer it for sale.[5] All the equal-time rule says is, *if* the broadcaster *does* let one candidate use his station, then he must afford equal opportunities to opposing candidates. But if that first candidate never uses the station, the broadcaster's programming will remain totally unaffected by the equal-time rule.

An obvious question arises: can a broadcaster avoid equal time altogether by arbitrarily refusing air time to any candidate? The answer is no. The reason does not lie in the equal-time rule itself, but in the broadcaster's duty to satisfy the political programming needs in his service area. Before the equal-time rule is ever triggered, a broadcaster is obliged to exercise reasonable judgment in deciding how much air time he will allocate for use by candidates. (Chapter 3 explains political programming responsibilities more fully.)

We now have a general perspective on the equal-time rule. It remains for us to follow the operation of the rule in detail. Since the rule has many corollaries and exceptions, an overall checklist will be helpful at this point to focus our further inquiry. Basically, there are five questions that must be answered in any equal-time situation:

(1) *Has there been some use of a broadcast station by a legally qualified candidate?* This question lies at the threshold. Unless it can be answered in the affirmative, there is no true equal-time situation, and the rule will remain inoperative. Two subquestions are prompted by the legal terms "use" and "legally qualified candidate": namely, *what constitutes the use of a station?* and *who is a legally qualified candidate?*

(2) *Who is entitled to equal time?* Here again the concept of the "legally qualified candidate" is pivotal. Only a legally qualified candidate running for the same public office as the candidate who uses the station has a right to equal time. We will discover that it is not always easy to determine whether two candidates are actually opponents for the same office.

(3) *Has a timely request for equal time been made?* The right to equal time may be lost if a request is not made before the legal deadline.

(4) *How is equal time measured?* For instance, how long should it be? When should it be scheduled? How much, if anything, should it cost? What studio facilities ought to be available? Subquestions like these suggest the multifaceted contours of equal time.

(5) *What controls may a broadcaster exert over the administration of the equal-time rule?* We have already seen that a broadcaster has some discretion as to when his station may be used in a way that triggers the equal-time rule. Under proper circumstances, he can also arrange for a candidate to "waive" — that is, forgo —

his right to equal time. However, the broadcaster has absolutely no power of censorship over programming covered by the equal-time rule.

Broadcasts Subject to Equal Time

To trigger the equal-time rule, there must be some *use* of a broadcast station by a candidate. What is a use? The FCC interprets this term broadly: "The word 'use' is synonymous with 'appearance' and . . . is essentially the same as the word 'exposure.' These words seem to import a meaning of showing publicly or offering to the public view or ear."[6] At a minimum, a candidate must be either seen or heard over a broadcast station.

It is not enough that a press release issued by a candidate is read over the air by some station announcer. In such a broadcast, the candidate is not seen or heard; no appearance, or use, occurs. On the other hand, suppose a candidate records an audio tape in which he discusses his role in a regional flood control project. He sends the tape to a local radio station, which broadcasts it. Now the candidate's own voice is heard over the air. There has clearly been a use of the station.[7]

In the case of television, the candidate's visual presence on the screen is a use, regardless of whether his voice is also heard. Consider three common television shots of candidates. (1) The camera pans a group of candidates seated in the studio while a noncandidate, who is off-camera, reads a political spot announcement. (2) A silent film of a candidate is shown while a noncandidate reads a spot off-camera. (3) A photograph of a candidate appears on the screen while a noncandidate reads a spot off-camera. In all of these shots, there is a use of the station, because the candidate is seen. The fact that a noncandidate is heard as the voiceover makes no difference.[8]

The candidate must be identifiable when he appears on television or radio. Only if the candidate's image or voice is identifiable will there be a use. A key distinction must be made, however, between being *identifiable* and being *identified*. Even if a candidate is not specifically identified on the air, there can still be a use if he is identifiable to the viewer or listener.

For example, Senator Jones visits a state college campus to film commercials for his upcoming reelection campaign. He is filmed conversing with a group of student supporters. In the actual finished commercial, the audio portion is an off-screen narration, so none of the students is heard. Nor are any of them identified by, for example, the narrator or a caption flashed on screen. Later on, after the film clip is already running on television as part of Senator Jones's campaign, one of the students seen in the film becomes a legally qualified candidate for public office. Are the student's opponents entitled to equal time based upon his appearance in Senator Jones's commercial?

The answer is yes if the student-candidate is visually *identifiable*, even though he is not specifically *identified* as, say, Senator Jones is.[9] "Local candidates frequently appear," the FCC has declared,

> at rallies or on other occasions with supporters or major candidates of the same party. The presentation by one candidate, A, in his campaign of film clips showing A's appearance with supporter[s] or colleagues, B and C, obviously can redound to B's and C's benefit, if they should campaign for local office in the area. . . . [A] political party could present on behalf of candidate A (who is identified) a paid broadcast consisting of film clips where A appears with his party colleagues, B and C, local candidates who are well known in the area but not identified by name in the film. In such circumstances, the opponents of B and C . . . should be able to purchase comparable time if the "equal opportunities" requirement . . . is to be maintained.[10]

Inevitably, close questions arise as to whether a candidate is, in fact, identifiable. In 1970 the National Urban Coalition sponsored a public-service spot on television.[11] It consisted of a 118-second film featuring a group of about 120 people, many of whom were leading personalities drawn from politics, sports, and entertainment. The group was seen and heard singing together the song "Let the Sun Shine In." No member of the group was identified by name; nor was his voice separately audible. Former Supreme Court Justice Arthur Goldberg, one of the 120 singers, was visible in two video shots: (1) for approximately 4.2 seconds in a long-range group shot of about a hundred; and (2) for approximately 2.8 seconds in a medium-range shot of about six people in which only the lower half of his face was visible.

At the time the film was to be shown — although, ironically, not at the time it had been made — Goldberg was a candidate for the Democratic nomination for governor of New York. The Urban Coalition asked the FCC whether either or both of the shots of Goldberg would require a station to afford equal time. The commission said no.

> With respect to video shot number 1, we note that the duration of the shot was too fleeting and the camera range too distant for Mr. Goldberg to be readily identified in a group of approximately 100 persons. Concerning shot number 2, we note that the camera angle caught only a partial view of Mr. Goldberg's face for a fleeting moment so he is not readily identifiable.

The criterion seems to be, then, whether or not a candidate is readily identifiable to the general public, rather than identifiable to some sophisticated observer, who knows precisely what to watch for.

The same criterion applies to voice identification. It is not infrequent that broadcast personalities or newsmen become candidates and, while campaigning, keep working at their stations. If such a candidate continues on as an unidentified radio announcer or an unidentified off-camera television announcer, the question is whether his voice is readily identifiable by listeners. If so, then the commercials, weather reports, newscasts, announcements, program "intros" and "exits," and so on, read by the announcer-candidate are uses subject to equal time. This often subtle determination is initially up to the reasonable good-faith judgment of the licensee who employs the candidate. Some of the variables the licensee should consider include how many years the candidate has been on the air, how long he was on each day, whether he used to be identified by name, whether he has been on the air right up to the time of his candidacy, or whether there was an interval preceding his candidacy when he was off the air, whether the candidate's on-the-air activities are being curtailed at all during his candidacy. These factors should indicate whether the candidate's voice "remains 'identified' to a substantial degree because of the particular circumstances."[12]

In general, every appearance on radio or television, no matter how brief or perfunctory, constitutes a use. There is, however, an old legal maxim, *de minimis non curat lex* (the law does not take notice of trifles). And this *de minimis* principle has its application to the equal-time rule. Remember how the FCC characterized Arthur Goldberg's appearances as "too fleeting." Such appearances — of, say, a fraction of a second to a few seconds — succumb to the *de minimis* principle. They are simply too negligible, too insubstantial, to be considered uses. Beyond a few seconds, though, the *de minimis* principle affords no escape from the equal-time rule. An appearance of even eight seconds is considered to be a use. "As is well known," the FCC has observed, "an 8-second period can constitute an effective commercial message and is, in fact, employed in political campaigns."[13]

The equal-time rule does not distinguish between a candidate's political and nonpolitical appearances. Both are uses of a station. There are no exceptions for so-called public-service or educational or entertainment appearances. A use occurs whether the President kicks off a Community Chest campaign, a senator broadcasts a weekly report to his constituents, a mayoral candidate lectures on local government, a candidate for borough council emcees a television dance party, a businessman-candidate does television commercials for his automobile dealership, or a Baptist minister, running for Congress, officiates at religious services that are broadcast weekly.[14] No broadcaster has the authority to evaluate the political utility of a candidate's appearance as a basis for granting or denying requests for equal time. As harsh as it may seem to some, if an actor-turned-candidate, while campaigning, rides off into the sunset on a "Late Show" revival of one of his westerns, the candidate's opponents will be entitled to equal time.[15]

Broadcasts Exempt from Equal Time

IN GENERAL. We know that any broadcast appearance by a candidate is ordinarily a "use" requiring equal time. There are, however, some important exceptions. In 1959 Congress exempted four categories of news coverage from the equal-time rule.

> Appearance by a legally qualified candidate on any —
> (1) bona fide newscast,
> (2) bona fide news interview,
> (3) bona fide news documentary (if the appearance of the candidate is incidental to the presentation of the subject or subjects covered by the news documentary), or
> (4) on-the-spot coverage of bona fide news events (including but not limited to political conventions and activities incidental thereto), shall not be deemed to be use of a broadcasting station. . . .[16]

Since there is no use of a station, the equal-time rule is not triggered; therefore, opponents of a candidate who makes an exempt appearance gain no right to air time.

Congress repeated one key phrase, *bona fide,* in each of the four exempt categories. The intent behind this phrase was to prevent political favoritism by broadcasters. "To state a rather extreme case," commented Congressman Oren Harris on the House floor in 1959, "the exemption . . . would not apply where the program, although it might be contrived to have the appearance or give the impression of being a newscast, news interview, or on-the-spot coverage of news events, is not presented as such by the broadcaster or network in good faith, but in reality has for its purpose the promotion of the political fortunes of the candidate making an appearance thereon."[17] A news program that is not bona fide constitutes a use of the station. The program is in no way illegal and may be aired freely, but equal time will be required.

The bona fide standard aims at testing a broadcaster's motives.

Any test of motivation can, of course, be highly subjective. Not surprisingly, the FCC resorts to certain objective criteria in order to assess a broadcaster's good faith: for example, what is the format, nature, and content of the program under scrutiny? Has the format, nature, or content changed since the program's inception? When was the program initiated? Who initiated it? Who produces and controls the program? Is the program regularly scheduled? If so, at what time and day of the week is it broadcast?[18]

While this list is not exclusive, it does reveal the general drift of the commission's inquiry. Answers to these questions are likely to indicate two things: the impact a program may have upon political fortunes because of its prominence and the degree to which the program has undergone any adaptation or special preparation for a particular political event or candidate. A program may appear to weigh so heavily in one candidate's favor that the counterweight of equal time seems advisable — at least, in the commission's judgment. In such a case, the program will be deemed a use of broadcast facilities rather than bona fide news coverage.

What we have, in effect, is a balancing test. On the one hand is the interest of broadcasters in journalistic freedom; on the other is the candidates' interest in evenhanded coverage by the media.[19] As arbiter of so-called bona fide news coverage, the FCC can keep its thumb on the scale that supposedly balances broadcasters with candidates. The commission has stated: "We fully recognize that the 1959 amendments were designed by Congress to be remedial in nature and to permit broadcast licensees to carry out more effectively their journalistic role. Further, we do not believe that the exemptions should be so narrowly construed as to stifle innovative news presentations."[20] Nonetheless, equal time remains the general rule, and the four news exemptions are administered as discrete exceptions to that rule. Each exemption has, as we shall see, its own set of qualifications; these must be satisfied if a candidate's appearance is to escape its normal status as a use requiring equal time.

A final admonition is in order: exempt news coverage of candidates, while immune from the strictures of equal time, is not free of all regulation. When Congress enacted the exemptions, it also added a clear proviso:

> Nothing [in the four news exemptions] shall be construed as relieving broadcasters, in connection with the presentation of newscasts, news interviews, news documentaries, and on-the-spot coverage of news events, from the obligation imposed upon them under [the Federal Communications Act] to operate in the public interest and *to afford reasonable opportunity for the discussion of conflicting views on issues of public importance.*[21]

This proviso is a congressional affirmation of the FCC's fairness doctrine, which requires balanced programming on controversial public issues. An election generally raises a controversial issue: namely, who should be elected? If one candidate has the opportunity to express his view on this issue during a news program, a reasonable opportunity should be provided for conflicting views. Thus, the fairness doctrine acts as a regulatory backstop when the equal-time rule is rendered inoperative (see pages 162–168).

NEWSCASTS. The "bona fide newscast" is the first class of program on which a candidate may appear without triggering the equal-time rule. In general, any newscast coverage featuring a candidate falls within the exemption. There are exceptions, however. When Congress enacted this exemption, it was concerned about the potential for political favoritism. Congress intended to withhold the exemption from so-called news stories that fulfilled no legitimate journalistic purpose and served only to enhance a candidate's image: "The appearance of the candidate must have been decided upon by the broadcaster for the purpose of aiding bona fide news coverage rather than for the purpose of advancing the political fortunes of the candidate."[22] It is possible, therefore, that certain promotional "puffs" passed off as news stories may not escape the equal-time rule, even though they are presented during a bona fide newscast.

In practice, the FCC will not second-guess a broadcaster's news judgments. It is well known that candidates frequently thrust themselves into dramatic settings, or strike out boldly against opponents, in a calculated attempt to attract media attention. However, a broadcaster enjoys wide journalistic discretion in deciding which candidate activities are newsworthy and deserve coverage on newscasts.[23] The broadcaster should at least bear in mind Congress's admonition: "The length of time of the candidate's appearance must not be disproportionate considering the length of the newscast and the significance of the event."[24] If a candidate's appearance is disproportionately long, it might conceivably lose an otherwise exempt status.

Certain news stories are permeated by such a high degree of candidate control — as opposed to journalist control — that they fall short of the requirements for exemption. Anxious to be seen or heard on newscasts, candidates sometimes record their own words and activities on film or audio tape. The film is then sent to television news departments — the tape to radio news departments — with the hope it will be run as "news" during a regular newscast. There is no doubt that such "canned news," if broadcast outside a bona fide newscast, would constitute a use of the station and trigger the equal-time rule. Can an obviously nonexempt broadcast attain exempt status merely by being included in an exempt program — like a bona fide newscast? The FCC says no: "To hold otherwise would be inconsistent with the legislative intent and would result in a subordination of substance to form."[25] Therefore, a candidate whose opponent is seen or heard in a canned news story is entitled to equal time.

(Lest there be any doubt, the exemption is not lost when printed press releases, supplied by a candidate, are either read or commented upon by a newscaster. The reason is already known to us: since the candidate, himself, is neither seen nor heard during the newscaster's reading of the press release, there is no use of the station; hence, the equal-time rule remains inoperative, and the question of exemption never arises.)

Can newsworthy excerpts from an ordinary nonexempt program be aired during a bona fide newscast without triggering the equal-time rule? In general, the answer is no. For example, a congressman's "Report to the People," broadcast weekly as a public service, constitutes a use of the station. If excerpts from that program are run during a newscast, they will also trigger the equal-time rule.[26]

This result may not always hold true, however. Certain excerpts may be exempt when run in a newscast, even though the program from which the excerpts came would not be exempt. We will learn shortly that candidates' debates and press conferences can be broadcast under the exemption for on-the-spot coverage of bona fide news events. To qualify for this exemption, the debate or press conference must be carried live and in its entirety. If only portions of the event are aired, or if it is taped and shown on a delayed basis, there will be no on-the-spot exemption. There could, however, be an exemption for excerpts from a debate or press conference carried as news stories on a bona fide newscast.[27]

NEWS INTERVIEWS. The "bona fide news interview" is the second class of program on which a candidate may appear without triggering the equal-time rule. In general, such a program explores the news through questions put to a newsworthy guest. Familiar examples of the bona fide news interview are ABC's "Issues and Answers," CBS's "Face the Nation," and NBC's "Meet the Press."

News interviews should not be confused with talk shows; the latter, designed chiefly to entertain, do not come within the present exemption. Sometimes close distinctions must be made in order to determine whether a program is basically a news interview or a talk show.

In 1973 the FCC had to decide if the "Lou Gordon Program" over WKBD-TV (Detroit) was essentially a news interview show.[28] "The first segment of the show," explained the commission,

> consists of a question and answer period. Mrs. Gordon asks her husband selected questions submitted by viewers previous to the taping of the show. The second segment consists of interviews between Mr. Gordon and one or more guests. The guests include government officials, newsmakers, sport celebrities, entertainers, authors and other categories of guests. Mr. Gordon uses both segments to present his personal opinions upon the subjects being discussed.

The commission characterized this format as a "melange." Within the melange, however, the entertainment ingredient struck the commission strongly. Lou Gordon's guests in the years 1972–1973 had included George Blanda (football player), Sidney Poitier (actor), Sybil Leek (self-styled witch), Irving Wallace (author), Xaviera Hollander (prostitute-turned-author), Rudy Vallée (entertainer), Graham Kerr (chef), Maharishi Mahesh Yogi (guru), Tempest Storm (burlesque queen), Barbara Howar (author), and Dick the Bruiser (wrestler).

The commission concluded that the "Lou Gordon Program" was not the type Congress intended to exempt, since "it does not deal solely, or even predominantly with news matters. The fact that the moderator continuously interjects his own personal opinions additionally takes it out of the category of 'Meet the Press' or 'Face the Nation.' " Other talk shows the FCC has excluded from the interview exemption include NBC's "Tonight" show and the "Barry Gray Show" over WMCA radio in New York City.[29]

Assuming a program is a news interview rather than a talk show, it must fulfill three requirements in order to qualify as "bona fide" in the judgment of the FCC. First, it must be regularly scheduled. Second, its content and format must be determined, and its participants selected, by the broadcaster — not the candidate. Third, the broadcaster's decisions should be made in the exercise of good faith news judgment: that is, without political favoritism.[30]

What is a regularly scheduled program? In general, it is one broadcast at uniform intervals (for example, daily or weekly) for a fixed amount of time (for example, one half-hour). However, so-called regular scheduling should not be regarded as a straitjacket on licensee discretion. The FCC has, over the years, recognized that broadcasters must be allowed to exercise their editorial judgment regarding changes in scheduling. Therefore, occasionally lengthening a news interview or moving it to a different time slot will not affect the program's exempt status.[31]

Consider a 1973 ruling on the "People in the News" segment of the "Sunday" show on WNBC-TV (New York City).[32] "Sunday" was initiated to create a two-hour "magazine format," within which a number of different program features could be presented. One of these was "People in the News." It carried on the news interview functions of several prior WNBC-TV programs, including "Newslight," "Man in Office," "Open Circuit," and "Direct Line." Since the format surrounding "People in the News" allowed flexibility, that particular segment frequently varied in its own scheduling. WNBC-TV admitted to the commission, "The 'People in the News' interviews on any particular Sunday can be and have been extended to any appropriate length from several minutes to one hour, and may present any number of interviewees either in joint appearance or separately in individual segments."

Despite these irregularities, the FCC decided that the "People in the News" segment was a regularly scheduled news interview:

> The Commission has held that changes in program length or time periods in and of themselves do not justify the conclusion that such programs are not regularly scheduled news interviews. . . . Thus, the question here is whether the evolving of the four bona fide news interview programs ("Newslight," "Man in Office," "Open Circuit," and "Direct Line") into "People in the News" and presenting it as a segment of the "Sunday" program can be considered such a change that the program would not be an exempt interview. We do not believe that the changes are such as to remove the exemption. The format and content of "People in the News" does not appear to differ substantially from its predecessor programs.

Clearly the commission is willing to afford broadcasters reasonable leeway in meeting the standard of regular scheduling.

Beyond a certain point, however, irregularities in scheduling have not met with the commission's favor. In 1964 the question arose whether press conferences called by candidates could be considered regularly scheduled news interviews.[33] The press conferences at issue happened to be those of President Johnson, held while he was running for reelection, as well as those of his Republican opponent, Senator Barry Goldwater. At least one of the commissioners believed that the conferences should be exempt, based upon a broad interpretation of regular scheduling:

> It seems most reasonable to construe "regularly scheduled" as meaning "recurrent in the normal and usual course of events" rather than as "recurrent at fixed and uniform

time intervals." . . . There is not, and cannot be, any question that Presidential news conferences have been held over many years, are recurrent in the normal and usual course of events, and are regular in every meaning of the term except the most narrow.

The majority of the commission, however, clung to a narrow view of "regularly scheduled":

It is no answer, we think, to state that [presidential press] conferences are called at some time, even if not at definite intervals. So also are press conferences called at some time by all major candidates for important office during political campaigns; yet there is not the slightest reference or implication in the lengthy Congressional consideration of the subject that such press conferences were to be considered "regularly scheduled news interviews." . . . Congress clearly knew how to exempt as a news interview such an important and significant aspect of a political campaign — the candidate's press conference — had it intended to do so.

While a candidate's press conference is not a regularly scheduled news interview, it may be exempted on other grounds. As we shall shortly see, a live broadcast of a candidate's press conference can qualify as on-the-spot coverage of a bona fide news event.

Not surprisingly, the FCC has refused to exempt the one-shot interview, sometimes billed as a "special news interview." Say a candidate makes a campaign stop in Buffalo, and a local broadcaster astutely sets up a half-hour interview. The program is special in the sense that it is unprecedented — not a regular edition of any established series. Such a one-shot interview will fall short of the FCC's standard for regular scheduling.[34]

Can an interview series be considered as regularly scheduled before it has even premiered? In 1972 the commission answered no but seemed to leave the door ajar for future exceptions.[35] Pittsburgh's WIIC-TV was about to launch a series called "Know Your Congressman." Each biweekly broadcast would feature two of the five Pittsburgh-area congressmen. Despite WIIC-TV's plans, the commission declined to exempt the series prospectively, noting that rulings of exemption had traditionally been limited to programs broadcast "over a substantial period of time in the past." (By a "substantial period," the commission meant a few years.)

"Know Your Congressman" was scheduled to begin just eleven weeks before Pennsylvania's primary elections. This inauspicious timing disturbed the commission and influenced its decision. After all, the program would feature incumbent congressmen; they might derive a distinct advantage over their challengers in the rapidly approaching primary. "Know Your Congressman" epitomized the fear expressed by some congressmen in 1959 that interview shows might spring up just before local elections, avoid the equal-time rule, and have the effect — if not the purpose — of favoring one candidate over another. This fear led Congress to insist upon regular scheduling.[36]

The second requirement for a bona fide news interview is control over program format and content. The broadcaster and his personnel must determine every aspect of the interview, whether editorial or technical — including the choice of a newsworthy guest, the selection of panelists, the scope and nature of the questions, and the production, direction, and editing of the program. If a broadcaster's exclusive control is compromised through participation by a candidate — for example, in planting questions or insisting upon reading a prepared statement — the interview will probably not be considered bona fide.[37]

A candidate's press conferences, for example, are usually not sufficiently under the control of the broadcasters to satisfy the FCC. The candidate normally retains control "in significant part." He schedules the conference, decides how many announcements to make, and determines when the conference will be thrown open to questions. The fact that attending newsmen formulate their own questions does not wrest enough control for the broadcasters.[38]

There is no necessity that all interviewers be broadcast personnel or newsmen. Nonprofessionals and even members of the general public can ask questions if that is the format planned and controlled by the broadcaster: for example, Sacramento's KFBK broadcast "Phone Forum," on which regular guests, including candidates, were questioned over the telephone by members of the listening audience. The program's moderator screened incoming calls by means of a four-second tape-delay device. Irrelevant or obscene calls were rejected, and the supporters or opponents of any guest candidate were not allowed to monopolize air time. Under these conditions, the broadcaster maintained sufficient control to make the interview bona fide.[39]

The phone-in format on KFBK's "Phone Forum" should not be confused with an equally popular, but nonexempt, format known as the "open mike." The aim of an open-mike format is to air the views of callers, who discuss subjects with the moderator or an occasional guest. In contrast, a phone-in news interview seeks primarily to elicit the response of newsworthy guests; it uses the phone-in device merely to supply questions. The open-mike format does not even constitute an interview, let alone a bona fide one.

The third requirement for a bona fide news interview is good faith news judgment. When a broadcaster determines such things as scheduling, guests, panelists, content, and format, he should be motivated by a desire to cover the news and inform the public — not to advance the political career of any candidate. During the 1959 congressional debates, the fear was expressed that a news interview, especially at the local level, could be rigged to enhance a candidate's image. Or, if panelists opposed a candidate, their interview of him might turn into a politically motivated fishing expedition into the candidate's past.[40] Senator John Pastore even went so far as to warn candidates themselves against converting a news interview into a political soapbox: "If [a] Senator . . . appeared on 'Meet the Press,' and, when asked questions, all he talked about was his previous record and how good a Senator he had been, I would say that would not be an exempt appearance. . . ."[41]

There is some doubt about how far a broadcaster may go in the name of good faith news judgment. At what point do news judgments weigh so heavily upon political fortunes that they can no longer escape the equal-time rule? This question was dramatically raised, but not thoroughly resolved, during the 1972 race for the Democratic presidential nomination. In the eight-day period preceding California's "winner-take-all" primary on June 6, 1972,

Senators Hubert Humphrey and George McGovern were chosen by the networks to appear jointly on "Meet the Press" (NBC), "Face the Nation" (CBS), and "Issues and Answers" (ABC). CBS and ABC expanded their joint interviews from one half-hour to an hour and shifted them to more desirable time slots.

Congresswoman Shirley Chisholm, another Democratic presidential candidate in the California primary, demanded equal time from CBS and ABC. She complained to the FCC that the joint appearances on "Face the Nation" and "Issues and Answers" should not be considered bona fide news interviews; they had been purposely lengthened, rescheduled for larger audiences, and converted from an interview format to a debate between Humphrey and McGovern.

The FCC ruled against Congresswoman Chisholm on the ground that CBS and ABC had exercised good faith news judgment.

> We believe that licensees may properly exercise editorial judgment as to the length and placement of regularly scheduled news interview programs, as they have exercised judgment with respect to these programs over a period of many years, without destroying the exemption accorded such programs. . . . The networks have at various times in past years increased the length of the programs in order to accommodate subject matter which in their judgment required more extensive than normal treatment, and they also have broadcast the programs at other than their usual time periods, apparently because they believed that extraordinary interest on the part of the public in particular broadcasts required that the programs be broadcast at times when larger than usual audiences might view and hear them. . . .
>
> We think it would constitute too narrow a view of [the exemption] to hold that a news interview otherwise meeting the statutory test of a bona fide news interview, and which has been regularly presented over a considerable period of time, loses its exempt status when the licensee occasionally puts it on at a different time because of its news judgment that the particular program is unusually newsworthy. . . .
>
> To hold otherwise would tend to discourage the fullest presentation of the news and to unduly limit that discretion which is so essential a part of the function of broadcast li-

censees. In every case where one or two candidates were presented on a regularly scheduled news interview program which varied in length or time of broadcast from the norm for that program, the licensee would be required to make equal time available to all other candidates, even though no change of substance relevant to the statutory purpose of preventing political favoritism was present.[42]

Congresswoman Chisholm appealed this ruling to federal court and won relief.[43] The court decided that the Humphrey-McGovern interviews looked suspiciously like nonexempt debates.

> We base this conclusion on a number of factors, not the least of which is the apparent concerted effort by the three networks in promoting and scheduling the three programs within an eight day period immediately prior to the California primary. Individual program format changes in themselves might not be decisive, but the carefully coordinated and scenarioed network series of the three encounters between the two leading contenders has been widely recognized for what . . . the series appears to us now — debates, though filtered through the somewhat altered format of pre-existing news interview programs.

The court ordered equal time for Congresswoman Chisholm on CBS and ABC, and the FCC reluctantly executed the order.

It should be noted that the court's decision was not actually a reversal of the FCC. Instead, the court merely afforded Chisholm what is technically known as "interim relief," without deciding the case on its merits. As a result, the opinion is more a hint of possible judicial interpretation than a binding precedent. Although the FCC obeyed the court, it adheres to its own reasoning in the original denial of equal time: changes in time and format, if occasional and justifiable, will not deprive a news interview of exemption so long as, in the words of the commission, there is "no change of substance relevant to the statutory purpose of preventing political favoritism." In all probability, good faith news judgments will continue to be accorded considerable leeway, as one was, for instance, when the FCC evaluated WNBC-TV's "People in the News" segment.[44] Still, it must be admitted, the exact limits on journalistic judgment are unsettled.[45]

NEWS DOCUMENTARIES. The "bona fide news documentary" is the third class of program on which a candidate may appear without triggering the equal-time rule. Perhaps the best definition of a news documentary was offered by the FCC in 1970: "News documentaries, by their very nature, depict news events, social conditions, political or economic subjects, etc., without fictionalization and generally use films, tapes, etc., of past events as documentation."[46]

The commission announced its definition in a case involving the educational television show "The Advocates." Produced by WGBH-TV (Boston) and KCET (Los Angeles), "The Advocates" employed a courtroom format. Two advocate-attorneys developed opposing sides of an issue by examining and cross-examining guest witnesses. The stations contended that "The Advocates" ought to qualify as a news documentary because it documented an issue in the news through an explanation of the issue's historical and logical context. The FCC decided, however, that the program's "debate-type" format precluded its designation as a news documentary.

Not every appearance on a news documentary is exempt from equal-time requirements. The appearance must be "incidental to the presentation of the subject or subjects covered by the news documentary." Senator Pastore clarified this requirement on the floor of the Senate in 1959.

> Only the other day the President of the United States, while in Europe, signed a resolution which permitted the building of a memorial to a former President of the United States, Franklin Delano Roosevelt. Let us assume that at the time when the memorial is completed and is being dedicated — and the dedication ceremonies will constitute a news item of current value — in showing that ceremony or news event, or whatever it might be termed, there is presented a cutback respecting the life of Franklin Delano Roosevelt, leading up to the building of the memorial. In the process of broadcasting that background, it so happens that they show the distinguished senior Senator from Alabama, Lister Hill, nominating President Franklin Delano Roosevelt, for his third term.

> At that time, Senator Hill, of Alabama, might have been
> a candidate for reelection; but his appearance was only inci-
> dental to the news documentary regarding the dedication of
> the memorial, which included the background of the life of
> Franklin Delano Roosevelt.[47]

We may safely speculate that Senator Hill's appearance would not
have been exempt from equal time if the documentary had dealt
predominantly with his role in President Roosevelt's career.[48]

In determining which candidates will appear during a news
documentary, and for what length of time, a broadcaster must use
good faith news judgment and exhibit no political favoritism. In
1962, for example, CBS presented a one-hour news program on the
off-year elections.[49] Entitled "The Fifty Faces of '62," it included a
historical review of off-year elections, coverage of conventions, and
flashbacks to newsworthy aspects of the 1962 campaigns. Appearing on the program were voters, students, and private citizens, as
well as some twenty-five political figures, none of whom was on
camera for more than two or three minutes. One of the political
figures was Republican Congressman Charles Halleck, who was
up for reelection. Halleck appeared in his capacity as minority
leader of the House. He discussed his party's prospects in the
upcoming election, without ever mentioning his own candidacy.

The FCC decided that "The Fifty Faces of '62" was a bona fide
news documentary, and Halleck's participation in the program was
exempt from equal time. "The determination as to who was to
appear on the program was made solely by CBS News on the basis
of its bona fide news judgment that their appearances were in aid
of the coverage of the subject of the program and not to favor or
advance the candidacies of any of those who appeared, such appearances being incidental and subordinate to the subject of the
documentary."

ON-THE-SPOT NEWS COVERAGE. "On-the-spot coverage of bona fide
news events" is the fourth class of program on which a candidate
may appear without triggering the equal-time rule. In general, two
requirements must be fulfilled before a program can qualify for
this exemption. First, a bona fide news event must have been the

basis for the on-the-spot coverage. Second, the broadcaster, in providing on-the-spot coverage, must have been motivated by good faith news judgment, rather than political favoritism.

What is a bona fide news event? Congress used this broad term to encompass the wide range of current events that are of genuine news value. The event may be no more momentous than a ribbon-cutting ceremony for a new bridge. Or, perhaps, the mayor of Chicago is televised while marching in the annual Saint Patrick's Day parade; the parade is a bona fide news event.[50]

In 1963 the FCC decided that certain courtroom proceedings held in Gary, Indiana, constituted a bona fide news event.[51] For fourteen years radio station WWCA had been broadcasting "Gary County Court on the Air," consisting of live coverage of actual trials in progress. Along with litigants and attorneys, one of the participants was, of course, the presiding judge. In 1963 the judge who had presided for the preceding seven-and-a-half years, Judge A. Martin Katz, became a candidate for mayor of Gary.

In view of candidate Katz's continuing appearances on the courtroom program, were his opponents in the mayoral race entitled to equal time? The FCC said no. "Gary County Court on the Air" qualified as on-the-spot coverage of a bona fide news event. The event was the courtroom proceedings, which the commission characterized as "the operation of an official governmental body."

Special reports to the nation by the President have been broadcast live without triggering the equal-time rule. On October 18, 1964, in the midst of the Johnson-Goldwater campaign, President Johnson addressed the nation.[52] He announced the United States government's response to the recent downfall of Soviet Premier Nikita Khrushchev and the explosion of a nuclear device by the Chinese. The three television networks carried President Johnson's address live. However, the networks denied a request for equal time from Senator Barry Goldwater, the Republican candidate for President.

The networks' denial of equal time was upheld by the FCC. According to the commission the networks had exercised reasonable news judgment when they accorded on-the-spot coverage to Johnson's address. The President had made a report to the nation regarding specific, current, international events affecting the nation's security. He had spoken officially in his capacity as Chief Executive, upon the recommendation of the National Security Council. The President had set forth United States foreign policy for the benefit of all Americans as well as other nations. Under these circumstances, President Johnson's very words constituted an act of office and, as such, were a bona fide news event, warranting on-the-spot coverage. That coverage was exempt from equal time.

Only one category of news event was specifically mentioned by Congress as being bona fide: namely, "political conventions and activities incidental thereto." For example, a candidate's press conference at the convention site, or an acceptance speech by the victorious nominee, would be a bona fide news event.[53] In 1972 this category of news event underwent a novel test in the wake of the dramatic Eagleton affair.[54] On July 13, 1972, the Democratic National Convention nominated Senator Thomas Eagleton as the party's vice-presidential candidate. By the end of the month, however, revelations about Eagleton's medical history forced him to withdraw from the race. With the convention long over, the Democratic National Committee called a special meeting for August 8, 1972, to choose a new nominee.

On August 5 at 7:30 P.M. (EST), the party's presidential candidate, Senator George McGovern, went on the air live over ABC, CBS, NBC, and the Mutual Broadcasting System. In a sixteen-minute address, he announced that R. Sargent Shriver was his personal choice to replace Senator Eagleton. (Indeed, Shriver was nominated at the August 8 meeting of the committee.)

The FCC decided that the August 8 meeting constituted a "political convention." The meeting had many elements similar to those in a regular convention, "including disputes as to which members should be seated, nomination of a Vice Presidential candidate, voting for the Vice Presidential candidate and an acceptance speech." Senator McGovern's August 5 address was an activity incidental to the so-called mini-convention and was, therefore, an exempt news event.

Other events of an equally political nature may also qualify as bona fide news events. Two prominent examples are debates between candidates and press conferences held by candidates. Prior to 1975, candidates' debates and press conferences were subject to equal-time requirements according to the then prevailing FCC decisions. On September 25, 1975, however, in *Aspen Institute Program on Communications and Society*,[55] the commission overruled its long-standing precedents and declared that both debates and press conferences could qualify for exemption.

One of the prior decisions overruled by the commission, *Robert Wycoff*,[56] arose during the 1962 gubernatorial race in California. On September 30, 1962, Governor Edmund G. Brown, the Democratic incumbent, debated his Republican challenger, Richard M. Nixon. The debate, which lasted one hour, was held in San Francisco before the annual convention of United Press International. NBC stations carried the debate live, in its entirety, because NBC regarded the debate as singularly newsworthy. The network, however, had absolutely no control over the debate itself; all arrangements and ground rules had been made by UPI. In the FCC's view (as of 1962), NBC's broadcast did not constitute on-the-spot coverage of a bona fide news event; as a result, the Prohibition Party's candidate for governor of California, Robert L. Wycoff, was entitled to equal time.

In another 1962 decision, *The Goodwill Station, Inc.*[57] — also overruled in 1975 — the commission held that live coverage of a debate between leading gubernatorial candidates in Michigan was not exempt from equal time. The debate in this case was sponsored by the Economic Club of Detroit, a weekly luncheon club of business and civic leaders. As was its past practice, the club in 1962 invited the two principal gubernatorial candidates — Republican and Democratic — to debate key issues following a club meeting. On October 8, 1962, the Democratic candidate, then-Governor John B. Swainson, and his Republican challenger, George Romney, having accepted the club's invitation, met and debated. Immediately after the debate, the candidates were questioned by the members of the club.

Detroit radio station WJR broadcast the debate and question-and-answer period live, in their entirety. Like NBC in the *Wycoff* case, WJR chose to cover the Swainson-Romney debate because of the station's judgment that the confrontation between the two leading candidates was exceptionally newsworthy. WJR had no control over the content of the debate. The FCC decided WJR's broadcast did not constitute on-the-spot coverage of a bona fide news event. Consequently, WJR had to give equal time to James Sim, the Socialist Labor Party candidate for governor. (In the previous gubernatorial election, the Socialist Labor Party had received 1,479 votes out of a statewide total of 3,225,991.)

In its 1975 *Aspen Institute* decision, the FCC overruled both *Robert Wycoff* and *The Goodwill Station, Inc.* The commission declared that if it were confronted in the future with "situations presenting the same factual contexts" as in *Wycoff* and *Goodwill*, it would exempt the broadcast debates before it as on-the-spot coverage of bona fide news events. Unfortunately, the commission did not specify exactly what it meant by situations presenting the same factual contexts as in the two overruled cases. Nevertheless, from our familiarity with *Wycoff* and *Goodwill*, we may infer that the same factual context presented in those cases would recur whenever five elements coalesce:

(1) *A debate between candidates is held.* Although the candidates in *Wycoff* and *Goodwill* happened to be running for the governorship, candidates on any level — local, state, or national — will presumably be included within the purview of the *Aspen Institute* decision. And that decision will probably be followed even though three or more candidates debate, rather than the two candidates opposing each other in *Wycoff* and *Goodwill*.

(2) *The debate is a newsworthy event.* Both NBC in *Wycoff* and WJR in *Goodwill* resorted to on-the-spot coverage, because they had concluded, in the exercise of their journalistic judgment, that the debates in question were events with important news value. Such journalistic judgments are hardly susceptible to objective verification; possibly the volume of coverage accorded a debate by other news media may tend to substantiate — or discredit, as the case may be — the broadcaster's news acumen. As a practical matter, the FCC is not likely to second-guess a broadcaster's judgments regarding newsworthiness; in its *Aspen* decision, the commission clearly conceived its role in administering the on-the-spot news exemption to be one of encouraging news coverage of political campaigns, rather than restricting it. Nevertheless, a given debate might be so patently devoid of any current news interest that the commission would question the broadcaster's news judgment or his good faith.

(3) *Sponsorship and control of the debate is not in the hands of the broadcaster.* The debates in both *Wycoff* and *Goodwill* were arranged by nonbroadcast organizations; neither NBC nor WJR had any control over the content of the debates. This "factual context" common to *Wycoff* and *Goodwill* would clearly be altered in any future situation where, say, a broadcaster set up a debate and staged it in his studio.[58] Given the intrusion of such a significant degree of control by the broadcaster, the resulting debate, although a perfectly legitimate and worthwhile form of programming, would not constitute a bona fide news event.

(4) *The broadcaster covers the debate live and in its entirety.* Apparently, if a debate is taped and broadcast on a delayed basis — unlike the live coverage of the Nixon-Brown and Swainson-Romney debates — or if live coverage is selective, omitting parts of the debate, there would be a significant change from the factual contexts in *Wycoff* and *Goodwill.* Consequently, the exemption for on-the-spot coverage would no longer be applicable. (It is possible, however, that taped portions of a debate might still be broadcast in some other exempt format — for example, within a bona fide newscast.)

(5) *The broadcaster acts in good faith, without political favoritism toward the debaters, when he provides on-the-spot coverage.* This element, present in both *Wycoff* and *Goodwill,* is actually the second overall prerequisite for the on-the-spot news exemption (discussed below).

In *Aspen Institute,* the FCC also decided that press conferences held by candidates for any public office could be broadcast live as on-the-spot coverage of bona fide news events. "Thus," explained the commission, "routine presidential press conferences, as well as press conferences by governors, mayors, and, indeed, any candidates whose press conferences are considered newsworthy and subject to on-the-spot coverage may be exempt from [equal time]."

The broadcast must be *live,* and it must cover the press conference *in entirety.* (As in the case of debates, however, taped portions of a press conference might be broadcast on a delayed basis in some exempt format other than on-the-spot coverage — for example, within a bona fide newscast.)

The significance of *Aspen Institute* is not limited to its strict holding — namely, that the live broadcast of candidates' debates and press conferences may be exempt from equal time. Underlying the decision is an important change in the FCC's conception of the on-the-spot exemption. Prior to *Aspen* the FCC required more than just a bona fide news event as the basis for exempt on-the-spot coverage; the appearance of a candidate during that coverage had to be *incidental to* the news event being covered. For example, the appearance of a candidate in the annual Saint Patrick's Day parade was incidental to the parade; the news event was the parade, not the candidate's appearance as a marcher. Or recall the 1963 case precipitated by "Gary County Court on the Air." The appearance of Judge Katz during that program was incidental to a bona fide news event — the official operations of the court.

If, instead of being incidental to a news event, the candidate's appearance *was* the event, there could be no exemption — prior to *Aspen* — for on-the-spot coverage of that event. For example, in *Wycoff* and *Goodwill* the sole event covered was the appearance of the candidates in debate; they *were* the event. Therefore, no on-the-spot exemption was available. (One notable deviation from this pre-1975 approach lay in the FCC's acceptance of special presidential addresses to the nation as bona fide news events in and of themselves.)

In *Aspen Institute* the FCC abandoned the requirement that a candidate's appearance must be incidental to a bona fide news event: "[A] program which might otherwise be exempt," said the commission, "does not lose its exempt status because the appearance of the candidate is a central aspect of the presentation, and not incidental to another news event." This principle could logically apply to candidate activities other than debates and press conferences. For example, a candidate's speech might be considered newsworthy enough to merit live coverage. Indeed, the

FCC has already exempted live coverage of a select category of speeches — namely, special presidential reports to the nation. However, the FCC insisted in *Aspen* that it was not expanding the on-the-spot exemption unduly, because its ruling was strictly limited to debates and press conferences. Whether the FCC will adhere to this arbitrary limitation when confronted, say, with live coverage of some particularly newsworthy activity, other than a debate or press conference, remains to be seen.

The FCC's abandonment of its "incidental-to" requirement makes administration of the on-the-spot exemption a highly subjective process. Under the old "incidental-to" test, there was, at least, some room for objectivity. The commission did not have to evaluate a candidate's appearance in terms of its intrinsic newsworthiness. Instead, that appearance was judged in a larger context — that is, in terms of the relationship between the appearance and some other extrinsic news event (like a parade or a courtroom trial). If the candidate's appearance was not incidental to an event of independent news value, the on-the-spot exemption was unavailable.

Following *Aspen,* broadcasters are free to determine whether a candidate's appearance — in a debate or press conference — is sufficiently newsworthy *in and of itself* to warrant live coverage. If asked to review that news judgment, the FCC will no longer have any point of reference extrinsic to the candidate's appearance. So the commission will fall back upon a broad subjective criterion, *reasonableness,* to review a news judgment that was largely subjective in the first place. Broadcasters will be afforded reasonable latitude in the formulation of their judgments regarding which, if any, debates or press conferences merit live coverage.

It was the FCC's hope in *Aspen* that broadcasters would be encouraged to increase news coverage of political campaigns. If live coverage does increase, it will most likely redound to the benefit of major candidates — that is, candidates whom broadcasters or special-interest groups regard as major. Suppose a large labor union or an association of bankers sponsors a debate between two candidates whom the union or association regards as the only viable contenders. Other candidates for the same office are not invited to participate, because the sponsor does not consider their positions to be "in the mainstream." If a broadcaster decides the scheduled debate does, indeed, pit the two front-runners in a newsworthy confrontation, the entire debate may be aired live without triggering the equal-time rule. Not only will the less prominent candidates be excluded from the debate, but they will also lose their chance for equal time. The same exclusion would occur if the press conference of a leading candidate were broadcast under the on-the-spot exemption.[59]

In our discussion thus far, we have focused on the first requirement for the on-the-spot exemption — namely, that a bona fide news event must be the basis for the coverage. The FCC's second general requirement relates to a broadcaster's motivation for employing on-the-spot coverage: the broadcaster must exercise his news judgment in good faith, not out of political favoritism. If it can be proven that in covering a news event live the broadcaster intended to promote the interests of a particular candidate, then the exemption will be lost.[60] Admittedly, proving the existence of bad faith is difficult, unless there is evidence of gross favoritism or, perhaps, a pattern of preferential treatment.[61]

Let us suppose the FCC's two requirements for bona fide on-the-spot coverage are satisfied by some live broadcast. Can the broadcast's exemption be lost if the candidate uses the coverage to his political advantage? The FCC said no in 1972, while exempting Senator McGovern's August 5 speech about a new vice-presidential nominee. That speech lasted sixteen minutes. However, in the estimation of the Republican National Committee, only one minute had been devoted to the actual announcement regarding Sargent Shriver; the other fifteen minutes had allegedly been exploited by McGovern for his own political advantage.

The FCC rejected the notion of dissecting a bona fide news event into exempt and nonexempt segments.

> Once the program is determined to be exempt . . . because it is on-the-spot coverage of a news event, the fact that a candidate uses the program for his political benefit does not make the program any less exempt. It is the nature of the news event which must be the controlling factor. It would be an unbearable burden for the networks during

"live" on-the-spot coverage of an important news event to have to make constant journalistic judgments as to which parts of the event are "news" and which are purely "political." The ramifications of such a burden as it relates to the broadcasting of news are staggering.

This line of reasoning would appear to have increased significance in light of the *Aspen Institute* decision. For if any news event is likely to have a highly political content, it is the press conference or debate featuring candidates in the heat of a campaign. Assuming that live coverage of the debate or press conference were determined to be exempt, the exemption would apparently not be lost merely because the candidates sounded more like politicians than impartial newsmakers.

Legally Qualified Candidates

The term "legally qualified candidate" serves a dual function. First of all, it determines whose broadcast appearances will trigger the equal-time rule. Only a legally qualified candidate, who is personally seen or heard on the air, can activate the rule. The equal-time rule remains inoperative if some noncandidate substitutes for the candidate. It makes no difference whether the noncandidate is a political party boss, a partisan campaign worker, or even a member of the candidate's immediate family. His appearance without the candidate will not create any equal-time rights, regardless of how much the candidate may benefit from the appearance. (The noncandidate's appearance may, however, trigger the FCC's *political party doctrine,* discussed in Chapter 3.)

Second, the term "legally qualified candidate" determines who can demand equal time from a broadcaster. Only a legally qualified candidate ever gains the right to equal time. Broadcasters are not obliged to fulfill a noncandidate's or a political party's request for equal time.[62] (We shall see, however, that a candidate, in using his equal time, may have noncandidates appear with him.)

Who is a legally qualified candidate? The FCC defines the term to include essentially any person who

(1) has publicly announced his candidacy, and

(2) meets the qualifications necessary to hold the office he seeks, and either

(3) qualifies for a place on the ballot, or

(4) is eligible to be voted for by write-in voting.[63]

To apply this definition in particular cases, the FCC usually refers to local laws in the state where the election is being held. "For, a person may be a candidate for public office and still, under applicable State law, not be a 'legally qualified' candidate."[64] Of course, local election laws vary widely. Sometimes their meaning is unclear; then the FCC will consult relevant interpretations by the state's courts. In the absence of any judicial precedent, the commission often relies upon rulings by the state's attorney general or other official in charge of elections.

The FCC created the necessity for a public announcement of candidacy in order to avoid prolonged uncertainty over equal-time rights and obligations.

> For example, incumbents often are eligible to run again, and, prior to a determination to seek another term, they may take many preliminary steps of varying nature (e.g., frequent trips to the election State, with speeches, conferences with financial sources, and potential delegates). Many incumbents later bear out previous widespread predictions in the press and do decide to run again, making a public announcement to this effect; in other instances the decision has been made not to run. To attempt to make findings on whether or when the incumbent has become a candidate during this usual, oft-repeated, and varying preliminary period would render [the equal-time rule] unworkable. There would be a continual series of complex factual hearings, whose resolution, in view of the nature of the issue, would be most difficult and indeed might remain stubbornly speculative. While we have used the case of an incumbent as an example, similar illustrations could be made with a nonincumbent political figure during this preliminary pre-announcement period.[65]

Without some starting signal like the public announcement of candidacy, broadcasters would have to gamble in their coverage of would-be candidates, never knowing whether the equal-time rule might, in fact, be triggered.

For example, on December 19, 1967, ABC, CBS, and NBC carried an hour-long television interview, entitled "A Conversation with President Johnson."[66] At that time, the President had made no public announcement regarding a possible second term, and during the program he declined to speculate on whether he would run for reelection. Nevertheless, Senator Eugene McCarthy, who was already challenging Johnson for the Democratic Party's nomination, demanded equal time.

The networks turned McCarthy down, and the FCC agreed with them on the ground that President Johnson had yet to announce his candidacy. A federal appeals court affirmed the commission's ruling. The court, however, hinted that the public announcement standard could not always be applied mechanically "without, in some instances at least, resulting in unfairness and possible constitutional complications." It is conceivable that an unannounced candidate who is acting and speaking very much like a candidate, and making broadcast appearances with highly political overtones, may delay his announcement to the point where he illegally deprives his opponent of the opportunity to express his views and be heard by the electorate. While President Johnson may have appeared to have been using such dilatory tactics, the ultimate irony came a few months after his December 1967 interview when he announced that he would not seek his party's nomination for the presidency.

Since April 7, 1972, candidates for presidential nomination may find that their actions speak louder than any public announcement of candidacy could. The new Federal Election Campaign Act directly affects unannounced candidates for presidential nomination. Suppose such a candidate makes a campaign expenditure for the use of some communications medium — for example, a broadcast station, newspaper, magazine, outdoor advertising facility, or, under certain circumstances, telephone service — on behalf of his candidacy. That expenditure will be regarded as though it were a public announcement of candidacy. For the purposes of equal time, this so-called announcement will be deemed to have taken place on one of two possible dates: either the date of the broadcast or publication for which the expenditure was made, or January 1 of the year in which the presidential election is being held, whichever date is later. It should be noted that the same consequences will result even if the campaign expenditure is made by some second party on behalf of the unannounced candidate.[67]

Assuming a candidate has publicly announced, he must also be eligible to hold office if elected. Obviously qualifications vary with the office as well as the state or district where the election is being held. Typical qualifications may include a specified minimum age, a period of residency, and citizenship. Sometimes there are formal requirements such as filing a report of the candidate's financial interests.[68]

A candidate who chooses to have his name placed on the ballot must satisfy the necessary prerequisites. For example, a state may specify official forms to be filed or, perhaps, a minimum number of signatures to be submitted on a petition. If a candidate cannot be voted for until he has met conditions such as these, then he must fully comply, before the FCC will consider him a legally qualified candidate.[69]

The term "legally qualified candidate" embraces write-in candidates as well as those whose names are officially printed on the ballot. Here again, local law must be consulted to establish whether some method of write-in voting is legitimate and can result in a valid election. The mere fact that write-in voting is permitted does not mean that any man-in-the-street who announces his candidacy automatically earns the right to equal time. *Not every write-in candidate is a legally qualified candidate.* In order to be considered legally qualified, a write-in candidate must do one of two things: either he must prove that he has been duly nominated by a recognized political party or he must make a substantial showing that he is a "bona fide candidate" for nomination or election.[70]

Some hard questions arise over which write-in candidates are, in fact, bona fide candidates. Usually the candidate marshals evidence that his campaign is serious and sustained. For example, the candidate may demonstrate that he has issued press releases, handed out campaign leaflets, held rallies and press conferences, addressed civic groups, and canvassed door to door. Added weight will be given to the candidate's efforts if he has a staff and, perhaps, a campaign headquarters. Any media exposure he attracts is further evidence that he is a bona fide candidate.[71]

There are some hidden equal-time pitfalls in the choice between seeking a place on the ballot and mounting a write-in campaign. Suppose candidate Jones intends to petition for a place on the ballot. He campaigns actively and collects signatures for his petition. Midway in his campaign, while he is still several thousand signatures short, Jones has occasion to request equal time when one of his opponents makes a broadcast speech. Jones claims he is seriously engaged in a petition drive, which he expects will succeed in placing his name on the ballot; if the drive fails, Jones then plans to campaign as a write-in candidate. At the moment of his request for equal time, is Jones a legally qualified candidate?

The FCC says no.[72] During the petition drive, Jones will not be considered a legally qualified candidate until he succeeds in having his name actually placed on the ballot. The fact that Jones may launch a write-in campaign at some future date does not afford him any fallback position while he is still petitioning to get on the ballot. In effect, by pursuing the more difficult of two paths, Jones is now caught in the middle without any rights to equal time. What's more, if he does switch to a write-in campaign, none of the activities from the petition drive (for example, speeches, leaflets, canvassing) can be used to show he is a bona fide write-in candidate; instead, Jones will have to rely on activities engaged in after he actually launched his write-in campaign.[73]

Whether or not a candidate is on the ballot, he bears the burden of proof whenever he seeks equal time from a broadcaster or complains to the FCC about noncompliance with the equal-time rule: "A candidate . . . shall have the burden of proving that he and his opponent are legally qualified candidates for the same public office."[74] Notice two important points about this burden. First, the candidate seeking equal time must prove not only that he is legally qualified, but that his opponent is also. Without this latter proof, there is no ground for concluding that the equal-time rule has been triggered. (Remember, only a legally qualified candidate can trigger the rule.)

Second, the candidate seeking equal time must also prove that he and his opponent are competing for the same public office — that is, they are candidates of the same class or character. Prior to a primary election, for instance, only candidates for a particular party's nomination are considered to be opposing candidates for the same office. Thus several Republicans seeking the party's nomination for governor are opposing candidates until the primary. They are running against each other and not against any Democrats who may simultaneously be vying for their own party's gubernatorial nomination. For equal-time purposes, the Democratic nomination is not the same public office as the Republican nomination. If, therefore, a Democratic gubernatorial hopeful makes a broadcast appearance, Republicans contending for their party's gubernatorial nomination gain no right to equal time. The same reasoning would apply prior to party conventions if they were being held instead of a primary.[75]

After the nominating process has been completed, the equal-time perspective changes. Now the Republican nominee and the Democratic nominee for any given office — as well as third-party nominees and bona fide write-in candidates for that office — are considered to be opposing candidates. It is not always obvious, however, exactly when this point is reached during a campaign. Often the intricacies of local election laws require close scrutiny to determine when two or more candidates are actually opposing each other for the same public office.

Take a simple illustration. A state primary will be held on June 20. Mary Smith is seeking the Republican nomination for state comptroller, and Joseph Jay is running for the same nomination on the Democratic ticket. Both Smith and Jay are running unopposed in their respective primaries. However, up until June 1 at the latest, anyone may register with the secretary of state as a write-in candidate for either the Republican or Democratic nomination for comptroller. Suppose no write-in candidates have registered as of May 28, when Joseph Jay makes a broadcast address. Is Mary Smith entitled to equal time?

The answer is no.[76] On May 28 Smith and Jay were not opposing candidates for the same public office, even though they were unopposed for their respective parties' nomination for comptroller. Smith and Jay will not become opponents for the same office until one of two conditions is fulfilled: no write-in candidate for either the Republican or Democratic nomination for comptroller registers before the June 1 deadline; or, if such a write-in candidate should register in time, both Smith and Jay go on to win their respective primaries.

One final point is in order regarding a candidate's burden of proof. He does not have to demonstrate that he is at all likely to be nominated or elected. Legal qualifications alone count — not political prospects nor, for that matter, political orientation. Broadcasters cannot deny equal time on the basis of subjective determinations that a legally qualified candidate is a dark horse or a fringe radical or just an eccentric. The FCC has warned that the equal-time rule covers all legally qualified candidates — no if's, and's, but's, or maybe's: "There is simply no room . . . to make determinations as to degrees of intent, or qualification, or 'seriousness' — nor should there."[77]

Requests for Equal Time

Every candidate is responsible for asserting any rights to equal time that he acquires during a campaign. A broadcaster has no affirmative obligation to seek out the candidate and offer him an opportunity to use the station. Instead, the broadcaster can simply wait for the candidate to initiate contact and make a request.

Ordinarily, a broadcaster does not even have to notify a candidate when his opponent uses, or plans to use, the station. This information should be given, however, if some candidate asks the broadcaster for it. FCC rules do require the broadcaster to keep a public record of all equal-time transactions: "Every licensee shall keep and permit public inspection of a complete record of all requests for broadcast time made by or on behalf of candidates for public office, together with an appropriate notation showing the disposition made by the licensee of such requests, and charges made, if any, if the request is granted."[78] This record must be maintained for at least two years.

Exceptional circumstances may arise, requiring a broadcaster to initiate contact with some candidate in order to allow the candidate to assert his rights and use them effectively. On April 12, 1970, just two days before the city council election in Oceanside, California, local station KUDE-AM broadcast a discussion among three of the seven opposing candidates.[79] James Spurling, a candidate who was neither invited to participate nor notified of the broadcast, complained to the FCC. The commission decided

> that the licensee acted contrary to the spirit of [the equal-time rule] in giving free time to [three] of the seven candidates only two days before election, without acquainting the other candidates with the fact in time for them to assert their [equal-time] rights and to prepare material for broadcast pursuant to such rights. Although a licensee ordinarily has no obligation to inform one candidate that time has been given or sold to a competing candidate, when a gift of time is so close to election day, failure to notify the opposing candidate or candidates can effectively nullify the statutory right to equal opportunities. . . . We believe timely notice is called for in such situations. . . .

Roughly speaking, timely notice would be unnecessary for an appearance that occurs several days before the election in question. For instance, five days prior to the 1972 Democratic presidential primary in New York, Senator George McGovern appeared on WNET-TV in New York City. The FCC decided that WNET-TV did not have to contact McGovern's opponents but could simply wait for their requests. Five days afforded "ample time" for these candidates to exercise their equal-time rights.[80]

To facilitate orderly programming, broadcasters must be able to settle their legal obligations to candidates within some reasonable time frame. Therefore, FCC rules require a request for equal time to be submitted to the broadcaster "within one week of the day on which the first prior use, giving rise to the right to equal opportunities, occurred."[81] *If the candidate fails to make a timely request, the right to equal time will be lost.*

Notice the critical event referred to in the rule: the first prior use giving rise to equal-time rights. The meaning of "first prior use" can best be conveyed through an example. Suppose A, B, and C are legally qualified candidates for the same public office. On April 5, A broadcasts a campaign speech over hypothetical station WWW. On April 12, B requests equal time from WWW. The request is granted, and, as a result, B uses WWW on April 15. The next day, April 16, C requests equal time. Must WWW grant C's request?

The answer is no. The first prior use, which gave both B and C the right to equal time, occurred on April 5, when A made his speech. B's request was, therefore, timely, coming within one week of April 5. By April 16, however, when C made his request, more than one week had passed since the first prior use. It makes no difference that, in the interim, there was a *subsequent* use: B's April 15 speech. That use could not start the seven-day clock running over again for C's benefit. If WWW had granted C's request, C's appearance would have started the clock again for A and B; for them, C's appearance would have constituted another first prior use, giving them new rights to equal time.[82]

The FCC's so-called seven-day rule gives the broadcaster a rule of thumb for his scheduling expectations following a candidate's appearance. "The licensee must be prepared, upon request, to afford the other candidate or candidates opportunities for the use of his station's facilities equal to the uses allowed the opponent during the 7-day period preceding the date of such request."[83] Thus, if candidate Jones's opponent, Smith, telegrams WWW on August 8 requesting time equal to that afforded Jones, the request sweeps backward to cover all uses of WWW that Jones made from August 1 through August 7. The retroactive effect of Smith's request is automatic; he does not have to refer specifically to the seven-day rule. It is enough that he requested time equal to Jones's. That message alone will put WWW on notice that it must provide Smith with air time equal to that enjoyed by Jones during the seven days preceding August 8.[84]

The seven-day rule may inspire some imaginative but inadvisable dilatory tactics by candidates. Suppose election day in the

Jones-Smith race is August 10. Just two days before, Smith, his campaign chest bulging with equal time earned during the prior week, telegrams WWW demanding, in effect, a day-before-election-day blitz of the station's air time. In all probability, WWW would be justified, if it claimed inability to accommodate Smith. The FCC frowns upon eleventh-hour requests for equal time:

> The thrust of this so-called "eleventh hour rule" is that a licensee will not be expected to accommodate last-minute equal opportunities requests made by parties who have sat on their [equal-time] rights in situations where the grant of such request would seriously interfere with the licensee's duty to program in the public interest, or where such a grant would give the last-minute purchaser an unfair advantage over prior-use candidates by allowing the purchaser to saturate broadcast time during the last few days before an election.[85]

A request made several days or a week before the election will ordinarily create no difficulties a broadcaster is unable to solve through acceptable changes in schedule. However, last-day or next-to-last-day requests are likely to pose the objectionable consequences contemplated by the "eleventh-hour rule."

While stalling is, thus, held in disfavor and can, indeed, boomerang on a candidate, jumping the gun may be perfectly acceptable. Suppose a specific future use of WWW is announced a few days before air time. An opposing candidate may request equal time in advance of the scheduled broadcast. WWW cannot refuse to give equal time following the broadcast by claiming that the request should technically have been made within one week *after* use.[86]

Are weekly requests necessary when one station is running a long series of broadcasts by the same candidate? For example, candidate Jones purchases thirty one-minute spot announcements, which will air daily for one month on WWW. Jones's opponent, Smith, requests equal time on the basis of Jones's series. Must Smith repeat this request each succeeding week Jones's series continues? The FCC says no. As long as Smith's initial request refers to the pattern of Jones's broadcasts, WWW will be on notice that

Smith wants equal time not only for uses during the preceding seven days, but also for all subsequent uses that carry forward Jones's already established schedule.[87]

The seven-day rule can get tangled in events when, as is increasingly the case, candidates drop in and out of a political race at different times. To help broadcasters cope with equal-time requests from new entrants, the FCC added a proviso to its seven-day rule: "Where a person was not a candidate at the time of [the] first prior use, he shall submit his request within one week of the first subsequent use after he has become a legally qualified candidate for the office in question."[88] In other words, the critical event from which the new candidate's rights will be measured is the first use that occurs *after he has become a legally qualified candidate.*

For example, A, B, and C are all legally qualified for the same public office as of August 31; but D, the fourth man in the race, does not become legally qualified until September 15. On September 1, A uses WWW for a campaign speech. B requests equal time on September 6 and, as a result, speaks over WWW on September 16. The next day, September 17, both C and D request equal time. WWW turns them both down.

Did WWW act legally? In regard to C's request, we know the answer is yes. For as far as C was concerned, A's September 1 speech was the first prior use; therefore, C's September 16 request exceeded the seven-day rule. Not so with D, however; WWW violated D's right to equal time. D's right, unlike C's, depended upon the date of *B's speech* (September 16) rather than the date of A's speech (September 1). B's speech was the "first subsequent use" after D had become a legally qualified candidate (on September 15). So D's request, made the day after B's speech, was well within the bounds of the seven-day rule.[89]

Aside from the operation of the seven-day rule, there is another deadline that cuts off the right to equal time — namely, the date of the election or primary, as the case may be. Once the election itself has been held, all possibility of equal time for formerly competing candidates terminates. A broadcaster is under no obligation to honor a request for equal time made after the election is over.

However, the broadcaster cannot circumvent his legal obligations by deliberately ignoring a timely request until after the election.[90]

Equal Opportunities

The equal-time rule speaks in terms of affording opposing candidates "equal opportunities" in the use of broadcast facilities. FCC regulations are quite specific: "In making time available to candidates for public office no licensee shall make any discrimination between candidates in charges, practices, regulations, facilities, or services . . . or make or give any preference to any candidate for public office or subject any such candidate to any prejudice or disadvantage. . . ."[91] Despite this seemingly rigid standard, the hard fact is that "absolute and pure equality of opportunity is impossible of achievement."[92] Therefore, in many cases the FCC settles for substantial compliance with the equal-time rule. "The intent and purpose [behind the rule] are fulfilled . . . when broadcast facilities are made available under conditions which amount to the closest approximation to 'equal opportunities.' "[93]

In general, a candidate must have the opportunity to use a station for the same length of time as his opponent. If candidate Jones gives a twenty-five-minute speech over hypothetical station WWW, his opponent, Smith, should have the same opportunity Jones had for twenty-five minutes of air time on WWW.

Computing equal time is relatively straightforward when a candidate appears alone during his own program. But suppose the candidate participates in a broadcast involving other people. Is the entire length of the broadcast subject to equal time? The answer depends upon the length of the broadcast and the nature of the candidate's participation.

The FCC computes equal time differently for spot announcements than for program-length presentations. Roughly speaking, the commission regards any broadcast that lasts two minutes or less as a spot announcement. If, at any time during a spot announcement, the candidate is either identified or identifiable by means of his voice or image, then the entire spot will be considered a use of the station. As a result, the candidate's opponent will be entitled to equal time lasting as long as the spot announcement.

For example, a sixty-second spot announcement on behalf of candidate Jones runs on WWW. During the first forty-five seconds, Jones is neither seen nor heard. Instead, an announcer reads various endorsements of Jones's candidacy. Only in the last fifteen seconds does Jones introduce himself and ask listeners for their support on election day. Since Jones is actually heard — in this instance, identifying himself and speaking during 25 percent of the spot announcement — his opponent will be entitled to sixty seconds of equal time from WWW.[94]

To be considered a program-length presentation rather than a spot announcement, a broadcast must last five minutes or longer. Even though the candidate does not appear throughout the program, the entire length of the program will be subject to equal time if certain conditions have been met. First, the candidate must have maintained control and direction over the program. Second, his personal appearance, either visual or vocal, must have been (1) substantial in length, (2) integrally involved in the program, and (3) the focus of the program.

For example, candidate Jones presents a ten-minute film on WWW-TV. We see Jones addressing rallies, shaking hands in factories, and conversing with tenants at a local housing project. Some of the footage is of people other than Jones (for example, factory workers, tenants); indeed, there are some shots of buildings and city streets in which Jones is neither seen nor heard. Nevertheless, he constantly reappears or is heard in a voiceover narration. The film was produced under his direction, and he is clearly at its focal point. Under these circumstances, the entire ten minutes is subject to equal time — not merely those discrete shots in which Jones is actually seen or heard.[95]

The result would be different if a candidate's appearance were incidental to a program-length format that featured some other central figure. Say the candidate was one of several guest speakers at a testimonial dinner carried over a local station. Out of the entire hour-long program, only six minutes were consumed by the candidate, who took no further part in the proceedings. The candidate's six minutes — not the entire hour — would be subject to equal time.[96]

A more difficult problem would arise if the candidate's appearance, instead of being readily separable from the rest of a program (like the six-minute speech in the last hypothetical situation), were intertwined with it and yet, at the same time, not its focal point. For example, a candidate is a guest on an entertainment talk show. He is interviewed by the host for just sixteen minutes. (The entire show runs ninety minutes.) Clearly, no more than sixteen minutes will be subject to equal time. However, will the entire sixteen minutes be counted? Or will those discrete moments when the talk-show host is seen or heard and the candidate is not be subtracted from sixteen minutes in order to compute equal time?

There is no hard-and-fast answer. The FCC will weigh each case on its facts. Particular attention will be paid to such variables as the degree of control that the candidate had over the course of the interview and the extent of the editorial discretion that the broadcaster exercised in regard to the interview. Certainly, if the candidate had no say over the questions asked and more or less had to follow the dominant part played by the talk-show host, the sixteen minutes were substantially beyond the candidate's control. He should, therefore, argue that only those minutes and seconds when he was seen or heard be used to calculate the equal time due his opponent.[97]

Suppose a broadcast is longer than a spot announcement but shorter than a program — that is, it runs over two minutes but under five minutes. This intermediate-length broadcast falls within a gray zone where the FCC has set no hard-and-fast rules for computing equal time. Therefore, the candidate requesting equal time would probably be best advised to analyze his opponent's broadcast as though it were program-length. If the opponent controlled the broadcast, and his appearance was substantial in length and central to the broadcast, the candidate requesting equal time should insist upon the full amount of time consumed by his opponent's broadcast.[98]

Sometimes one candidate is the nominee of more than one party. Say candidate Jones is both the Democratic and Liberal nominee for United States senator. If Jones's Republican opponent broadcasts for five minutes over WWW, is Jones entitled to a double helping of equal time: five minutes for Jones qua Democrat, and another five minutes for Jones qua Liberal? The FCC says no; each candidate deserves only one helping regardless of how many nominations he holds.[99]

Opposing candidates must be treated equally when it comes to the use of station facilities: for example, microphones, videotaping equipment, teleprompters. Whatever facilities one candidate is allowed to use, his opponents should be entitled to use on equal terms.[100] Still, technical discrepancies are occasionally unavoidable, in which case a candidate may have to be satisfied with substantially similar opportunities, rather than equal opportunities.

For example, during Senator Birch Bayh's 1968 campaign for reelection in Indiana, he and his Republican opponent videotaped a debate on WPTA-TV (Fort Wayne). An Indianapolis station, WISH-TV, arranged to have a copy of the tape made for its own rebroadcast later that night. Due to technical failure in WPTA-TV's videotape machine, the video portion of two minutes and fifty seconds of Senator Bayh's closing remarks was lost; the accompanying audio portion remained unaffected. When WISH-TV aired the tape, it substituted a still picture of the senator during the defective video segment. Regrettably, even this device broke down, and WISH-TV had to flash a slide on the screen reading "Technical Difficulties," while Senator Bayh's voice was still being broadcast without interruption. The FCC decided Senator Bayh was not entitled to use WISH-TV over again to reread the two-minute-and-fifty-second segment on camera. The station had made a reasonable effort to cope with its technical setbacks. There had been no substantial discrepancy between the so-called equal opportunities afforded Senator Bayh and his opponent.[101]

The time periods afforded opposing candidates must be comparable in quality. One segment of air time is comparable to another if it is generally as desirable as the other in terms of value and impact. Notice that the operative word here is *comparable*, not *equal*. We have moved from the quantitative realm — Is A's use as long as B's? — to the qualitative realm — Is A's use as valuable or effective as B's? In terms of quality, one use can never really equal another.[102]

There are some rough guidelines that help determine whether different time segments are, at least, comparable, though not equal. Opposing candidates are entitled to air their segments within corresponding time periods. These overall periods are ordinarily established by the broadcaster when he breaks up his broadcast day in order to set rates for the sale of air time. For instance, WWW might divide its day into the following periods: prime time (7:30 to 11 P.M.), class "A" (5 to 7:30 P.M.), class "B" (9 A.M. to 5 P.M.; 11 to 11:30 P.M.), and class "C" (7:30 to 9 A.M.; 11:30 P.M. to sign-off). If candidate Jones utilizes thirty-second spot announcements on WWW during prime time, his opponent, Smith, cannot be relegated to running his spots in, for example, the late-night hours following prime time (the class "B" period). WWW must allow Smith equal time during the same period Jones used the station.

A comparable time period does not mean exactly the same moment in the schedule previously used by an opponent. So if Jones's campaign commercials ran at exactly 8:37 P.M., Smith has no right to insist that his commercials also run at 8:37 P.M. As long as the overall time periods used by Jones and Smith are comparable — for example, both use prime time — they have enjoyed equal opportunities.[103]

Suppose WWW finds that it is sold out of upcoming prime time when Smith seeks to purchase his equal-time spots. WWW still has no excuse for shunting Smith into less desirable time periods (for example, class "A" or "B"), when audiences are smaller. A broadcaster, in planning his programming, must leave enough leeway to accommodate unforeseen events, such as requests for equal time. If the broadcaster schedules himself too tightly, he may be obligated to cancel prior arrangements in order to fulfill his equal-time obligations.[104]

Can equal time be subdivided and distributed throughout a broadcast day according to the candidate's wishes? The FCC said no in 1970 during the race for United States representative from New York's nineteenth congressional district.[105] Democrat Bella Abzug was running against Republican Barry Farber. A well-known radio personality, Farber hosted an interview show over WOR from 8:15 to 9 P.M. Monday through Friday. WOR offered Abzug her own late-night forty-five-minute program, but she demanded, instead, the right to use up her equal time in one-minute spot announcements. (Since Farber was not paying for his time, neither would Abzug be.)

WOR balked at the economic discrepancy Abzug's proposal would have occasioned. The station's one-minute rate during the evening was $60 per spot; forty-five of the Abzug spots would have had a value of $2700 each evening. In comparison, Barry Farber's entire show time cost $965.25 nightly. (If the Abzug messages were to run throughout an entire day, the total value of such a package would have been $4600.) What's more, WOR argued, Abzug would achieve greater audience impact than Farber, because a message repeated throughout the day affords multiple exposures as the audience constantly changes.

The FCC decided that an equal opportunity for Abzug lay somewhere between her demands and those of WOR:

> We cannot consider as reasonable Mrs. Abzug's request for spot announcements. Specifically, we believe it would be unreasonable for a licensee to be required to afford an opposing candidate only short time segments such as 60-second announcements when the first use consisted of program-length segments. We agree that granting the request by Mrs. Abzug that she be given only spot announcements would give her more than the equal opportunities which [the law] requires. On the other hand, we do not believe that [WOR] can insist that Mrs. Abzug use only 45-minute segments at times specified by [the station] on a take it or leave it basis. In this case, Mrs. Abzug's equal opportunities would appear to consist of the opportunity to use program segments which may or may not be shorter than the program segments used by Mr. Farber.

The commission made it incumbent upon the broadcaster and the candidates to work out the mechanics for equal time through good faith negotiations.

In general, a candidate cannot insist that he be allowed to appear on the same program his opponent appeared on. For example, if candidate Jones does a guest shot on a prime-time variety show, his opponent, Smith, is not necessarily entitled to appear on that show some other night. This limitation is not absolute. As is frequently the case, a rule of reason must prevail between the parties. Conceivably the audience impact of Jones's appearance may have been so great as to eliminate any other comparable way in which Smith can receive an equal opportunity, other than appearing on the same variety show.[106]

The commission has refused to direct that all opposing candidates for one office must be put on a single show together. In 1965 there was a four-way race for the New York City Democratic mayoral nomination. WPIX-TV scheduled a half-hour face-to-face debate between the two front-runners, Abraham Beame and Paul Screvane.[107] Fifteen minutes of free air time was scheduled separately for each of the other two contenders, Paul O'Dwyer and William F. Ryan. The latter two candidates complained of their treatment as also-rans. They claimed WPIX-TV was, in effect, giving Beame and Screvane an unfair advantage because (1) the debate format would attract a larger audience than individual appearances; (2) direct confrontation between opponents in a debate is a more effective means of demonstrating one's qualifications than in a speech by a lone candidate; (3) the segregation of Beame and Screvane as front-runners, with all its attendant publicity, amounted to a prejudgment that the candidacies of O'Dwyer and Ryan were not viable.

The FCC disagreed. O'Dwyer and Ryan had no right under the equal-time rule to appear on the same broadcast with their opponents. They had been afforded equal opportunities when WPIX-TV offered each of them fifteen minutes of air time. It is certainly arguable that such treatment violates the FCC's prohibition against giving any "preference" to a candidate or subjecting him to any "prejudice or disadvantage." Arguable though this contention may be, the commission has stated: "It does not appear that [separately] scheduled broadcasts, solely by virtue of the fact that a debate with 'major' party candidates may have a larger audience than separate or joint appearances of 'minor candidates,' will result in 'prejudice or disadvantage' so as to constitute a violation of the rules."[108] What we have, in effect, is a "separate-but-equal" approach to political broadcasting; it highlights one important inequality subsumed under the misnomer "equal time."

The Cost of Air Time

In general, a broadcast that triggers the equal-time rule also establishes how much, if anything, equal time will cost an opposing candidate. When one candidate uses a station without cost, his opponent is entitled to equal time free of charge. For example, hypothetical station WWW gives candidate Jones free time for a campaign speech as a public service; or, perhaps, Jones makes a guest appearance on a WWW variety show, which is sponsored by a commercial advertiser. In either case, the broadcast costs Jones nothing. Therefore, his opponent, Smith, has a right to free equal time on WWW.

But suppose a labor union supporting Jones buys him air time on WWW for a speech. The broadcast is not a free one, since Jones's campaign supporters are paying WWW's regular rates. When Smith requests equal time, WWW must give him an opportunity to purchase comparable air time at the same rates afforded Jones's supporters. WWW is neither obligated nor permitted to give Smith equal time free of charge or at a reduced rate; such rate discrimination between candidates would violate the equal-time rule.[109]

How much can a station charge a candidate whose broadcast triggers the equal-time rule? In general, the candidate is entitled to the same rates a comparable advertiser would enjoy. The FCC's regulations state: "A candidate shall, in each case, be charged no more than the rate the station would charge if the candidate were a commercial advertiser whose advertising was directed to promoting its business within the same area as that encompassed by the particular office for which such person is a candidate."[110] For example, WWW broadcasts from Capital City to the entire state.

The station charges its advertisers two different rates: "local," a low rate for businesses whose products or services are confined to the immediate metropolitan area of Capital City; and "national," a higher rate for businesses taking advantage of the station's coverage beyond the city. Candidate Jones is running for United States representative from a congressional district that encompasses not only Capital City but outlying towns as well. If Jones wishes to buy time on WWW, he will find himself on the same footing with so-called national advertisers, who are selling to the market beyond the immediate metropolitan area; Jones will be charged the national rate.[111]

All discount privileges that a station offers its advertisers must be made available on equal terms to candidates. For example, WWW sells both preemptible and nonpreemptible spots; the former are sold at a discount, because they are subject to cancellation in order to make room for the latter. A candidate, if he wanted preemptible spots, would be entitled to purchase them at the same discount granted any commercial advertiser.[112]

There is an important exception in this parallel treatment accorded candidates and advertisers. In 1972 the Federal Election Campaign Act prescribed special low rates for candidates during certain critical periods of a campaign. These rates are available to every legally qualified candidate for public office with one exception: candidates for nomination by a convention or caucus of a political party. For instance, a person campaigning to have a party convention nominate him for state office or choose delegates favorable to him for the party's national nominating convention would not be entitled to the special low rates.[113]

Under the Act, the low rates apply to broadcasts made during (1) the forty-five days preceding the date of a primary or primary runoff election, and (2) the sixty days preceding the date of a general or special election.[114] During these forty-five or sixty days, if a candidate uses a station, the charge for air time must not exceed "the lowest unit charge of the station for the same class and amount of time for the same period." The term "class of time" refers to the categories of air time the station sells: for example, preemptible and nonpreemptible spots. The term "amount of time" refers to the unit of time purchased: for example, thirty seconds, one minute, an hour. The term "period" refers to some particular segment of the broadcast day; normally the station divides its broadcast day into several segments, such as prime time (7:30 to 11 P.M.), class "A" time (5 to 7:30 P.M.), class "B" time (9 A.M. to 5 P.M.; 11 to 11:30 P.M.).

An illustration using all these terms will show how the lowest-unit-charge formula works. Suppose candidate Jones wishes to buy a single, one-minute, nonpreemptible spot during prime time on WWW. For a spot of the same class (nonpreemptible) and amount of time (one minute) in the same period (prime time), WWW charges commercial advertisers $15. Ordinarily, if Jones's spot were to run before the forty-five- or sixty-day periods, he would have to pay $15, just like a comparable commercial advertiser. Within the purview of the Federal Election Campaign Act, however, Jones may get better terms than would an advertiser in his position. Assume that WWW also offers its most favored advertisers a package of five hundred spots like the one Jones wants for a total price of $5000; this price is the station's lowest on one-minute, nonpreemptible, prime-time spots. In that case, the lowest unit charge to Jones for his one spot would be $10 rather than $15. The lowest-unit-charge formula gives Jones the benefit of the bulk discount, even though he is not buying the five hundred spots required of an advertiser.[115]

The lowest unit charge is simply the lowest possible unit price a candidate might have paid had he been the broadcaster's most favored commercial advertiser. This charge may be based upon rates listed on the broadcaster's rate card. Sometimes, however, the broadcaster uses his rate card merely as a point of departure; once in negotiation with advertisers, the broadcaster may yield rates even lower than those on his card. For example, WWW might find itself with some unsold air time during the critical forty-five- or sixty-day period. To avoid a total loss, WWW sells the time to an advertiser at a rock-bottom bargain price, which is lower than the price reflected on the rate card. This unique sale will become the basis for the lowest unit charge on sales to candidates of the same class and amount of time for the same period.[116]

Censorship Prohibited

A basic objective behind the equal-time rule is "to permit a candidate to present himself to the electorate in a manner wholly unfettered by licensee judgment as to the propriety or content of that presentation."[117] Toward this end, Congress prohibited any censorship of material broadcast under the rule. The prohibition applies whenever a candidate uses a broadcast station — whether that use triggers the equal-time rule or is made as a result of some prior use by an opponent; in either case, the broadcaster has no power of censorship.[118] Regardless of how well intentioned or judicious a broadcaster's directives to a candidate may be, if they impinge upon the candidate's complete freedom of expression, they are likely to be branded as censorship.

There are many different forms of censorship. One of the most obvious is canceling a scheduled appearance. Suppose hypothetical station WWW agrees to sell candidate Jones one half-hour for a speech. Before air time, however, WWW decides Jones's speech is objectionable or, perhaps, libelous. When Jones insists upon his right to say whatever he pleases, WWW cancels his appearance. The cancellation is blatant censorship, coming as it does after arrangements for air time have already been settled.[119]

Even requiring Jones to submit an advance script as a precondition to making his speech would be censorship. A broadcaster may *request* submission of an advance script to help plan out the program (for example, for duration, lighting, sound). The request is permissible as long as it represents a practice applied uniformly to Jones's opponents. However, Jones cannot be forced to submit his speech in order to get air time.[120]

It is censorship for a broadcaster to establish some standard for orthodox campaign appearances and then insist that every candidate live up to that standard. A candidate may wish to devote all his air time to an exposition of party doctrine. If so, he cannot be compelled to describe his personal qualifications for office simply because the broadcaster believes some discussion of qualifications is appropriate. Nor can a candidate's presentation be restricted to subject matter covered by his opponent in a previous appearance.[121]

During the 1972 Democratic primary for United States senator from Georgia, the candidate of the National States Rights Party ran the following ad on radio and television:

> I am J. B. Stoner. I am the only candidate for U.S. Senator who is for the white people. I am the only candidate who is against integration. All of the other candidates are race mixers to one degree or another. I say we must repeal Gambrell's civil rights law. Gambrell's law takes jobs from us whites and give those jobs to the niggers. The main reason why niggers want integration is because the niggers want white women. I am for law and order with the knowledge that you cannot have law and order and niggers too. Vote white. This time vote your convictions by voting white racist J. B. Stoner into the run-off election for U.S. Senator. Thank you.[122]

Despite complaints from civil rights leaders, the FCC refused to order local broadcasters to censor Stoner's commercial. As offensive as the commercial was to many listeners, it did not raise any clear and present danger of imminent violence. Therefore, Stoner's constitutional right to free speech could not be curtailed by licensee censorship.

A broadcaster cannot prohibit a candidate from having other people appear with him so long as certain conditions are met. First, the candidate must maintain control and direction over the program. Second, his personal appearance, either visual or vocal, must be (1) substantial in length, (2) integrally involved in the program, and (3) the focus of the program.

In a 1968 Florida race for county tax collector, a candidate scheduled for equal time on WJHG-TV (Panama City) showed up at the studio accompanied by a high-school chorus, the proud winner of a prize automobile, and various dignitaries from business and politics.[123] The candidate intended to beguile viewers with a homemade variety show. No doubt taken aback by the entourage, the station manager refused to let anyone appear with the candidate. This refusal, according to the FCC, constituted censorship. The candidate had clearly planned to be the show's focal point, reappearing frequently as emcee to introduce, interview, and thank his supporting cast. He was, therefore, entitled to have the guests appear with him.

Once it is conceded that other people may appear with the candidate, their roles as well as his cannot be censored. The broadcaster loses all right to prior approval over the form and content of the entire show. This total ban does not apply if the candidate's appearance is merely an incidental inclusion in a program featuring some other person as its central figure. For example, the candidate makes a guest appearance on a late-night talk show produced and controlled by others. Or, perhaps, he speaks briefly at a televised banquet just to introduce the evening's toastmaster. In these situations only the candidate's appearance — not the entire program — would be shielded from censorship.[124]

To go one step further, suppose the candidate does not participate at all in a program. Instead, some party leader speaks on the candidate's behalf, or a group of citizens express their opinions about the candidate, but he is neither seen nor heard throughout the show. The prohibition against censorship would then have absolutely no application. A broadcaster would be free to exercise his discretion regarding the show's form and content.[125]

It takes little imagination to guess at the legal dilemmas lurking in the ban against censorship. Someone may make defamatory remarks during a noncensorable program. The broadcaster is powerless to delete such objectionable material, because that would be censorship. Can he, nevertheless, be held liable for libel or slander? The United States Supreme Court answered no in the famous case of *Farmers Educational & Cooperative Union v. WDAY, Inc.*[126] Since a broadcaster is barred from censoring defamatory material, he must be granted immunity from liability.

Is a broadcaster cloaked with the same immunity in other kinds of lawsuits that arise from noncensorable programs — for example, copyright infringement, invasion of privacy, or violation of a union contract? In 1972 the FCC said yes: "We believe that in light of [the Supreme Court's decision] the courts would hold a licensee free from liability for any claim arising out of a 'use' by a candidate where the licensee was unable under the no-censorship provision . . . to prevent the act which gave rise to the claim."[127] As a result, the broadcaster is not allowed to compel a candidate to sign an indemnification form: an agreement to reimburse the broadcaster for any loss arising from the candidate's appearance. The FCC regards these forms as acts of censorship, because they tend to inhibit the candidate's freedom of expression.

In general, the immunity rule applies to any program that is noncensorable. This category, as we have seen, includes some programs featuring a candidate and his guests. Since these programs are noncensorable in their entirety, the broadcaster cannot be held liable for the words and acts of either the candidate or his guests.[128] If only part of a program is noncensorable (for example, the segment during which a candidate appears), there will be no immunity from liability occasioned by the censorable portion; the broadcaster is, after all, free to protect himself by exercising his editorial judgment. If some noncandidate substitutes entirely for the candidate, there is no bar at all to censorship, nor will there be any immunity for the broadcaster if a lawsuit results.[129]

Waiver of the Right to Equal Time

A candidate can waive his right to equal time. The waiver may occur involuntarily if, as we have seen, the candidate fails to request equal time quickly enough. It is also possible for a candidate to waive his right freely and knowingly. Such a voluntary waiver is, under the proper circumstances, legally binding upon the candidate.

Voluntary waivers are often useful to a broadcaster who wishes to schedule a joint appearance by all opposing candidates for one particular office. The broadcaster usually wants to organize and present the program without subjecting himself to any equal-time obligations, which will disrupt later programming. To avoid disruption, the broadcaster may seek equal-time waivers from the candidates invited to appear on the program.

Suppose there are four candidates in the Capital City mayoral race: Jones, Smith, Black, and White. Hypothetical station WWW offers one hour of free time to the four opponents for a joint appearance. The station justifiably makes its offer contingent upon the following condition: all the candidates must agree either to appear or to waive any right to equal time arising from an opponent's appearance on the program. Assume Jones, Smith, and Black agree to appear; White rejects WWW's offer and waives the right to equal time he would otherwise have gained from the appearance of his opponents. This waiver will be binding upon White. Following the joint appearance, he will have no legal right to equal time from WWW.

Assuming Jones, Smith, and Black have agreed to appear, WWW can seek a further waiver from them. The station may ask them to waive their right to equal time if, for any reason, they are subsequently unwilling or unable to appear on the program. Say all three candidates grant this waiver to WWW. Only Jones and Smith, however, actually participate in the hour-long program; Black cancels out at the last minute to fulfill other campaign commitments. Because of his waiver, Black will acquire no right to equal time.[130]

Sometimes when a station like WWW makes its initial offer, the candidates' responses vary widely. For example, Jones and Smith may accept WWW's invitation and be willing to waive their rights; but Black rejects the invitation outright; and White will appear only if a specific format is followed — a format WWW finds unacceptable. The proposed joint appearance, therefore, reaches an early impasse. The station must now decide what program, if any, will serve the community. If WWW feels that coverage of the Capital City mayoralty race is of sufficient public interest, it may decide to air a joint appearance between Jones and Smith and then give equal time to Black and White for their own use. On the other hand, WWW might withdraw its original offer entirely. The station's only obligation is to act in good faith and make a reasonable judgment considering the needs of the community it serves.

WWW's original offer to the candidates, in and of itself, created no rights to equal time. A mere offer by a broadcaster cannot trigger the equal-time rule; only actual use of the station can do that. Conversely, withdrawing the offer does not violate the equal-time rule — so long as the broadcaster exercises reasonable judgment.[131]

The FCC encourages good faith negotiations between the broadcaster and candidates when a joint appearance is proposed: "We believe it is reasonable and proper for a station and candidates to agree in advance on a format and procedures for a program on which several candidates will be appearing."[132] The broadcaster cannot simply pick some format, select the participants, specify a program length, set a date for taping and a time for broadcast, and so on, and then offer this package to the candidates on a take-it-or-leave-it basis. Such a dictatorial approach would constitute censorship, which is prohibited under the equal-time rule. It is entirely within a candidate's prerogative to reject any take-it-or-leave-it offer he finds objectionable.

What if the broadcaster, nevertheless, airs the program without the dissenting candidate? That candidate can legally demand equal time based upon his opponents' use of the station during their joint appearance. An unacceptable take-it-or-leave-it offer in no way diminishes the candidate's right to demand equal time after his opponents have taken advantage of the offer.[133]

A joint appearnace should follow any format that is agreed upon in advance. Otherwise, the waiver given by a candidate may no longer bind him. The FCC has stated: "Waivers given with full knowledge of the relevant facts concerning the broadcast (and assuming of course that the disclosed conditions [are] adhered to) [will] generally be binding."[134] If full disclosure has not been made, however, or if the disclosed conditions are not, in fact, carried out, an unfairly treated candidate will retain his rights under the equal-time rule.

For example, WWW proposes a joint appearance with all of the state's gubernatorial candidates: the Republican, Jones, the Democrat, Smith, and the third-party independent, Riley. Before the broadcast, the three candidates agree to a half-hour joint interview by a panel of WWW newsmen. The interviewers can ask questions of any candidate they choose. Candidates to whom a question is not addressed may respond if they are first recognized by the moderator. During the actual broadcast, most of the questions are directed at Jones and Smith, the two front-runners. Even though Riley constantly raises his hand, he is infrequently recognized and enjoys only four minutes of air time, while Jones uses twelve and Smith thirteen. In all likelihood, the imbalance will prove to be an unreasonable departure from the original ground rules. Despite Riley's waiver, he will be entitled to further air time from WWW in order to compensate for the disparity during the joint appearance.[135]

5
Fair Coverage of Public Issues

General Principles

THE FAIRNESS DOCTRINE. The FCC's fairness doctrine imposes a twofold duty on broadcasters: first, a broadcaster is expected to devote a reasonable percentage of air time to the coverage of public issues; second, coverage of these issues must be fair in the sense that a reasonable opportunity is afforded for the presentation of contrasting points of view.[1] The first duty is often referred to as the "affirmative obligation" imposed by the fairness doctrine; the second duty is known as the broadcaster's "balancing obligation."

The fairness doctrine represents the FCC's basic mechanism for promoting open debate on important issues. "The purpose and foundation of the fairness doctrine," said the commission in 1974, "is . . . that of the First Amendment itself: 'to preserve an uninhibited marketplace of ideas in which truth will ultimately prevail, rather than to countenance monopolization of that market, whether it be by the Government itself or a private licensee. . . .'"[2] Strict adherence to the fairness doctrine is regarded by the FCC as the single most important element in a broadcaster's service to the public.[3]

All commercial radio and television stations must abide by the fairness doctrine. The doctrine also covers programming originated by and carried over cable television (that is, so-called origination cablecasting).[4] The requirements of fairness apply generally to noncommercial educational radio and television stations, with one important exception: such stations have been prohibited by Congress from engaging in editorializing.[5] All other stations may express their editorial opinion on any public issue; indeed, the FCC encourages licensees to editorialize, so long as they abide by the balancing obligation of the fairness doctrine.[6]

The prohibition against editorializing is given only narrow application under current FCC interpretations. Noncommercial educational broadcasting is permitted, indeed, expected, to function as a vital public affairs medium, exploring and helping to solve controversial economic, social, and political problems. Noncommercial educational stations can employ the same investigative and reportorial techniques and formats utilized by broadcast journalists on commercial stations, such as documentaries, interviews, forum discussions. The one form of programming that cannot be indulged in is expression of the official opinion held by station management on any public issue.

Such formal editorializing must not be confused with personal views aired by employees of noncommercial educational stations. Anyone appearing on a noncommercial educational station as a reporter, moderator, or guest, et cetera, may express his personal opinion on public issues with the same freedom enjoyed by any other advocate who appears on a commercial or noncommercial station. However, the views expressed by the individuals appearing on a noncommercial educational station must not be represented as, or intended as, the official opinion of the station. The prohibition against formal editorializing would be violated if the station's management were presenting their own views on public issues in the guise of personal opinions aired by employees.[7]

THE BROADCASTER'S AFFIRMATIVE OBLIGATION. The broadcaster's "affirmative obligation" under the fairness doctrine is a highly general one. The FCC does not specify which public issues should be covered, nor how much time is reasonable for their coverage. Instead, the broadcaster has wide journalistic discretion in making the specific programming choices necessary to fulfill his affirmative obligation.

On occasion the commission has referred to certain issues of such overriding importance that a broadcaster could not omit them from his coverage without violating his affirmative obligation. In 1970, for example, the commission singled out the "burning issues" of Vietnam, pollution, and racial unrest.[8] Such critical issues are rare, however, and the commission will ordinarily refrain from identifying any issues that must be covered: "We have no intention of becoming involved in the selection of issues to be discussed, nor do we expect a broadcaster to cover each and every important issue which may arise in his community."[9]

It is possible that the commission might regard as unreasonable a licensee's failure to cover some issue of critical importance to a given community. In general, the issue's importance will be evidenced by (1) the amount of coverage the issue receives in the other media, for example, newspapers; (2) the degree of attention paid to the issue by public officials and community leaders; and (3) a substantive evaluation of the impact the issue has on the community at large.[10] For example, an issue upon which a community must vote — that is, a ballot proposition or public election — may pose a choice so critical to the community that the issue cannot be overlooked by a local broadcaster.[11]

THE BROADCASTER'S BALANCING OBLIGATION. The balancing obligation is, as its name suggests, a safeguard against one-sided coverage of public issues. It requires a broadcaster to afford *a reasonable opportunity for the presentation of contrasting views on controversial issues of public importance*.[12] Like the affirmative obligation, the balancing obligation is highly generalized in nature; it is up to the broadcaster to give specific content to this obligation through the exercise of his journalistic judgment.

The balancing obligation does not come into play until after coverage of some controversial issue has already been initiated. That coverage may occur during a variety of news and public affairs programs. For example, one side of a controversial issue might be presented in a station editorial, news report, news commentary or analysis, documentary, interview, forum discussion, phone-in program, or a spot announcement sponsored by some group with a point of view to express.

Assuming the balancing obligation is triggered by some program, no particular individual or group gains the right to provide the necessary balance. In this sense, the fairness doctrine operates differently from other FCC rules, like the personal-attack, political-editorial, and equal-time rules. These rules usually dictate the appropriate spokesman. The fairness doctrine does not. Instead, a broadcaster has great leeway in his choice not only of spokesmen but also of format, amount of time, and scheduling.

The mechanics of the balancing obligation are examined in the rest of this chapter. We will learn that many variables must be weighed in the balancing process. If successful, the process will result in a state of *rough balance* — not equality. Although the balancing process does not abide by any precise formula, it usually focuses upon three basic questions, which broadcasters and concerned citizens must seek to resolve.

(1) *What issue is at stake?* Assuming a program is suspected of having been one-sided, the initial task is to define the issue addressed by the program. This step seems simple enough. Indeed, it occasions few disputes when the program is straightforward, such as a station editorial in which a clear-cut position is taken. We shall see, however, broadcasters and listeners (and the FCC) may disagree on the exact issue raised by certain programs. To complicate matters further, some programs address two or more issues, each of which may include subissues.

(2) *Is the issue at stake a controversial issue of public importance?* Once the issue presented has been defined, it must be evaluated. Balance is required only for issues that are both controversial and of public importance. If an issue is of limited significance or subject to little debate, it will not trigger balancing obligations.

(3) *Has there been a reasonable opportunity for contrasting viewpoints?* Answering this question lies at the heart of the balancing process. Assuming one side of a controversial public issue has

been aired, the broadcaster must afford a reasonable opportunity for conflicting points of view; in short, he must be fair. To achieve balance, a broadcaster will adjust many different factors, including choice of program formats, scheduling, amount of time, charges — if any — and, not least of all, selection of responsible opposing spokesmen. In all the decisions he makes, the broadcaster enjoys wide discretion.

As we seek answers to the three basic questions in the balancing process, we will repeatedly encounter one overall standard: *reasonableness*. In general, the FCC contents itself with reviewing a broadcaster's judgments on fairness solely for their reasonableness and good faith. The commission constantly professes unwillingness to substitute its judgment for that of the broadcaster on questions of specific program content.

The Issue at Stake

DEFINING THE ISSUE. "To invoke the fairness doctrine," a federal judge has wisely observed, "it is not only necessary to define a controversial issue of public importance, but implicitly it is first necessary to define the issue."[13] Depending upon how the issue is defined, it may be deemed controversial and of public importance, or it may not. In the former case, the question of fairness must be pursued further to determine whether there has been a reasonable opportunity for contrasting viewpoints. If, however, the basic issue, as defined, is noncontroversial or unimportant, further fairness inquiry becomes unnecessary. Therefore, the first step in any fairness challenge — defining the issue — is often the most critical.

Defining the issue raised by a particular broadcast is easy when the issue is identified clearly on the air. Assume that the community served by hypothetical station WWW is in the midst of a heated debate over a school bond proposal on the upcoming election ballot. The president of WWW presents a station editorial in which he exhorts listeners, "Vote for the school bond measure as a constructive step toward upgrading local education." The basic issue of whether to vote for the school bond has been explicitly raised.

Suppose, however, WWW's president were to take no position on the merits of the bond proposal. He simply encourages listeners, "Vote your convictions." An irate listener seeks an opportunity to counter WWW's editorial by warning the audience, "Stay away from the polls and don't vote in this election." WWW refuses to allow this viewpoint to be aired; it maintains the issue of whether to vote at all has not been raised by the editorial.

The WWW listener disagrees with the station's assessment. He points out that local law requires more than fifty percent of the qualified freeholders to vote in a bond election in order for it to be valid. Because of this peculiarity in the election law, the question of whether to vote at all became an implicit issue when WWW editorialized. In at least one case of this nature, the FCC upheld the listener's definition of the issue at stake and decided the broadcaster had violated the fairness doctrine by failing to present the no-vote viewpoint.[14]

Let us carry our school bond example one step further. In its editorial, WWW never mentions the upcoming school bond election or alludes to it in any way. The editorial does, however, assert, in forceful terms, that the community urgently needs new school construction and a substantial increase in teachers' salaries. Thus, while WWW's editorial never explicitly states the ultimate matter in controversy — that is, passage of the school bond measure — it does present key arguments that implicitly support one side of the ultimate issue. (To facilitate school construction and salary increases, funding from the proposed school bond would first be required.) WWW would have to decide in good faith: did the editorial raise the issue of whether the school bonds should be authorized — a controversial issue — or did it merely question whether present school facilities and salaries were adequate — an issue that might not be at all controversial?

To resolve such a question, WWW or any of its concerned listeners should follow the analytical approach suggested by the FCC:

> The licensee's inquiry should focus not on whether the [broadcast] bears some tangential relevance to the school

bond question, but rather whether that [broadcast], in the context of the ongoing community debate, is so obviously and substantially related to the school bond issue as to amount to advocacy of a position on that question. If, for example, the arguments and views expressed over the air closely parallel the major arguments advanced by the partisans on one side or the other of the public debate it might be reasonable to conclude that there has been a presentation of one side of the ultimate issue, i.e., authorization of the school bonds.[15]

Needless to say, broadcasters may arrive at different conclusions when following the FCC's formula. The commission has said it will not disturb a broadcaster's determination as long as it is reasonable and arrived at in good faith.

The limits of reasonableness were dramatically tested in a recent fairness-doctrine battle touched off by an NBC news documentary.[16] On September 12, 1972, NBC-TV broadcast "Pensions: The Broken Promise." "The program had no set format," a federal judge was later to observe, "but its most prominent feature was a presentation of tragic case histories, often through personal interviews with the persons affected." An announcer opened the program, "Tonight NBC reports on Pensions: The Broken Promise," followed immediately by a series of remarks from unidentified men and women:

> WOMAN: There must be thousands maybe millions of them that's getting the same song and dance that my husband got. When they reach their time for retirement there is no funds to pay them. . . .
>
> MAN: Where does all this money go that's been paid into these pensions?
>
> MAN: The pension system is essentially a consumer fraud, a shell game and a hoax. As a matter of fact, when you say it's a consumer fraud, you pay it an undue compliment, because typically you think of consumer frauds in terms of short transactions, the purchase of an automobile, the purchase of a pair of pants, but with the pension system you really have a long term contract that doesn't perform. You have an insurance contract that can't be relied on. . . .

MAN: And I think it's a terrible thing in this country when men who work forty-five years have to eat yesterday's bread. And I don't want to compete on my old age against other old men on old age running down a supermarket aisle to get dented cans and stale breads. I don't want to look forward to it. So I really have nothing to look forward to at sixty-five.

After this opening, NBC's Edwin Newman picked up the narration: "This is a story about ordinary people with the modest hope to finish their working careers with enough money to live in dignity. That is a modest hope but it's one that is all too often not realized." Newman visited a Department of Labor building in Maryland, where annual reports on pension plans are filed. "There are millions of hopes and dreams in these files," he observed. "If experience is any guide, very many of the hopes will prove to be empty and dreams will be shattered and the rosy promises of happy and secure retirement and a vine covered cottage will prove to be false."

Newman's comments were echoed by those of various public figures, like consumer advocate Ralph Nader and former Pennsylvania Insurance Commissioner Herbert Denenberg:

NADER: We've come across in our questionnaires and other surveys, some of the most tragic cases imaginable. Where people who worked for twenty-five, thirty years and just because of a tiny quirk in the pension plan's fine print, they don't get anything.

DENENBERG: When you get to be sixty-five, you're out of work and you need a source of money and that's what a pension plan is supposed to do. Unfortunately, it's woefully inadequate. Over half the people have nothing at all from pension plans and those that do typically have only a thousand dollars a year so even if you have social security, most pension funds are inadequate.

"Many employees form their ideas about pensions," Newman continued, "by reading the slick brochures that their company or union gives them. Most of these booklets do make a pension seem a sure thing. The many restrictions and exclusions are buried in fine print or concealed by obscure language." To substantiate this point, Newman interviewed Senator Harrison Williams, chairman of the Senate Labor Committee:

> SENATOR WILLIAMS: I have all kinds of descriptions of plans here and all of them just suggest the certainty of an assured benefit upon retirement. Here's a man — this was from a brewery, sitting relaxed with a glass of beer and checks coming out of the air; well, you see, this gives a false hope, a sense of false security.
>
> NEWMAN: Senator, the way private pension plans are set up now, are the promises real?
>
> SENATOR WILLIAMS: The answer is, they are not.

Once more, the program cut to Herbert Denenberg for his overview of the pensions situation:

> It's almost an obstacle course and the miracle is when someone actually collects with the plan. There have been studies that indicate that most people won't collect. . . .
> You have to go to work for an employer, you have to stay with him, you have to stay in good health, you have to avoid layoffs, you have to take your money, turn it over to the employer, hope that he invests it safely and soundly, you have to hope that when you're age sixty-five the employer is still around and he's not likely to be in terms of the high mortality of business, so there's almost a sequence of miracles which you're counting on.

Much of the program was devoted to specific examples of pension plans that had failed. Newman narrated individual case histories of men and women who had lost their pension rights: plants closed down, taking pension rights with them; employees were prematurely fired, before they attained the age at which pension rights "vested," that is, became irrevocable; union members who moved from one local to another learned — too late — that pensions were not "portable" — that is, benefits earned through membership in one local could not be transferred to another.

"This has been a depressing program to work on," Edwin Newman concluded, but we don't want to give the impression that there are no good private pension plans. There are many good ones, and there are many people for whom the promise has become reality. That should be said.

There are certain technical problems that we've dealt with only glancingly [for example, vesting of pension rights, portability]. . . .

These are matters for Congress to consider. . . . They are also matters for those who are in pension plans. If you're in one, you might find it useful to take a close look at it.

Our own conclusion about all of this, is that it is almost inconceivable that this enormous thing has been allowed to grow up with so little understanding of it and with so little protection and such uneven results for those involved.

The situation, as we've seen it, is deplorable.

Edwin Newman, NBC News.

What issue was raised in "Pensions: The Broken Promise"? The FCC had to decide, because on November 27, 1972, a fairness-doctrine complaint was filed by Accuracy in Media, Inc. (AIM), a Washington-based organization which monitors the media. According to AIM, the program constituted a one-sided attack on the whole private pension plan system: "Nearly the entire program was devoted to criticism of private pension plans, giving the impression that failure and fraud are the rule in the management of private pension funds."

NBC characterized "Pensions" much differently: "The program constituted a broad overview of some of the problems involved in some private pension plans. It did not attempt to discuss all private pension plans. . . . Rather, it was designed to inform the public about some problems which have come to light in some pension plans and which deserve a closer look." The network's view of "Pensions" was significantly narrower than AIM's: while AIM saw a broadside against all pension plans, NBC saw only probes at some plans.

Defining the issue was critical to the ultimate question of fairness. Assuming AIM's definition was accepted — that is, "Pensions" attacked the entire pension system as a fraud and a failure — the program had presented one side of a controversial public issue, and further program balance would probably be required. If, on the other hand, "Pensions" merely investigated some problems existing in some pension plans, the program could not be considered controversial: the individual tragedies in "Pensions" were not themselves subject to controversy; exposing them merely illustrated a truism — that is, some evils exist within certain pension plans. Consequently, NBC argued, further program balance under the fairness doctrine would be unnecessary.

The FCC analyzed the case in terms that did not bode well for NBC: "The specific question properly before us here is . . . not whether NBC may reasonably say that the broad, overall 'subject' of the 'Pensions' program was 'some problems in some pension plans,' but rather whether the program did in fact present viewpoints on one side of the issue of the overall performance . . . of the private pension system." Thus, the commission seemed fully prepared to bypass NBC's determination, regardless of whether it was reasonable. At stake was a question of fact: Had "Pensions" actually presented one-sided views on the performance of the entire pension system? If so, then the issue of overall performance had, in fact, been raised, as AIM contended.

After its own review of the "Pensions" transcript, the commission concluded that views broadly critical of the entire pension system had, in fact, been presented. Only a few positive views had been expressed — for example, part of Edwin Newman's closing commentary. The result, in the commission's judgment, was a one-sided presentation on the overall performance of America's private pension system. Since this broad issue was considered a controversial one, the commission ruled that further programming would be necessary to achieve balance.

NBC appealed to federal court. On September 27, 1974, a three-judge panel of the Court of Appeals for the District of Columbia reversed the FCC by a vote of 2 to 1. Speaking for the majority, Judge Harold Leventhal relied upon the principle, often espoused by the FCC, that a licensee's judgments under the fairness doctrine will not be disturbed as long as they are reasonable and made in good faith. This principle, he said,

> has distinctive force and vitality when the crucial question is the kind raised in this case, i.e., in defining the scope of the issue raised by the program, for this inquiry typically turns on the kind of communications judgments that are the stuff

of the daily decisions of the licensee. There may be mistakes in the licensee's determination. But the review power of the [FCC] is limited to licensee determinations that are not only different from those the agency would have reached in the first instance but are unreasonable.

The court found no basis for questioning the reasonableness of NBC's judgment:

> In our view, the present record sustains NBC as having exercised discretion, and not abused discretion, in making the editorial judgment that what was presented, in the dominant thrust of the program, was an exposé of the abuses that appeared in the private pension industry, and not a general report on the state of the industry.

Judge Leventhal warned against confusing a sharply aimed exposé with an overall critique:

> A report that evils exist within a group is just not the same thing as a report on the entire group, or even on the majority of the group. An exposé that establishes that certain policemen have taken bribes, or smoked pot, or participated in a burglary ring, is not a report on policemen in general. It may be that the depiction of abuses will lead to broader inferences. Certainly, severe deficiencies within an industry may reflect on the industry as a whole. . . . But the possible inferences and speculations that may be drawn from a factual presentation, are too diverse and manifold — ranging, as they inevitably must, over the entire span of viewer predilections, characteristics and reactions — to serve as a vehicle for overriding the journalistic judgment.

In short, a broadcast journalist does not have to balance off an exposé "solely because the facts he presents jar the viewer and cause him to think and ask questions as to how widespread the abuses may be."

Judge Leventhal recognized that "Pensions" had precipitated "the first case in which a broadcaster has been held in violation of the fairness doctrine for the broadcasting of an investigative news documentary that presented a serious social problem." Precisely because "Pensions" involved *investigative journalism,* self-restraint on the commission's part was essential.

> Investigative reporting has a distinctive role of uncovering and exposing abuses. It would be undermined if a government agency were free to review the editorial judgments involved in the selection of theme and materials, to overrule the licensee's editorial "judgment as to what was presented," though not unreasonable, to conclude that in the agency's view the expose had a broader message in fact than that discerned by the licensee and therefore, under the balancing obligation [of the fairness doctrine], required an additional and offsetting program.

Here NBC had determined that "Pensions" would expose specific abuses its reporters had uncovered. There was no controversy over the existence of these abuses. The commission, however, substituted its judgment for NBC's and decided that "Pensions" actually raised an entirely different issue. As enlarged by the FCC, the "Pensions" issue attained controversial status. Therefore, NBC News incurred the burden of presenting opposing views on the escalated controversy. If such governmental intrusion were allowed to go unchecked, future attempts at investigative journalism might be inhibited. It was chiefly to avoid inhibiting broadcast journalism that the court reversed the FCC.

ISSUES AND SUBISSUES. We have proceeded thus far on the tacit assumption that any given broadcast will raise only one issue. While this characteristic is true of many programs, it is not universally so. A program may address two or more discrete issues, each deserving of a separate balance of opinion in order to achieve fairness. As the FCC warned in 1970: "The licensee could not cover an issue, making two important points in his discussion of that issue; afford time for the contrasting viewpoint on one of these two points; and on the other point, reject fairness requests on the ground that it is a 'sub-issue.' "[17]

On the other hand, some aspects of a program may be nothing

more than subissues within the overall discussion. The fairness doctrine does not require that independent balance be achieved on each subissue. Therefore, distinguishing subissues from primary issues becomes a critical exercise. The FCC offers no formal guidelines. However, a look at one recent ruling may prove helpful.

On May 8, 1972, President Nixon instituted a new war policy in Vietnam, which consisted of mining the harbor at Haiphong and other North Vietnamese ports. On May 11 and 16, WNET-TV (Newark–New York City) devoted two editions of its show "Free Time" to the views of antiwar advocates such as Jane Fonda and Daniel Ellsberg.[18] These broadcasts prompted a complaint from one viewer, Horace Rowley III; he insisted that WNET-TV air contrasting views to offset opposition to the new mining policy expressed on May 11 and 16.

WNET disagreed with Rowley's contention that the mining policy was a distinct issue raised by the programs in question. The new mining policy, WNET claimed, was but a subissue, included within the primary issue of overall escalation in the Vietnam War.

> The two "Free Time" offerings in May were not exclusively devoted to mining of North Vietnamese harbors. They also discussed at length, Vietnam history, the administration's escalation policies, the effects of a prolonged war in Southeast Asia, the ability of the President to lead our country, the air war, student unrest, the P.O.W. issue, and a host of other issues associated with current foreign policy.
> In this connection, we believe that a discussion of the mining of Haiphong, and other North Vietnamese ports is part of the larger, more important issue of the Government's policy of military escalation (which dates as early as March 6 [1972] and which achieved prominence on April 10 [1972] with the announcement that the government was resuming B-52 raids — a tactic last employed in November, 1967). . . . Both the primary issue [escalation] and the sub-issue [mining] were extensively discussed over our facilities.

The FCC accepted WNET's definition of the primary issue raised by the "Free Time" broadcasts. "In applying the fairness doctrine," the commission wrote to Rowley, it is sometimes difficult to determine whether only one general issue exists or whether another distinct but related issue arising out of the general issue should be treated separately. . . . For the purposes of this discussion, we can assume that the controversy over the bombing and mining is sufficiently separable from the general controversy over the Vietnam war to be treated as a distinct issue under the fairness doctrine. However, we do not feel it was unreasonable for WNET to conclude that the bombing and mining policy announced by President Nixon on May 8 was part of the larger issue of military escalation of the war which dated back to March and April of 1972. WNET notes that on April 10 the government announced renewed B-52 bombing raids in North Vietnam. Therefore, while the bombing and mining of North Vietnam could perhaps be treated as a separate controversial issue we do not agree with your conclusion that this issue need necessarily be isolated from other events in the way you urge.

Thus, out of three potential issues — United States involvement in Vietnam, escalation of the war, and mining North Vietnamese harbors — only two could be segregated as primary issues for the purposes of the fairness doctrine. Escalation presented an issue worthy of its own treatment apart from the other primary issue (United States involvement in general). Not so, however, with the narrower mining controversy, on which Rowley had requested an independent balance of opinion. That controversy was merely a subissue within the primary issue of escalation, and on this latter issue, WNET had fulfilled its obligation to present contrasting viewpoints.

Controversial Issues of Public Importance

IN GENERAL. The fairness doctrine applies only to issues that are both *controversial* and *of public importance*. No precise definition of these two terms can be offered. "Given the limitless number of potential controversial issues," said the FCC in 1974, "and the varying circumstances in which they might arise, we have not been able to develop detailed criteria which would be appropriate in all cases."[19] Therefore, the commission relies, at least initially, upon the reasonable good faith judgment of broadcasters, who must identify controversial issues of public importance on a case-by-case basis.

Some general guidelines, however, can be laid down. The controversial nature of an issue can be determined rather objectively. Highly relevant to the broadcaster's judgment — as well as that of an aroused listener or viewer — will be his measurement of the degree of attention paid to an issue by public officials, community leaders, and the media. From this measurement, the broadcaster or listener should be able to tell whether an issue is "the subject of vigorous debate with substantial elements of the community in opposition to one another."[20]

A determination of public importance depends upon an essentially subjective evaluation of "the impact that the issue is likely to have on the community at large."[21] Suppose the issue requires the community to make some choice, be it social, political, or economic, et cetera. An election would necessitate such a choice; a labor boycott would prod consumers to decide whether they should stop patronizing a store or product. If some decision is called for, the broadcaster or listener ought to ask himself whether the outcome of that decision will have a "significant impact" on society or its institutions.

When identifying controversial public issues, the broadcaster, as well as the citizen, must look to substance rather than label or form. "It is immaterial," the commission has said, "whether a particular program or viewpoint is presented under the label of 'Americanism,' 'anti-communism' or 'states' rights,' or whether it is a paid announcement, official speech, editorial or religious broadcast."[22] What counts is the substance of the issue presented — not the category or format of the program dealing with the issue.

For example, a broadcast address by an elected official can present one side of a controversial issue, although the address may be officially billed as a nonpartisan "report to the people." Such an official characterization should not be blindly accepted, even if the President himself is reporting to the nation. Instead, the address —

whether it be presidential, senatorial, gubernatorial, or mayoral — must be objectively analyzed; if it actually discusses controversial issues in a partisan one-sided manner, then, the fairness doctrine will be triggered.[23]

During 1961 about fifty radio stations were carrying a syndicated program entitled "Living Should Be Fun."[24] It featured the well-known nutritionist Carlton Fredericks. After many listener complaints regarding the controversial nature of the show, the FCC investigated. In response to commission inquiries, some of the fifty stations maintained that a program dealing with good health and a nutritious diet should not be considered a discussion of a controversial issue.

The FCC, however, took a closer look at the actual substance of "Living Should Be Fun" and came to a different conclusion.

> We do not say that "Living Should Be Fun" in its entirety dealt with controversial issues; nor do we say that controversial issues were discussed on each individual program. However, neither can we agree that the program consisted merely of the discussion of the desirability of good health and nutritious diet. Anyone who listened to the program regularly — and station licensees have the obligation to know what is being broadcast over their facilities — should have been aware that at times controversial issues of public importance were discussed. In discussing such subjects as the fluoridation of water, the value of krebiozen in the treatment of cancer, the nutritive qualities of white bread, and the use of high potency vitamins without medical advice, Fredericks emphasized the fact that his views were opposed to many authorities in these fields. . . .

Clearly, it was unreasonable for the radio stations to conclude, solely on the basis of the program's general theme or outlook, that it had not raised any controversial issues.

Beyond these generalizations about controversial public issues, we may now examine some more specific criteria, which the commission, over the years, has developed.

LOCAL AND NATIONAL ISSUES. Both local and national issues may be subject to the fairness doctrine. On a local issue, fairness obligations arise solely within the broadcast service area, where the issue is controversial and of public importance. A national issue, on the other hand, is likely to be the cause of public controversy in most, if not all, areas served by broadcasters. Therefore, the fairness doctrine must be satisfied whenever one side of such a national issue is presented by some local broadcaster.[25]

Can the broadcaster excuse himself from airing the other side of an issue on the ground that the issue, while a matter of national controversy, has not yet become controversial locally? The probable answer is no. Referring to a local broadcaster, whose treatment of a controversial national issue had been less than evenhanded, the FCC stated in 1962: "A licensee cannot excuse a onesided presentation on the basis that the subject matter was not controversial in its service area, for it is only through a fair presentation of all facts and arguments on a particular question that public opinion can properly develop."[26] In other words, the local broadcaster ought to encourage the "disinterested formation of public opinion" in his service area by covering national issues fairly.

Sometimes a broadcaster may mistakenly overlook the fact that an issue has become controversial within his local service area. On May 6, 1970, then-Governor Ronald Reagan made an address over California radio and television stations.[27] He announced a four-day closure of California's state colleges and universities because of campus disruptions following the killing of four students at Ohio's Kent State University. Reagan also called for the closing of all private colleges in California.

One California broadcaster declined to balance the views expressed by the governor. The broadcaster insisted that in his service area the school closure was not a controversial issue, because no colleges in the vicinity were affected by Reagan's order. However, this fact did not, according to the FCC, remove the closure issue from the realm of local controversy.

> The closing of all state universities and colleges and the Governor's request that all private schools consider similar action appears to have been likely to affect, and result in controversy, in all parts of the state. We think that the

speech, whether categorized in terms of the necessity, wisdom or legality of the closing of California institutions or in other terms, must by all reasonable standards be considered a discussion of a controversial issue of public importance to the people of California and that the fairness doctrine is therefore applicable to the issues presented therein.

The broadcaster's judgment that no controversial issue had been raised in his area was clearly unreasonable.

A local controversy can spring up over an issue that is admittedly noncontroversial nationally. Consider a 1970 dispute in Dayton, Ohio.[28] Station WLWD-TV aired a presidential address, public service announcements, and an editorial supporting the charity drive conducted by the United Appeal. A local organization, the United People, opposed this viewpoint, believing instead that people ought to give directly to their favorite charities, rather than through the United Appeal. According to United People, the United Appeal did not allocate its funds equitably in Dayton, and the Appeal's governing board lacked any representation by poor people, factory workers, or youth.

WLWD-TV maintained that support of the United Appeal raised no controversial issue, because the United Appeal was nationally recognized and accepted. The FCC ruled WLWD's decision had been unreasonable. No attempt had been made by the station to refute the evidence of a local controversy presented by United People. "The licensee's position," observed former FCC Chairman Dean Burch, "comes down to the assertion that the United Appeal has long-established national and local acceptance. That is undoubtedly true, but that does not gainsay the showing that in Dayton a significant controversy has emerged at this time."

NEWSWORTHINESS AND PUBLIC IMPORTANCE. The public importance of a controversial issue should not be equated with the issue's newsworthiness. The degree of news coverage — broadcast or print — accorded to an issue is just one factor to be considered when determining the issue's public importance. That factor is by no means conclusive.[29]

The distinction between public importance and mere news-worthiness was dramatized recently in Los Angeles.[30] On Sunday, February 16, 1969, the *Los Angeles Times* ran a front-page profile of a local Communist, Dorothy Healey. Entitled "Patriot-Marxist — L.A.'s Number One Red Finds the U.S. Isn't All Bad," the article portrayed Healey in many respects as an upstanding American, who had been subjected to government harassment.

The *Times's* article provoked an angry retort the following day over local station KTTV-TV. Enraged by both the substance of the article and its prominent position on page one, KTTV commentator George Putnam blasted the *Times* and Healey during the station's news report:

> If I were a soldier or a sailor or a Marine or a young American in the Air Force, serving in Vietnam — wondering if I would live just one more day — if I were a young lad back from Vietnam, lying in one of our Veterans' hospitals — a leg gone — an arm missing — blind — or faceless — from the horrors of that war . . . I would be shocked into rage by the story that appeared in the number one column on the number one page of Sunday's *Los Angeles Times.*
>
> The *Los Angeles Times,* which chose not to even mention Abraham Lincoln's birthday — devoted more words to their "patriot-Marxist," Dorothy Healey, in their Sunday edition . . . than any other news item or topic. Yes, more space for the Communist Dorothy Healey than the Communist violations of the Tet New Year's observance — or the Berlin crisis — or the tinderbox in the Middle East, or any other top news.
>
> Now listen, if you will, to just a portion of what the *Los Angeles Times* has to say about . . . Dorothy Healey. "In some ways," says the *Times,* "Dorothy Healey might be considered an exemplary American — she owns her home, pays her taxes, cares for her aged mother, and dotes on her scholarly son. She professes a sincere patriotism, and she rarely missed a meeting of the P.T.A." . . .
>
> Mrs. Healey tells of the night she heard the report read concerning Joseph Stalin's horrors. The report released by Nikita Krushchev. And Mrs. Healey tells the *Times* that she sobbed all night long. She just never believed those stories.
>
> One can't help but wonder if she might have lost another

night's sleep had Krushchev told us of his own extermination of millions of Ukrainians by systematic starvation. Wonder if she ever heard about that? . . .

Well, in that lengthy and boring *Times* story she tells of her home and her office being bugged — of telling her visitors never to mention their names when they visit her. Actually Mrs. Healey should be right at home with such tactics — because they're all too commonplace among the Communists. . . .

Dorothy Healey may be the *Los Angeles Times'* kind of exemplary American, who professes sincere patriotism — she may be the *Los Angeles Times'* kind of patriot — but she sure as hell is not mine. And, my fellow Americans, I trust she is not yours.

And if you are as shocked as I am by this insult to American patriotism, I urge you to let the *Times* hear your voice — loud and clear.

Healey complained to the FCC. She contended Putnam had attacked her character and integrity during his discussion of a controversial issue of public importance — namely, her role as a Communist in the community. Therefore, under the fairness doctrine, KTTV should have recognized her as the appropriate spokesman to answer Putnam's personal attack. The commission, however, refused to upset KTTV's judgment that Healey's role as a Communist was not an issue of public importance in Los Angeles. Consequently, the station had not acted unreasonably in denying Healey an opportunity to respond.

Healey appealed to federal court, where the FCC's decision was upheld. The court emphasized the distinction between newsworthiness and so-called public importance.

Merely because a story is newsworthy does not mean that it contains a controversial issue of public importance. Our daily papers and television broadcasts alike are filled with news items which good journalistic judgment would classify as newsworthy, but which the same editors would not characterize as containing important controversial public issues.

Indeed, George Putnam had specifically criticized the *Times* for overrating the newsworthiness of Dorothy Healey's story.

"Even if we considered that the Putnam broadcast was primarily or substantially directed against . . . Healey personally," the court continued,

> there still was raised no controversial issue of public importance. In effect, the *Los Angeles Times* wrote a long article to prove that even an American Communist could be a nice, normal, ordinary housewife. The TV licensee's commentator disagreed; he questioned whether she really is a nice, normal ordinary person. We fail to see the "controversial issue of public importance" here. . . . Healey has had favorable publicity on the front page of the Sunday *Los Angeles Times,* followed by six minutes . . . of substantially unfavorable publicity on the television station. Would any other Los Angeles housewife, similarly written and broadcast about, because of any other unusual aspect of her personal life, automatically become a controversial issue of public importance? We doubt it. In effect [Healey's] rationale is: I am a Communist. I am (or was) a Communist leader in the Los Angeles area. Therefore, I am important. I am controversial. What I say and do is therefore a controversial issue of public importance.
>
> [Healey] may be newsworthy — this is a question we leave to the editorial judgment of the *Times* and the licensee — but we cannot see that this 57-year-old Communist housewife and her PTA activities, her children and their families, qualify as a "controversial issue of public importance" under the fairness doctrine.

The court concluded by warning that a decision in Healey's favor might have undermined the basic purpose of the fairness doctrine.

> To characterize every dispute on this character as calling for a rejoinder would so inhibit television and radio as to destroy a good part of their public usefulness. It would make what has already been criticized as a bland product disseminated by an uncourageous media even more innocuous. It would discourage any radio-television commentary on newspaper editorials or news items. It would in every way inhibit that "robust public debate" that the fairness doctrine was born to enhance.

. . . By elevating this Los Angeles housewife to the dignity of a "controversial issue of public importance," we would insure that the licensees and the FCC would be swamped by complaints under the fairness doctrine, and that the licensee's only defense would be to eliminate everything controversial from the air. Obviously the American people would be the loser.

PRIVATE DISPUTES. The fairness doctrine cannot be invoked to secure balanced discussion of controversies that concern only limited or private circles within society. Resolution of such controversies is unlikely to have a significant impact upon the public at large. Therefore, airing both sides of these private controversies would do little to advance the high purpose behind the fairness doctrine — namely, to keep the public informed on matters of concern to major segments of the community.[31]

On September 19, 1972, during a pre–football game broadcast of "The NFL Today," CBS sports commentator Tom Brookshier discussed pension rights for former professional football players.[32] Brookshier argued that these players deserved to be included in the current retirement plan of the National Football League Players Association (NFLPA). Brookshier's opinion aroused the NFLPA, which was then fighting a lawsuit over pension rights brought by former professional players (members of the National Football League Alumni Association). NFLPA asked CBS for an opportunity to present a contrasting viewpoint on the issue Brookshier had raised — namely, whether former players should share in pension rights which accrued to present-day players. "In its own context — the playing of professional sports," said the NFLPA, "the issue presented herein is in fact a controversial one and could have a direct impact on both the players and the fans of professional football."

CBS disagreed, and the FCC upheld the network's judgment.

. . . NFLPA and the Alumni Association are engaged in a dispute wholly private in nature and only incidentally related to or of interest to the public. . . . The [evidence] submitted by the NFLPA in the form of newspaper copy show[s] that there is interest in the matter by the nation's sportswriters and their readers, but not the kind of controversy which would raise the issue to one of public importance. . . . Even the NFLPA concedes that, at best, the issues involved are fairly well concentrated within the confines of the professional football sports world and fans of the game.

CBS had acted reasonably, therefore, in deciding the pension issue was not one of public importance.

A private controversy will not attain public importance simply because it receives some media coverage. Consider the persistent opposition to Darwin's theory of evolution by religious fundamentalists. In 1971 WSPA-TV (Spartanburg, South Carolina) broadcast two series: one entitled "The New Science," the other, "Monkeys, Apes, and Man."[33] A viewer, H. B. Van Velzer, complained that the series supported the theory of evolution, and WSPA-TV should, therefore, present the contrasting viewpoint — that is, a rejection of Darwinism in favor of the biblical interpretation of creation.

"Any dispute that may exist as to the theory of evolution," responded WSPA-TV, "fails to rise to sufficient public importance to invoke the fairness doctrine in the area served by WSPA-TV. . . ." The station cited surveys it had made within its service area to ascertain community needs and interests: not a single person had identified the theory of evolution as an important public issue.

According to Van Velzer, however, the very fact that the series had been broadcast three times a week for five months and had been highly acclaimed indicated the public importance which WSPA-TV must have attached to the subject of evolution. The FCC quickly disposed of this argument: "Merely because a particular subject is considered of informational or educational value and interest to the viewing public and is therefore presented in the licensee's programming does not necessarily indicate that such a subject constitutes a controversial issue of public importance. . . ."

Van Velzer's documentary evidence of a public controversy included letters to the editor of South Carolina's *Greenville News*. The FCC was not impressed by the tenor of these letters.

Although the letters to the editor of the *Greenville News* . . . would appear to indicate that there are differing private views on the theory of evolution among certain members of your community, such letters and views do not in and of themselves evidence a substantial public controversy regarding the subject within the purview of the fairness doctrine. . . . This is not to say that the particular religious views which you and others in your community hold are inconsequential or lightly dismissed. However, the issue here is not the general significance of such private views, but the reasonableness of the licensee's determination that no controversial issue of public proportion inheres in the theory of evolution as presented in its programming.

WSPA-TV, according to the FCC, had exercised its discretion in a reasonable manner when it found no controversy of "public proportion."

MINOR SHADES OF OPINION. Not every shade of opinion broadcast activates balancing obligations under the fairness doctrine. The FCC recognizes that "if every statement, or inference from statements or presentations, could be made the subject of a separate and distinct fairness requirement, the doctrine would be unworkable."[34] The commission would be forced to pass judgment on thousands of complaints that some remark — or the mere inference to be drawn from a remark — had not been fairly balanced by other programming. Such an incessant review could easily surpass the commission's capacities. What's more, it might discourage attempts at provocative programming. "A policy of requiring fairness, statement by statement or inference by inference, with constant Governmental intervention to try to implement the policy, would simply be inconsistent with the profound national commitment to the principle that debate on public issues should be 'uninhibited, robust, wide-open.' . . ."[35] Thus, the fairness doctrine, if applied with excessive zeal, could defeat its own purpose of promoting diversity of opinion.

To avoid this counterproductive effect, the commission follows a *de minimis* principle: below a certain threshold, controversial viewpoints expressed on the air fail to create the imbalance in programming that precipitates fairness obligations. While the critical cutoff point has never been precisely set by the commission, it seems to depend upon the degree of advocacy or emphasis with which broadcast remarks are made. One side of some controversial issue must be espoused; simply dispensing neutral information is not enough. "Merely because a particular subject is considered of informational or educational value and interest to the viewing public and is therefore presented in the licensee's programming does not necessarily indicate that such subject constitutes a controversial issue of public importance. . . ."[36]

Usually, when only passing reference is made to some controversy, no significant imbalance in programming results, and the fairness doctrine cannot be invoked. Newscasts, for example, frequently do no more than touch upon controversial issues in the course of reporting current events. On July 21, 1972, during the "David Brinkley's Journal" segment of "NBC Nightly News," commentator Brinkley remarked on the retirement of Otto Otepka from the Subversive Activities Control Board (SACB):

> What follows is another moral saga of the bureaucratic life in Washington. Nine years ago, a man named Otto Otepka was a minor security official in the Department of State when a Senate sub-committee was investigating the loyalty of State Department employees. Otepka said the committee was not getting the whole truth, as he saw it, so he slipped the committee some State Department classified papers. But he was caught at it, and there was a loud, raucous controversy. It is interesting to note now, by the way, that the same people who were outraged when Daniel Ellsberg put out classified papers thought it was fine when Otepka put out classified papers. Anyway, the State Department fired him. He appealed the firing and it dragged through hearings and appeals for five years, while in the meantime he remained on the payroll, doing nothing, at full salary – $17,000. However, three years ago President Nixon came into office and ended this by giving Otepka a better job at $36,000 a year – a member of the Subversive Activities Control Board. *That is an agency which does nothing whatsoever, has no reason to exist, and it holds on in spite of attempts to abolish it.* Its members are supposed

to be confirmed by the Senate, but for three years the Senate just never got around to voting on Otepka one way or another, and so he stayed on there, doing nothing. Now after three years of no work at $36,000 a year, coming after five years of no work at $17,000 a year, he is retiring at the age of 57. His pension is computed on his three highest earning years, or $36,000. So he will retire on a pension of $24,000 a year for life, or $7,000 more than he ever made when he was working. It's the end of another continuing series on the bureaucratic life in Washington.[37]

Admittedly, Brinkley's characterization of SACB as a do-nothing agency evinced a one-sided viewpoint. His disparagement also happened to coincide with congressional consideration of a bill to continue appropriations for SACB. Not surprisingly, a viewer complained that Brinkley had presented only one side of a controversial issue, thereby incurring balancing obligations.

The FCC disagreed. "The specific issue on the facts presented here," began the commission,

> is whether Mr. Brinkley's remarks were so related to a question of the SACB's performance and continued existence and to the SACB appropriation bill before Congress as to evidence a discussion of a controversial issue of public importance, and the reasonableness of NBC's judgment that they were not.

The commission concluded that Brinkley's commentary was not sufficiently closely related to the SACB issue:

> It must first be observed that aside from . . . one specific reference to the SACB in passing, the Brinkley commentary was focused on the personal history and retirement of Mr. Otepka as what the commentator termed "another moral saga of bureaucratic life in Washington" and not on the Board itself or its record. Secondly, Mr. Brinkley did not comment upon nor even mention the SACB appropriation bill in his remarks. Thus, although the commentary touched upon the work and continuation of the SACB, it did so only incidentally during a discourse on Mr. Otepka's career and retirement. Thus, it is not believed that Mr. Brinkley's remarks were addressed more than incidentally to the SACB.

There was no necessity, under the fairness doctrine, to offset the particular shade of opinion toward SACB expressed by Brinkley in passing.

FCC intervention to secure perfect fairness in the Brinkley situation would not have been in the public interest. "For, under the guise of enforcing the fairness doctrine," the commission conceded, "we cannot become the national arbiter of the fairness or accuracy of every observation, statement or casual comment in the tens of thousands of newscasts by thousands of broadcast licensees." Such pervasive intervention by government in the journalistic process would conflict with both the goal of the First Amendment as well as the public interest standard.

The *de minimis* principle has been applied to entertainment programming as well as news and public affairs. A typical example arose in 1969 over "Romper Room."[38] This children's program was carried five mornings a week over KTVU (Oakland, California). On each show the children recited grace: "God is great, God is good. Let us thank Him for our food. Amen." A viewer complained that recitation of the prayer raised a controversial issue of public importance: "To say, 'God is great' and 'God is good' . . . is clearly tantamount to saying 'There is a God, and therefore atheism is mistaken.' "

The FCC disagreed. It reasoned that a mere passing reference to an issue in the course of an entertainment program did not amount to advocacy of a particular viewpoint on the issue. Therefore, KTVU incurred no fairness obligations. The commission has applied the same reasoning to religious programming in which church services are aired; broadcasting a service does not, in and of itself, raise any controversial issue.[39]

In general, the commission has not delved into broadcast entertainment in order to discover the presentation of controversial issues. In 1972, George Corey, a student at Suffolk Law School, brought a complaint against three Boston television stations — WBZ-TV, WNAC-TV, and WSBK-TV.[40] Corey objected to the scenes of violence in children's programming. He claimed that by merely showing violent episodes, the stations had "unfairly presented violence as something worthwhile for young children to watch without indicating that exposure to such stimuli may be detrimental. . . ." Corey urged that a contrasting viewpoint be presented — perhaps, in the form of a public-service notice: "Warning: Viewing of violent television programming by children can be hazardous to their mental health and well being."

"We cannot agree," ruled the commission,

> that the broadcast of violent episodes during entertainment programs necessarily constitutes the presentation of one side of a controversial issue of public importance. It simply is not an appropriate application of the fairness doctrine to say that an entertainment program — whether it be Shakespeare or an action-adventure show — raises a controversial issue if ·it contains a violent scene and has a significant audience of children. Were we to adopt your construction that the depiction of a violent scene is a discussion of one side of a controversial issue of public importance, the number of controversial issues presented on entertainment shows would be virtually endless (e.g., a scene with a high-powered car; or one showing a person taking an alcoholic drink or cigarette; depicting women in a soft feminine or light romantic role).

The commission seems clearly disinclined to recognize controversial issues implicit in entertainment programming.[41]

Reasonable Opportunity for Contrasting Views

IN GENERAL. If one side of a controversial issue is aired, there must be a reasonable opportunity for the broadcast of contrasting views. What constitutes a reasonable opportunity? The term has never been sharply defined by the FCC. The commission expects a spirit of cooperation on the part of broadcasters, rather than adherence to any set of rigid procedures.

As early as 1949, the FCC emphasized the need for broadcasters to play a conscious and positive role in encouraging presentation of opposing viewpoints:

> We do not believe . . . that the licensee's obligations to serve the public interest can be met merely through the adoption of a general policy of not refusing to broadcast opposing views where a demand is made of the station for broadcast time. If, as we believe to be the case, the public interest is best served in a democracy through the ability of the people to hear expositions of the various positions taken by responsible groups and individuals on particular topics and to choose between them, it is evident that broadcast licensees have *an affirmative duty generally to encourage and implement the broadcast of all sides of controversial public issues* over their facilities, over and beyond their obligation to make available on demand opportunities for the expression of opposing views.[42]

The broadcaster's affirmative duty should not be discharged in a "stingy, narrow fashion":

> What is called for is a generous, good faith effort. . . . With such an effort, fairness will be markedly served; without it, the result is simply to short change the public interest in a most vital area. A licensee who can and should be as outspoken and hard-hitting as he wishes in presenting his view of an issue should be equally vigorous in getting the other side before the public. . . . It follows also that the licensee should be most cooperative in making available appropriate station facilities and resources to those responding to his offer of time. The cooperative attitude or atmosphere of the station in this vital area is thus of great importance.[43]

The duty to afford a reasonable opportunity for conflicting views is nondelegable; it rests squarely with each licensee. A broadcaster must evaluate his controversial-issue programming and determine whether and when balance is actually achieved. He cannot rely blindly upon assurances from others that a particular program has "built-in balance," which obviates the need to air opposing views. Nor can he proceed on the vague assumption that a supposed liberal "tone" in network programming will somehow offset the more conservative "tone" of local programming. Such casual reliance upon outside sources would be incompatible with the fairness obligations of a broadcast licensee.[44]

Can a broadcaster acquit himself of his responsibilities by pointing to the coverage that other media — print as well as broadcast — have given to a controversial issue? The FCC says no. It recognizes that citizens receive their information on public issues from a variety of sources. Still there are sound reasons for each broadcaster to comply with the fairness doctrine through his own programming:

> We believe that the requirement that *each* station provide for contrasting views greatly increases the likelihood that individual members of the public will be exposed to varying points of view. . . . Since the fairness doctrine does not require balance in individual programs or series of programs, but only in a station's overall programming, there is no assurance that a listener who hears an initial presentation will also hear a rebuttal. . . . However, if all stations presenting programming relating to a controversial issue of public importance make an effort to round out their coverage with contrasting viewpoints, these various points of view will receive a much wider public dissemination.[45]

In the discussion that follows, we will consider how a reasonable opportunity for contrasting views can best be facilitated. Few hard rules exist in this area. The FCC recognized in 1949 that

> there can be no one all embracing formula which licensees can hope to apply to insure the fair and balanced presentation of all public issues. Different issues will inevitably require different techniques of presentation and production. The licensee will in each instance be called upon to exercise his best judgment and good sense in determining what subjects should be considered, the particular format of the programs to be devoted to each subject, the different shades of opinion to be presented, and the spokesmen for each point of view. In determining whether to honor specific requests for time, the station will inevitably be confronted with such questions as . . . whether the viewpoint of the requesting party has already received a sufficient amount of broadcast time, or whether there may not be other available groups or individuals who might be more appropriate spokesmen for the particular point of view than the person making the request.[46]

When reviewing any of these decisions, the FCC will not substitute its judgment for that of a licensee. Instead, the commission looks only for reasonableness and good faith on the part of broadcasters.

MAJOR SHADES OF OPINION. The fairness doctrine does not require air time for every conceivable viewpoint on a controversial issue.[47] Instead, the selection of viewpoints to be aired is left within the broadcaster's discretion. His choice will be relatively easy if the issue in question involves few contrasting views. For example, a straightforward ballot proposition may arouse only narrow pro and con opinions. Accordingly, a broadcaster could provide a reasonable opportunity for contrasting views simply by presenting two opposing spokesmen, whose remarks adequately reflect the essential public debate.

Not all issues, however, are so elementary. Some involve many different viewpoints — often called "shades of opinion" by the FCC. Consider the national controversy that raged for years over American conduct of the Vietnam War. Our participation in the war clearly constituted a controversial issue of public importance. What were the contrasting viewpoints on that issue? Certainly they were more varied than might have been suggested at times by the often simplistic confrontation between hawks and doves.

Any reasonable analysis of the war issue would have to have included at least four widely debated points of view: namely, that we should have escalated our military effort in Vietnam; that we should have maintained our commitment without escalating; that we should have decreased our commitment through gradual phased withdrawal of troops; or that we should have withdrawn at once. Given such an array of important contrasting views, a broadcaster would have been remiss in his fairness obligations had he limited his coverage of the war issue to the "victory-at-all-cost" position versus the "out-now" position; there were simply too many significant shades of opinion in between, which could not have been ignored.[48]

In affording a reasonable opportunity for conflicting viewpoints, how is a broadcaster to decide which shades of opinion to present?

There is no hard formula to follow. The FCC merely points out a general direction:

> In evaluating a "spectrum" of contrasting viewpoints on an issue, the licensee should make a good faith effort to identify the *major* viewpoints and shades of opinion being debated in the community, and to make a provision for their presentation. In many, or perhaps most, cases it may be possible to find that only two viewpoints are significant enough to warrant broadcast coverage. However, other issues may involve a range of markedly different and important policy alternatives. In such circumstances, the broadcaster must make a determination as to which shades of opinion are of sufficient public importance to warrant coverage, and also the extent and nature of that coverage.[49]

While a broadcaster is not required to present relatively insignificant views, he can, of course, do so, giving air time to even small minorities within the community.

OVERALL PROGRAMMING AND SPECIFIC FORMATS. Contrasting viewpoints on any given issue may be presented in many different formats. Identical formats are not required: a station editorial on one side of the issue need not necessarily be balanced by an editorial on the other side, nor must an interview with one spokesman be offset by an interview with an opponent. What counts, instead, is a station's *overall programming on each issue.* So long as a balanced presentation is achieved on an overall basis, individual variations in format are irrelevant.

On October 9, 1969, WMAL-AM (Washington, D.C.) editorialized against the upcoming observance of "Vietnam Moratorium Day" (October 15, 1969).[50] No direct rebuttal — that is, an editorial reply — was ever presented. On the eve of the moratorium, however, WMAL carried a special forty-five-minute broadcast, which included statements by such moratorium supporters as Senators George McGovern and Edward Kennedy and Dr. Benjamin Spock, as well as quotes from Mrs. Coretta King and students at moratorium headquarters. During the week of the October moratorium, WMAL's live broadcasts covered the antiwar rally at the Washington Monument, the protest staged at Selective Service headquarters, and the candlelight march around the White House. On moratorium day itself, WMAL carried various highlights, including school teach-ins and a special nighttime session of the House of Representatives where several congressmen spoke out against the war. Considering WMAL's overall programming on the moratorium issue, the FCC concluded that the station's performance had been reasonable — despite the lack of any specific rebuttal to the October 9 editorial.

The broadcaster is responsible for choosing an appropriate format for the contrasting viewpoints presented. Choice of format calls for deliberate planning, not happenstance. A broadcaster cannot simply hope that some relevant remarks turn up on a phone-in show. Nor can he rely on the possibility that a pertinent question may be asked on a general interview show — that is, one not intended to deal with the issue in question.[51]

The FCC does not prescribe which formats a broadcaster must choose: "Different issues will inevitably require different techniques of presentation and production."[52] Selection of the appropriate format is left to the broadcaster's reasonable good faith judgment. A broadcaster may employ a variety of formats while covering the same issue: for instance, newscasts, editorials, phone-in shows, interviews, debates, and public-service announcements. Many of these programs will be locally produced; some may originate with a network. If a local station carries a network program that presents a contrasting viewpoint on an issue raised by the station, the network program may be counted toward the achievement of balance.[53]

On March 8, 1970, WBBM-TV (Chicago) presented a report on sex education in the local public schools.[54] The National Coalition on the Crisis in Education objected to the report on the grounds that it favored the pro–sex education viewpoint. Nevertheless, the coalition rejected WBBM's invitation to participate in a discussion program on sex education pro's and con's. "A discussion format," the coalition wrote WBBM, "with representatives of both viewpoints, and one which will include the answering of questions submitted by viewers . . . simply will not allow us an opportunity for an uninterrupted and relevant presentation of our objections to [your March 8] program. . . ." The FCC, however, found WBBM's format choice to be entirely reasonable. Round-table and forum discussions are often excellent outlets for a wide cross-section of differing opinions.[55]

Sometimes one viewpoint may clearly outweigh another because of the different formats employed. On November 4, 1969, the citizens of Seattle voted on an excess levy proposition, aimed at funding local public schools.[56] During the week preceding election day, Seattle's KING-TV covered the pro's and con's on the levy issue. On October 31, the station aired a fifteen-minute in-depth feature, which was openly prolevy. Between November 1 and 3, a short prolevy editorial was repeated fourteen times. The only coverage of the antilevy views came on the November 1 evening news in the following brief item:

> Levy opponents roughly fall into six categories — ranging from those who object to what is "happening" in education today — that is, those who call themselves traditionalists and oppose new learning strategies to those who simply want to ease their tax loads. Some school critics charge the Seattle administration is mismanaging the schools — tolerating disorder and wasting its funds. Others claim levy money really goes for "nonessential" education. And still a final group concurs that the schools are inadequately funded but suggests the defeat of Seattle's levy may prompt state voters to adopt tax reform.

The station manager and news staff felt that this report adequately summarized the basic positions taken by levy opponents.

The FCC disagreed. "It appears from a review of the news item," the commission wrote KING-TV, "that you merely categorized or labeled the different groups or opponents and did not "present contrasting views" in a meaningful way. The purpose of the fairness doctrine, i.e., to inform the public, is not fulfilled merely by citing the existence of different groups who oppose an issue without supplying some factual basis or reasons in support of their respective positions." The "skeletal nature" of this news coverage was egregious in light of the formats employed for the prolevy viewpoint: namely, an in-depth feature and an editorial repeated frequently so as to reach a wide audience. The disparity in formats chosen by KING-TV denied a reasonable opportunity for antilevy views.[57]

The presidential address to the nation, perhaps more than any other format, is likely to create a dramatic imbalance in overall programming on a controversial issue.

> Television has become, in recent years, a principal vehicle by which the President presents to the public his views on important issues of the day. Indeed, no single fact of our changing political life overrides the significance of the expansion of the President's ability to obtain immediate and direct access to the people through the communications media. For the words of the President, speaking as he does both in his constitutional roles of chief executive and commander-in-chief and in his extra-constitutional role as head of his party, carry an authority, a prestige and a visibility that have a counterpart in no other institution.[58]

The impact of so-called presidential television can prove difficult to offset through ordinary journalistic formats (for example, newscasts, interviews).[59]

During the seven months between November 3, 1969, and June 3, 1970, for example, President Nixon broadcast five addresses on his administration's conduct of the Vietnam War.[60] The shortest was fourteen minutes; the longest, forty-one minutes — November 3, 1969 (9:30 to 10:02 P.M.); December 15, 1969 (6 to 6:14 P.M.); April 20, 1970 (9 to 9:30 P.M.); April 30, 1970 (9 to 9:41 P.M.); June 3, 1970 (9:01 to 9:16 P.M.).

These addresses were designed to reach and influence maximum numbers of the American public. First of all, the speeches were scheduled for prime-time viewing hours; indeed, four of the speeches ran between 9 and 10 P.M. — an optimum hour within prime time. Second, competing programming was eliminated, since all three television networks, as well as radio outlets, carried the speeches simultaneously. Third, each speech was broadcast fully intact, there were no interruptions, nor was the President asked any questions before, during, or after each address. Fourth, the speeches were broadcast "live," imparting an urgent air of history-in-the-making. Fifth, the speeches were delivered in impressive settings, conducive to a favorable image of the President as he presented his views. Sixth, the speeches were delivered in a series of progress reports, each one updating the country on the status of the administration's policies.

Since the President had presented one side of a controversial issue, the fairness doctrine was triggered. Several groups — including Business Executives Move for Vietnam Peace and fourteen United States senators sponsoring an "Amendment to End the War" — complained to the FCC. They felt that the customary fairness-doctrine obligations could not adequately adjust the imbalance created by the presidential address. An equal-time type of approach was, therefore, urged. The complainants sought a ruling allocating a block of prime time following presidential addresses, in which a responsible spokesman could rebut the President's views without interruption or questions from interviewers. Only through such a format, uncontrolled by the broadcasters, and permitting direct access to the public, could the President's views be answered effectively.

The FCC declined to establish any automatic right of rebuttal following every presidential address. Instead, the commission adhered to a traditional fairness-doctrine approach. Considering overall network programming on the Vietnam War issue — exclusive of the five Nixon addresses — a rough balance had been achieved (for example, through newscasts, interviews, documentaries, and commentary analyzing presidential speeches). The dramatic additional ingredient here was the five speeches. Their impact compelled the commission to ask: "Are reasonable opportunities afforded [for contrasting viewpoints] when there has been an extensive but roughly balanced presentation on each side and five opportunities in prime time for the leading spokesman of one side to address the nation on this issue?"

The commission decided that, under the circumstances, a reasonable opportunity had not been afforded. The "sheer weight" on the side contributed to by the President had created a clear imbalance: "We believe that in such circumstances there must also be a reasonable opportunity for the other side geared specifically to the five addresses (i.e., the selection of some suitable spokesman or spokesmen by the networks to broadcast an address giving the contrasting viewpoint)."

The reasonable opportunity thus ordered was not supposed to equal the President's five speeches. All the commission required was one uninterrupted opportunity for rebuttal by a spokesman selected by the networks. The commission emphasized that its ruling was based on the "unusual facts" in the case: five prime-time addresses by the leading spokesman for one side of a particular issue. This unique source of imbalance called for the adoption of a special format that would not be required in other circumstances.

In subsequent cases the FCC has steadfastly refused to extend its ruling on the five Vietnam speeches. One case arose over four addresses President Nixon made in 1971 concerning the economy.[61] All of the addresses were carried live by ABC, CBS, and NBC. Three addresses were broadcast over radio and television, two aired during prime time. One of the non-prime-time addresses aired only on radio. The commission found that overall network programming had provided a reasonable opportunity for opposing views on the administration's economic policies. The commission refused to descend a "slippery slope" of *ad hoc* decisions like the one precipitated by the five Vietnam speeches.

> If, for example, we were now to hold that the broadcast of two prime-time Presidential addresses and two not in prime time . . . requires the networks to afford additional time for response despite other presentations on the issues without any showing of overall unfairness, what ruling would be appropriate if there were only one prime-time plus three non-prime-time addresses? or one prime-time plus two non-prime-time [addresses]. . . . A continuing series of *ad hoc* rulings by the Commission which necessarily constitute special departures from the general fairness weighing process would inevitably push the Commission further and further into the programming process.

Instead of more "special departures," like the one made to offset the five Vietnam speeches, the commission opted for traditional licensee discretion in achieving overall programming balance.

The courts have upheld the FCC's treatment of "presidential television" under the general balancing principles of the fairness doctrine. While the President's edge on media exposure is conceded, there is also a judicial recognition of the public interest in presidential communications.

> One of the primary sources for public information concerning the nation and its welfare is from the Presidential broadcast. While political scientists and historians may argue about the institution of the Presidency and the obligations and role of the nation's chief executive officer it is clear that in this day and age it is obligatory for the President to inform the public on his program and its progress from time to time. By the very nature of his position the President is a focal point of national life. The people of this country look to him in his numerous roles for guidance, understanding, perspective and information. No matter who the man living at 1600 Pennsylvania Avenue is he will be subject to greater coverage in the press and on the media than any other person in the free world.[62]

It is unlikely that the courts or the commission will mandate any format resembling an automatic right of reply to presidential addresses. However, the pervasiveness of "presidential television" deserves constant monitoring and effective checks. "If the words and views of the President become a monolithic force," warns federal Judge J. Skelly Wright, "if they constitute not just the most powerful voice in the land but the only voice, then the delicate mechanism through which an informed public opinion is distilled, far from being strengthened, is thrown dangerously off balance. Public opinion becomes not informed and enlightened, but instructed and dominated."[63] Without some form of meaningful balance, a danger exists that the President's word may gain a monopoly in our supposedly free marketplace of ideas.

OPPOSING SPOKESMEN. When one side of a controversial issue has been broadcast, who should the opposing spokesmen be? Rarely is there a clear-cut answer. In most circumstances, a variety of potential spokesmen will be available. The fairness doctrine does not dictate selection of any particular one. Instead, the choice is left to the sound discretion of broadcasters; they must act reasonably and in good faith.

Sometimes the broadcaster himself performs the function of an opposing spokesman. He covers significant contrasting viewpoints through his own personnel. For example, a newscaster may read a press release from some community organization, rather than interview a representative from that organization. The substitution of broadcast personnel for members of the public can be a reasonable choice, but it should not become standard operating procedure; for the fairness doctrine requires presentation of representative community voices as well as viewpoints.[64]

What's more, broadcasters must make reasonable allowance for *genuine partisans* who actually believe in the views they express. A broadcaster who insists upon acting as proxy for every impassioned spokesman fosters an unhealthy paternalism, which the FCC decries: "A licensee policy of excluding partisan voices and always itself presenting views in a bland, inoffensive manner would run counter to the 'profound national commitment that debate on public issues should be uninhibited, robust, and wide-open.' "[65]

Beyond these general guidelines, choice of an opposing spokesman is largely unregulated; it is a matter of discretion. To determine whether a person requesting air time is an appropriate spokesman, the broadcaster may inquire about the particular point of view held by the applicant. The purpose of such an inquiry must be legitimate: that is, to ascertain whether the applicant has a significant contrasting viewpoint, which has not been previously aired. If the applicant feels that demands made upon him are unreasonably burdensome, or unrelated to the goals of the fairness doctrine, he should complain to the FCC. In one case, for instance, a community leader was improperly rejected as a spokesman, because he refused to identify members of his organization.[66]

While the broadcaster has considerable leeway in picking appropriate spokesmen, he must not abuse his discretion. He cannot select opposing spokesmen in order to favor one viewpoint over another. Deliberately avoiding equally forceful presentations evinces bad faith and violates the fairness doctrine.[67]

Spokesmen should not be rejected for personal reasons unrelated to the policy behind the fairness doctrine. Say an unsuccessful job applicant at our hypothetical station, WWW, subsequently seeks air time over the station in order to express his views on some issue. Conceivably, WWW may suspect that the request was prompted by vengeful personal motives. Nevertheless, WWW cannot reject the request because of any animosity the applicant is thought to harbor. Personal motivation is irrelevant to the only valid consideration: that is, whether the public will be fully informed on a controversial issue.[68]

In a 1963 case, an Alabama radio station broadcast views critical of a proposed nuclear test ban treaty. Reply time was requested by a national organization, the Citizens Committee For A Nuclear Test Ban Treaty. The request was turned down, because the organization did not have a local chapter within the station's service area. Of course, the station had a right to exercise its discretion in selecting a local or regional or national spokesman — whoever was deemed most appropriate. However, rejecting the committee solely because it lacked a local chapter was unjustifiable — especially when the station's listeners were being deprived of a significant contrasting viewpoint.[69]

Is it an abuse of discretion for a broadcaster to reject the sole volunteer for reply time? The answer depends upon the efforts made by the broadcaster to locate an appropriate spokesman. Assume these efforts have been diligent, although unsuccessful. The broadcaster may then exercise his discretion and reject the sole volunteer, even though this decision means no contrasting views will be presented (see pages 151–153).

Is a broadcaster required to act as opposing spokesman himself, when no one else seems willing or qualified to do so? The answer is no. A broadcaster may choose to present contrasting views on his own, and he would serve his community well if he did; but there is no such requirement. The offer of reply time, however, should be kept open for the benefit of any latecomers.[70]

There is an important corollary to the rule that gives broadcasters the power to select opposing spokesmen: *No individual or group has the right to be the spokesman for a particular point of view.* The fairness doctrine is chiefly concerned with *what* is broadcast — not *who* broadcasts it.

> Whether the opportunity to appear is afforded to a particular individual or group is of no moment because the cornerstone of the fairness doctrine is not the right of any particular individual or group to speak but rather the public's right to be informed as to all significant points of view relating to an issue of public importance.[71]

While individuals and groups can and should vigorously seek the opportunity to reply, they cannot demand it. Thus, the president of the Husbands' Liberation Movement may believe he is the only person who can rebut claims broadcast by representatives from the Women's Liberation Movement, but a broadcaster could reasonably decide that some other man — or woman — would be more appropriate.[72]

No potential spokesman can exert veto power over controversial-issue programming. Consider a FCC case from 1950.[73] Chrysler Corporation was being struck by the UAW-CIO. Detroit radio station WWJ recognized that the strike raised a major controversy of national as well as local importance. The station sought to induce both Chrysler and the union to appear and air opposing sides of the issue: Chrysler said no; the union, yes. WWJ then refused to supply the union with the air time originally offered, because the management side would have been unrepresented.

The union complained to the FCC. The commission decided that WWJ had abused its discretion by allowing Chrysler virtual veto power over the proposed debate. Once a broadcaster has determined — as WWJ did — that a controversial issue is important enough to deserve coverage, programming plans should proceed according to the broadcaster's best judgment. No potential spokesman has the right — nor should he be conceded the power — to veto programming simply by refusing to broadcast his position. Given such an obstacle, the broadcaster need only make a reasonable effort to secure some substitute representation for the viewpoint being withheld. If no substitute can be found, the essentially one-sided program may still be aired; indeed, it should be, considering the importance of the issue involved. A reasonable opportunity for reply must remain open after the broadcast, in case the once-reluctant spokesman changes his mind, or someone else volunteers.[74]

NOTIFICATION TO OPPOSING SPOKESMEN. We have seen that a broadcaster himself may present significant contrasting views. If he does not intend to do so, however, he must actively seek out some responsible opposing spokesman; he cannot sit back and wait for volunteers. (In this sense, the fairness doctrine differs from the equal-time rule, under which candidates must take the initiative in requesting air time.)

The FCC does not prescribe steps for locating responsible spokesmen. "Our experience indicates," the commission observed in 1964,

> that licensees have chosen a variety of methods, and often combinations of various methods. Thus, some licensees, when they know or have reason to believe that a responsible individual or group within the community holds a contrasting viewpoint with respect to a controversial issue presented or to be presented, communicate to such an individual or group a specific offer of the use of their facilities for the expression of a contrasting opinion, and send a copy or summary of material broadcast on the issue. Other licensees consult with community leaders as to who might be an appropriate individual or group for such a purpose. Still others announce at the beginning or ending (or both) of programs presenting opinions on controversial issues that opportunity will be made available for the expression of contrasting views upon request by responsible representatives of such views.[75]

While the commission cited these examples with apparent approval, there was no attempt to endorse them as the only, or even the best, methods for achieving fairness. Instead, broadcasters are left to exercise their discretion, reasonably and in good faith, by choosing some method — or methods — for offering air time to opposing spokesmen. The choice is not irrevocable. A broadcaster does not have to adhere rigidly to one system of notification. Different forms of controversial-issue programming may well call for different means of notification. It might reasonably be expected, for instance, that the more elaborate and, perhaps, continuous the coverage on one side of a controversial issue, the more extensive and persistent the search for opposing spokesmen ought to be.[76]

Whatever form of notification is employed, it must clearly apprise a person of what is being offered: namely, an opportunity to present a contrasting viewpoint *on the air*. Merely sending someone a copy of a station editorial, for instance, without an accompanying explanation, would not be adequate notice. "The fairness doctrine is not so well known," the commission has said, "that persons receiving copies of station editorials know that they are being offered an opportunity to respond. . . ."[77]

One California station sent out copies of its editorials with the following statement printed at the bottom: "Responsible representatives of opposing viewpoints are given the opportunity to reply on the air. If you missed the broadcast of this editorial, we hope you will read it. Your comments are most welcome."[78] This offer is rather oblique. A recipient might easily assume that persons other than himself — that is, "responsible representatives" — get actual air time. He, on the other hand, has only the opportunity to submit "comments"; presumably, these are for the station's internal consumption, rather than broadcast. To avoid such a misunderstanding, a station should make its offers explicit and direct, whether they are announced on the air or mailed out.[79]

How prolonged an effort must a broadcaster make in order to find an opposing spokesman? There is no hard-and-fast answer. Suffice it to say, a broadcaster can be called upon to renew and intensify his search, if he has found no spokesman and, therefore, presented no contrasting viewpoint. The determining factor will be the reasonableness of the broadcaster's effort.

Suppose our hypothetical station, WWW, carries extensive programming on one side of a major controversial issue. On-air invitations to potential spokesmen elicit no response. As a result, contrasting viewpoints are never presented. A citizen, concerned with the one-sidedness of WWW's programming, files a fairness complaint with the FCC. Since WWW's effort appears unreasonably limited, the station may well be requested to supplement its unsuccessful on-air announcements with other forms of notification: for example, individual invitations to potential spokesmen.

At what point can a broadcaster abandon his unsuccessful search for a spokesman? In a 1972 decision, the FCC attempted to answer this question.[80] KNX-AM-FM (Los Angeles) broadcast an editorial, entitled "Judging the Judges," which sharply criticized specific decisions rendered by local judges. The editorial concluded with an invitation to reply: "This has been an editorial by [the] General Manager of KNX. Qualified representatives of opposing viewpoints are offered hereby an opportunity to reply over the station." Copies of the editorial with offers of reply time were sent to approximately 550 individuals and groups representing a wide spectrum of community opinion.

No one accepted the station's offer, but there was one volunteer: Thomas Slaten, a college student, who had not been offered time by KNX. The station decided that Slaten was not an appropriate spokesman and turned him down. Thereafter, KNX sent written invitations to the deans of three local law schools, the presiding judge of the Los Angeles Superior Court, the California Judicial Council, and the California and Los Angeles County bar associations. None of these individuals or groups accepted. As a result, "Judging the Judges" went unanswered.

Thomas Slaten, the sole volunteer, complained to the FCC. At issue, according to the commission, was the reasonableness — not the efficacy — of KNX's efforts. Had the station been sufficiently conscientious in its search for a responsible spokesman? The commission said yes.

> We cannot find that the licensee failed to comply with the requirements of the fairness doctrine. Although it rejected the only person volunteering to present contrasting views, on the grounds that he was not an appropriate spokesman, we are not disposed to second-guess a licensee

in judging the qualifications of a particular person as a spokesman, provided that the licensee appears to have made a reasonable effort, overall, to obtain responsible representation of contrasting views.

So KNX was not called upon to renew and intensify its efforts to locate a spokesman.

Lest the import of this decision be overlooked, remember that no opposing viewpoint was ever broadcast. KNX listeners received only one side of a controversial issue; perhaps they even concluded that everyone agreed with the station's opinion. This complete lack of balance was, nonetheless, condoned by the FCC.

Indignant over an apparent elevation of procedure over substance, former FCC Commissioner Nicholas Johnson dissented from the *KNX* decision.

> What the majority in this case seem to forget is that the fairness doctrine was not designed for the benefit of the licensee, or even for the benefit of the party who claims the right to respond. It is for the benefit of the viewing or listening public, and represents the obligation of the licensee, the public trustee of the airwaves, to inform the public as to the various viewpoints that may exist on controversial issues. This obligation is especially important when the viewpoint is one being directly advocated by the licensee itself. . . .
>
> For the fairness doctrine to operate to protect the public interest, there must be some indication that the licensee has actually presented some aspect of each side of a controversial issue. Merely soliciting replies to on-air editorials cannot be a major factor in a station's "good faith effort" to comply with the fairness doctrine, whether [the station] solicits from 500 or even 5000 persons or groups.
>
> The Commission often plays numbers games over fairness issues, in which it attempts to decide such questions as whether six and one-half minutes of news coverage might sufficiently balance some 15 one minute spots. But one game that has not been played until now has been the determination that a licensee has made a sufficient "effort" at fairness on the basis of the weight of its "extra-broadcast" activities, when the time presented on the air has been zero.

Despite Johnson's justifiable compunction over "balancing" one side with zero reply time, the commission seems comfortably disposed to accept such an equation as fair — provided reasonable efforts were made to locate an opposing spokesman.[81]

There is no requirement — at least, for commercial stations — that any program tapes, transcripts, or summaries be supplied to potential opposing spokesmen. While such a service would seem most conducive to an informed debate, the commission has not made it mandatory.[82] Noncommercial educational stations are, however, required to retain an audio recording of any program they broadcast in which a controversial issue of public importance is discussed. (The period of retention lasts for sixty days, starting on the date of broadcast.) Currently, the commission is in the process of formulating rules that will regulate public access to these recordings.[83]

COOPERATION WITH OPPOSING SPOKESMEN. Many spokesmen who receive air time under the fairness doctrine are unfamiliar with broadcasting technique. If they are treated with indifference or, worse still, abused by station personnel, these spokesmen may be unable to express their views effectively. As a result, the public will be deprived of adequate coverage on one side of a controversial issue.

It is no wonder, then, that the FCC urges broadcasters to cooperate fully with each opposing spokesman, regardless of whether his viewpoint conflicts with the station's. The broadcaster should volunteer technical assistance and production facilities whenever necessary. Any deliberate attempts to make one advocate look or sound better — or worse — than an adversary may deny one of these spokesmen the reasonable opportunity to which he is entitled.[84]

A broadcaster is also responsible for the attitude manifest toward various spokesmen by program personnel. Consider the role of a moderator on a talk show or phone-in program. He has the right to express his views as forcefully as he wishes. Such advocacy may often include vehement disagreement with guests or people who telephone to air their opinions. The FCC warns, however, that a moderator "cannot seek, in practical effect, to preclude or inhibit the presentation of views by verbally 'beating up' or harassing the participant with whom he disagrees, so that the program becomes a forum only for views compatible with those of the licensee or moderator."[85] The moderator of a phone-in show, for example, must not favor one side of an issue by routinely insulting or cutting off callers who espouse the other side.

In the *Brandywine–Main Line Radio* case, WXUR-AM-FM, a station with a distinctly conservative orientation, carried a daily interview program called "Delaware County Today."[86] Its moderator, Carl Mau, was accustomed to "roughing up" guests with whom he disagreed — or as Mau put it, he "took the American side" when guests voiced discontent with national affairs (for example, antiwar sentiment, black militancy).

Opposition to the black civil rights movement had been freely expressed over WXUR. However, the contrary point of view met with hostile treatment on "Delaware County Today." A civil rights advocate was interviewed by Mau in an openly antagonistic manner. Mau's questions were aimed less at eliciting his guest's views than disparaging them: for example, "Why is it that negroes can talk about the white people but a white person cannot talk about a negro?" "The population of Broadmeadows Prison is 95 percent negro male, and 75 percent female. How will you answer that one?" "Basically what do you people want? A handout?"

The FCC decided Mau's attitude — for which WXUR was, of course, responsible — effectively denied the civil rights advocate a reasonable opportunity for rebuttal. "Fairness cannot be achieved," the commission ruled, "when the expression of one view is deliberately treated in an antagonistic manner while the opposing view is given the opportunity for expression without any interference, harassment or even opposing argument." It is important to note that the commission was not condemning Mau's tactics in and of themselves. Harassing conduct is permissible, as are various rough-and-tumble formats, like talk shows and phone-in programs. However, if only one side of a controversial issue is subjected to abuse, the program cannot be counted toward the achievement of balance on the issue in question. In effect, the commission was suggesting reasonably similar treatment for opposing spokesmen.[87]

CENSORSHIP. The fairness doctrine, unlike the equal-time rule, does not flatly prohibit censorship. A broadcaster retains his customary programming prerogatives when presenting conflicting points of view: he can reject or delete material that fails, in his judgment, to serve the needs and interests of his community.[88] If this prerogative is exercised unreasonably, however, or in bad faith, it may be curbed by the FCC.

Consider a 1972 case. KMBC-TV (Kansas City, Missouri) offered some local spokesmen the opportunity to express their side of a controversial issue.[89] The offer, however, had several strings attached. "We will produce a program," KMBC-TV wrote to the spokesmen,

> containing whatever response you choose to make provided (i) the format and content of such response [do] not contain any defamatory, scandalous, or obscene matter or any matter contrary to law or any of the rules and policies of the Federal Communications Commission ("FCC"); (ii) the program will not subject us or any person to ridicule or public censure; (iii) the program will not contain any "personal attacks" as defined by the FCC; and (iv) the content of said program will be such that we will not be obligated to offer any other person or group time to respond thereto under the Fairness doctrine. . . .

The spokesmen who received this offer complained to the FCC. They objected to the "chilling effect" that KMBC's conditions had upon their freedom to formulate and present conflicting views with honesty and conviction.

The FCC approved the first of KMBC's four conditions: namely, that the reply contain no defamatory, scandalous, obscene, or other illegal material. Such a condition was not deemed improper so long as it was reasonably administered by the station. However, conditions (ii), (iii), and (iv) were too overbearing to comport with the aim of the fairness doctrine — that is, uninhibited debate on controversial issues. Regarding condition (ii), the FCC observed that ridicule is a perfectly legitimate form of argument, which KMBC-TV could not exclude arbitrarily and entirely from a fairness response. "Nor should a partisan spokesman be required to forswear all personal attacks," added the commission, referring to condition (iii), "no matter how germane or essential to discussion of an issue, or to himself decide in advance what the licensee's judgment will be on whether any particular language is a personal attack." Exclusion of personal attacks would be particularly inhibiting whenever the integrity of some person or group was the issue in controversy; then a condition like (iii) would force opponents to skirt the very heart of the debate.

The FCC approved the intent behind condition (iv), that is, to insure responsiveness in fairness replies: "We have recognized that licensees may properly insist that a Fairness Doctrine reply be responsive and germane to the issue(s) raised in the initial broadcast . . . in order that significant differing views may be presented without triggering a continuous cycle of response after response." However, condition (iv) had been stated much too vaguely to accomplish its limited objective without, at the same time, inhibiting the opposing spokesmen.

What disturbed the commission most about conditions (ii), (iii), and (iv) was the timing which had been imposed on them. Accompanying as they did KMBC-TV's initial solicitation of a fairness response, these conditions tended to exert a prior restraint upon views which the spokesmen contacted might otherwise have tried to express. The robust open debate that the fairness doctrine promotes is clearly hindered, the FCC concluded, "by the advance imposition of conditions which steer discussion away from relevant responsive material."

Any spokesman who feels that the scope or quality of debate is diminished because of restrictions imposed upon the expression of his views should resist the encroachment and, if necessary, complain to the FCC. While a broadcaster can, in his discretion, exert some limited control over the airing of conflicting points of view, he cannot unreasonably limit partisan debate and controversy.

TIME AND SCHEDULING. Many laymen mistakenly believe the fairness doctrine requires equal time for conflicting viewpoints. If one spokesman on a controversial issue gets, say, thirty minutes in prime time, it would seem only "fair" that his adversary should have thirty minutes also — and in the same time period. Such an equal opportunity comports with commonly accepted notions of "fairness."

Under the fairness doctrine, however, a strict equal-opportunities approach would be unworkable. "It would inhibit, rather than promote, the discussion and presentation of controversial issues in the various broadcast program formats (e.g., newscasts, interviews, documentaries). For it is just not practicable to require equality with respect to the large number of issues dealt with in a great variety of programs on a daily and continuing basis." Besides being impracticable, an equal-opportunities approach would involve the FCC too deeply in broadcast journalism.

> We would indeed become virtually a part of the broadcasting "fourth estate," overseeing thousands of complaints that some issue had not been given "equal treatment." We do not believe that the profound national commitment to the principle that debate on public issues should be "uninhibited, robust, wide-open" . . . would be promoted by a general policy of requiring equal treatment on all such issues, with governmental intervention to insure such mathematical equality.[90]

The fairness doctrine calls for reasonableness rather than equality. Reasonableness is measured on the basis of a station's overall programming on a given issue. That programming may derive from a local or a network source; it may include many different formats. Considering the "entirety of viewpoints" expressed on the issue, the key question under the fairness doctrine is: has a reasonable opportunity been afforded for discussion of conflicting views?[91]

Four basic criteria must be weighed when overall reasonableness is being determined: the total amount of air time devoted to each side of the issue; the frequency with which each side was presented; the scheduling of broadcasts on each side; and the size of the audience reached by each side during the various broadcasts. Any one of these factors, or some combination of them, may create an imbalance that is unreasonable.[92]

(1) TOTAL AMOUNT OF TIME. Besides rejecting an equal-time approach to the fairness doctrine, the FCC declines even to suggest some ratio — for example, three to one or five to one — for weighing relative coverage of contrasting viewpoints.

> We believe that such an approach is much too mechanical in nature and that in many cases our pre-conceived ratios would prove to be far from reasonable. . . . Moreover, were we to adopt a ratio for fairness programming, the "floor" thereby established might well become the "ceiling" for the treatment of issues by many stations, and such a ratio might also lead to preoccupation with a mathematical formula to the detriment of the substance of the debate.[93]

While the commission will not fix any ratios, it has indicated that an imbalance in time exceeding ten to one is clearly unreasonable.[94]

Although it seems inconceivable, there is at least one situation in which the commission may condone zero minutes for an opposing viewpoint. When a station has made a diligent but unsuccessful search for an opposing spokesman, the commission may be inclined to accept this effort — in lieu of any actual programming — as full compliance with the fairness doctrine (see pp. 151–153).

(2) FREQUENCY. The FCC recognizes that repetition of a particular viewpoint generally increases its impact. Not only is the viewpoint driven home, but it also reaches different audiences over an extended period of time. Thus, even though two sides of an issue receive comparable amounts of air time, an imbalance may still exist if one side is repeated with greater frequency than the other.[95]

(3) SCHEDULING. The time at which contrasting views are presented is up to the broadcaster. He does not have to schedule them for the same program. In 1973, for instance, the FCC specifically rejected a proposal that the "CBS Evening News" carry a back-to-back rebuttal whenever commentator Eric Sevareid presented one side of a controversial issue.[96]

There is no requirement that contrasting views be covered during the same series of programs. Suppose one side of a controversial issue is raised in "Close-Up," a half-hour public-affairs interview, which a local station airs each Sunday at noon. Contrasting views need not be presented on some future installment of· "Close-Up" as long as balance is achieved through the station's overall programming.[97]

How soon after one side of an issue is aired must opposing views be presented? "Within a time reasonably approximate to the initial presentation," says the FCC; one side does not have to follow the other immediately.[98] Reasonable proximity will vary with the circumstances. For example, the issue in question may be heading for certain resolution on a known date — like election day. Or, perhaps, the issue is peculiarly seasonal in nature — like the annual use of migrant laborers to harvest crops. Whenever public interest is thus focused within a limited time frame, opposing views should not be delayed until they are irrelevant or even moot. On the other hand, scheduling one viewpoint for a particularly strategic time — say, election eve — may unreasonably tip the scales against the view presented considerably earlier.[99]

Broadcasters have greater scheduling leeway when the issue is a continuing one. In the fall of 1969, KIRO-TV (Seattle) sent two of its newsmen to several Arab nations on a fact-finding mission.[100] Based upon the results of the trip, KIRO-TV broadcast six editorials between October 13 and November 3, 1969. These editorials presented Arab attitudes toward United States involvement in the Middle East crisis. The station informed its viewers that a news team would travel to Israel in December, after which trip Israeli views would be broadcast in a second series of editorials.

A viewer complained that both viewpoints should have been presented at the same time. By December, he argued, the earlier editorials would be forgotten. The FCC disagreed. The Middle East crisis represented a continuing issue, which KIRO-TV chose to comment on over a period of months. The station had provided a reasonable opportunity over a reasonable period of time, which is all the fairness doctrine requires for a continuing issue.[101]

(4) AUDIENCE. Broadcast audiences vary throughout the day. The size and makeup of an audience for a particular viewpoint de-

pends upon when and how often the viewpoint is broadcast. The audience level will generally be at its peak during prime-time evening hours in the case of television, or drive-time commuting hours in the case of radio. It would be unreasonable to give one viewpoint the advantage of prime-time or drive-time airing, while relegating opposing views to, say, early afternoon, when audience levels are reduced.[102]

FREE TIME. There is no requirement that all contrasting viewpoints be aired free of charge. If one side of a controversial issue is raised on a sponsored program, the broadcaster has a right to seek paid sponsorship for any reply time. A person requesting reply time may, therefore, be asked if he is willing to pay for it. Such an inquiry is legitimate, and the broadcaster is entitled to an answer. If the answer is no, the broadcaster can choose some other advocate who is willing to pay. Of course, this person should be selected in good faith on the basis of his qualifications as a responsible spokesman — not solely on the basis of his financial resources.[103]

While a broadcaster can ask for payment, he should not make it an absolute prerequisite; indeed, he should not even convey the impression that reply time is available strictly on a paid basis. Suppose the broadcaster writes to a spokesman who has requested air time. Besides asking if the spokesman is willing to pay, the letter recites at length economic reasons why the station is unable to give free time. The clear implication is: pay or be silent. Such an inquiry pushes the broadcaster's prerogative to extremes and may well result in denying a reasonable opportunity for reply.[104]

Under no conditions will the failure to secure paid sponsorship justify rejecting every spokesman and leaving the public uninformed as to contrasting viewpoints. Faced with such a prospect, the broadcaster would either have to present his own program balance or provide reply time *free of charge*. This rule, known as the *Cullman* principle, is based on the 1963 *Cullman* case in which the FCC declared:

> Where the licensee has chosen to broadcast a sponsored program which for the first time presents one side of a

controversial issue, has not presented (or does not plan to present) contrasting viewpoints in other programming, and has been unable to obtain paid sponsorship for the appropriate presentation of the opposing viewpoint or viewpoints, he cannot reject a presentation otherwise suitable to the licensee — and *thus leave the public uninformed* — on the ground that he cannot obtain paid sponsorship for that presentation.[105]

In short, an appropriate spokesman would have to be given free reply time to avoid the alternative of no contrasting viewpoints at all.

Even if there has been some coverage of contrasting viewpoints, the *Cullman* principle may still apply. Assume that Capital City institutes a system of rent control, under which increases in residential rents are strictly regulated. The new rent controls arouse widespread controversy. Our hypothetical station WWW covers the pro's and con's on the issue in its newscasts and public affairs programming. In addition, however, WWW carries a long series of spot announcements paid for by the Realty Owners' Association (ROA), attacking rent control as unfair and confiscatory. The United Tenants Coalition (UTC) requests time over WWW to answer ROA's ads. UTC cannot afford to pay for its reply time. Since WWW has already afforded balanced coverage to the controversy in its own programming, must it now give free time to UTC?

The probable answer is yes. WWW must decide whether ROA's ads resulted in substantially more exposure to the anti–rent control position than had been achieved in WWW's own programming. If such an imbalance exists, WWW will have to correct it with further programming. The *Cullman* principle would then be applicable, and WWW could not insist upon payment from opposing spokesmen like UTC.[106]

The *Cullman* principle also governs broadcast discussions of ballot propositions (for example, constitutional amendments, bond proposals, initiative or recall propositions, and referenda). Normally, coverage of a ballot proposition will involve a controversial issue of public importance. If one faction buys air time to make its case on the proposition, the station may be obliged to afford free time to an opposing faction. "It has been argued," the commission observed in 1974,

> that in the closing days of an election campaign, licensees may be overwhelmed by orders for large quantities of spot announcements favoring or opposing a proposition, and could be hard put to comply with the requirements of the fairness doctrine if only one side buys time. No licensee, however, is required to sell all the time an advocate of a proposition . . . may wish to buy . . . for a so-called "blitz." [The licensee's] clear obligation . . . is . . . to plan his programming in advance so that he is prepared to afford reasonable opportunity for presentation of contrasting views on the issue, whether or not presented in paid time.[107]

If a broadcaster fails to plan ahead, and then cannot find sponsorship for the presentation of contrasting views on the ballot proposition, free time will have to be carved out of the schedule during the campaign.

It is possible that ballot-issue advocates may take advantage of the *Cullman* principle. They may devote what funds they have to advertising in nonbroadcast media; when it comes to air time, they will wait until opponents buy time and then invoke *Cullman* to gain free time for their own views. The FCC recognizes this potential strategy but tolerates it in order to assure that the public will not be deprived of contrasting views on ballot propositions. Of course, *Cullman* does not guarantee equal time to ballot-issue advocates; so they may not wish to rely solely upon *Cullman* to gain broadcast exposure for their views.[108]

Fairness and Political Campaign Coverage

IN GENERAL. The fairness doctrine plays an important role in two categories of political programming. The first category includes broadcasts concerning ballot propositions (for example, initiative or recall propositions, referenda, bond proposals, and constitutional amendments). The second category is comprised of news coverage in which a candidate (for nomination or election) appears personally or is discussed by noncandidates (for example, newscasters, members of the general public).

The second category should not be confused with broadcasts falling under the equal-time rule. Normally, when a candidate himself appears, equal time is required; but appearances on news shows are exempt from equal-time requirements. *It is precisely these exempt appearances that are subject to the fairness doctrine.*[109] On news shows where a candidate is merely discussed, rather than seen or heard, the equal-time rule has no application; once again, however, the fairness doctrine does.[110]

Invoking the fairness doctrine can result in critical broadcast coverage to candidates as well as groups supporting or opposing various ballot propositions. Often these partisans cannot afford to purchase air time, so free news coverage — or free reply time — will be particularly valuable. Anyone consulting this discussion of political programming would be well advised to familiarize himself with the overall fairness doctrine. The general principles covered in this chapter apply to the programming discussed in this section — with certain nuances, to which we may now turn.

DEFINING THE ISSUE AT STAKE. In any fairness-doctrine analysis of political programming, the first step is identical to that taken in every potential fairness situation — defining the basic issue addressed by the broadcast. In the case of ballot propositions, this step has already been covered in detail (see pages 111–113).

What is the basic issue raised in broadcasts by or about candidates? The FCC has rejected the notion that simply by entering a political race a person's candidacy becomes an important issue in and of itself. Whether any individual candidate should be elected is not the basic issue for fairness-doctrine purposes; instead, each campaign for a nomination or office is thought to present one overall issue: who among all the candidates should be elected? Or, stated slightly differently: which candidate is best qualified to execute the office at stake?[111]

There may, of course, be numerous subissues. For example: did the incumbent's budgetary policies impair the government's ability to borrow money? Will the challenger's private law practice create a potential conflict of interest if he takes office? Normally, subissues like these are important components of the primary issue — namely, who should govern? If a candidate seeking to invoke the fairness doctrine complains about unbalanced coverage of a subissue, without connecting it in any way to the primary issue, his complaint may be dismissed by the broadcaster — and, ultimately, by the FCC. As in the usual fairness situation, broadcasters are not obliged to provide balanced programming on every subissue.

For example, Republican Governor Jones runs for reelection. Our hypothetical station WWW interviews him several times regarding his encouragement of increased strip mining in the state. Since these interviews occur on newscasts, the governor's challenger, business executive Sarah Smith, is not entitled to equal time. However, she seeks to increase news coverage of her campaign by invoking the fairness doctrine. She complains to WWW that its extensive interviews with Jones have presented one side of the environment issue and, thus, reasonable opportunity must be provided for a contrasting point of view — namely, hers.

WWW responds, however, that it has covered all sides of the "environment issue"; it cites several network documentaries, station editorials, and dozens of news stories examining a variety of environmental problems from air pollution to waste disposal. In all likelihood, WWW's assessment of overall balance would be reasonable. Protecting the environment, a subissue in the Jones-Smith campaign, is also a sweeping national and local issue to which WWW has devoted extensive noncampaign coverage.[112]

Smith's complaint would have had a better chance of success had she defined the so-called environment issue in terms more relevant to the gubernatorial campaign: for example, does the incumbent's policy toward strip mining betray his incapacity to administer the state's natural resources wisely and equitably for the benefit of all the state's citizens? When the issue is defined in this manner, WWW may readily concede that its coverage has been one-sided — that is, only the governor's unchallenged point of view. If WWW still declines to balance its programming on the "incapacity-to-administer" issue, Smith will have stronger grounds for complaint to the FCC.

The general ability-to-govern issue at stake in every election may be raised implicitly through news coverage of a particular candidate. The candidate need not be shown declaring that his wisdom and administrative skills represent an asset voters should weigh heavily. Such a message may be clearly implied. For example, a district attorney running for governor stages a series of news conferences to announce major indictments; a mayor's increasing ribbon-cutting activities are reported during his campaign for reelection; a presidential contender's canoe trip with his family is covered. In each instance, election issues are not explicitly raised. However, the candidate has been presented as, for example, upholding law and order, or encouraging new construction or devoting time to his family. These positive characteristics implicitly support one side of the ability-to-govern issue, because they enhance the candidate's image and tend to substantiate promises he may have made in the campaign. Thus, excessive news coverage of one candidate, even if ostensibly nonpolitical, can create an imbalance on the ability-to-govern issue. The fairness doctrine should be invoked to achieve balance.

CONTROVERSIAL ISSUES OF PUBLIC IMPORTANCE. Once the issue has been defined, the next question, as in the usual fairness situation, is whether the issue is controversial and of public importance. Broadcasters must make this determination reasonably and in good faith. In 1974 the FCC suggested a standard for evaluating the issues raised by ballot propositions and elections: "If the issue involves a social or political choice, the licensee might well ask himself whether the outcome of that choice will have a significant impact on society or its institutions."[113] The less significant the impact is judged to be, the less the public importance that attaches to the issue. Therefore, a broadcaster could conclude that certain ballot or candidate issues are not controversial or of public importance and do not trigger the fairness doctrine.

While such a conclusion may be reasonable in particular cases, it is unlikely to prove the norm. The FCC is inclined to view election issues as inherently controversial and in need of balanced coverage.

> The existence of an issue on which the community is asked to vote must be *presumed* to be a controversial issue of public importance, absent unusual circumstances. . . . It is precisely within the context of an election that the fairness doctrine can be best utilized to inform the public of the existence of and basis for contrasting viewpoints on an issue about which there must be a public resolution through the election process.[114]

In short, a presumption of controversiality arises on election issues: whether a ballot proposition ought to be adopted or rejected is presumably a controversial issue; a similar presumption attaches to the question, who among all the candidates should be elected? The presumption can, of course, be rebutted, given what the FCC characterizes as "unusual circumstances." This presumption will considerably lighten the burden of proof a complainant shoulders when he seeks to invoke the fairness doctrine.

REASONABLE OPPORTUNITY FOR CONTRASTING VIEWS. If a broadcaster's coverage of an election issue triggers the fairness doctrine, he must provide a reasonable opportunity for contrasting viewpoints. A reasonable opportunity for contrasting views on ballot propositions has already been discussed (see pages 141–142). In the case of issues concerning candidates, we have seen the controversial issue in most elections is, who among all the candidates should be elected? Contrasting viewpoints on this issue are represented by the individual candidates competing for the office (or nomination) in question. For example, each candidate seeking the presidency has his own viewpoint on who is best qualified to serve as President.[115]

The broadcaster's duty is to afford a reasonable opportunity for expression of these contrasting views. As in normal fairness-doctrine situations, a reasonable opportunity does not mean equal time. Instead, the broadcaster is expected to evaluate the relative significance of the various contrasting viewpoints. Through this evaluation he will determine how to allocate coverage to each viewpoint during the campaign period. A broadcaster may reasonably decide that the viewpoint of a fringe-party candidate on the issue of who should be elected does not merit as much coverage as that accorded the viewpoint of a major-party candidate – or, indeed, any coverage.[116]

For example, the FCC decided that ABC-TV, CBS-TV, and NBC-TV had not been unreasonable in providing only minimal coverage to the 1972 presidential campaign of Dr. Benjamin Spock.[117] Spock, the well-known pediatrician, author, and political activist, was the candidate of the People's Party. The party had held a national convention and was not narrowly devoted to a single issue or single election. Spock's campaign had attracted the attention of the press, and he was one of only four presidential candidates to be accorded Secret Service protection. Still the commission decided that Spock's fairness complaint seeking greater campaign coverage

> failed to show that the networks acted unreasonably or in other than good faith in determining that the view that Dr. Spock should be elected did not constitute a significant viewpoint on the issue of the 1972 Presidential election. The information before the commission is that Dr. Spock was one of twelve candidates seeking the Presidency and that he was on the ballots of only ten states, in total representing 25 percent of the nation's population. Although [the complaint] estimated Dr. Spock's strength at five to ten percent of the national electorate and stated that he had conducted "an extensive national campaign," this information consists merely of [the complainant's] own opinion. Considering these facts and circumstances, we cannot conclude that the networks' judgments as to the significance of Dr. Spock's candidacy were unreasonable.

The commission is chary of second-guessing a broadcaster's allocation of coverage to candidates, because the determination usually involves journalistic judgments as to newsworthiness. In this area, the commission will defer to the standards employed by broadcast journalists, unless there is evidence of deliberate news suppression.

As in general fairness situations, balanced coverage of candidates may be achieved through a station's overall programming. The broadcaster can exercise his customary discretion in selecting appropriate spokesmen as well as formats for the presentation of contrasting views. In this regard, two points bear mentioning. First, if one candidate appears personally in a station's news coverage, it may be unfair to offset that coverage by merely having a newscaster read stories about an opposing candidate. While the choice of spokesmen is up to the broadcaster, the FCC has suggested, "In a case involving political candidacies, the natural opposing spokesmen are readily identifiable (i.e., the candidates themselves or their chosen representatives)."[118] Opposing candidates are, after all, the only "genuine partisans" on the issue of who should be elected.

Second, a candidate should realize, before he seizes the opportunity to air his viewpoint, that his personal appearance may trigger the equal-time rule. As a result, his opponent(s) will acquire the right to equal air time. To avoid this consequence, the candidate ought to endeavor to present his views on a program exempt from the equal-time rule (for example, a newscast or news interview).

6
Advertising and the Fairness Doctrine

Introduction

If a broadcast advertisement takes a position on some controversial public issue, it may trigger the fairness doctrine. As a result, the broadcaster will be obligated to afford a reasonable opportunity for contrasting points of view. Exactly when this obligation will arise and how it must be discharged depend largely upon the general principles discussed in the preceding chapter. There are, however, important nuances, which deserve our closer attention.

Idea Advertising

Basically, three kinds of broadcast advertisements can create balancing obligations under the fairness doctrine: editorial ads, institutional ads, and public-service announcements. In the case of an editorial ad, some individual or group acquires air time to advocate one side of a controversial public issue. Say an antiabortion organization sponsors a sixty-second spot announcement; listeners are urged to support adoption of a constitutional amendment overriding the decision of the United States Supreme Court that facilitates legal abortions. For the purposes of the fairness doctrine, this ad should be treated just as a station editorial on the same subject would have been.[1]

So-called institutional advertising is usually part of an overall public relations effort on behalf of some business. The sponsor — be it an entire industry or an individual corporation or service — seeks to present a favorable public image of itself or its activities, as opposed to selling a particular product. Normally, such advertising does not argue points on controversial issues; thus the fairness doctrine is not triggered. Sometimes, however, the institutional advertiser subtly presents arguments in the ad which clearly advance one side of an important public issue. In such a situation, the broadcaster would incur a balancing obligation under the fairness doctrine.

How is a broadcaster or a concerned citizen to determine whether a particular institutional ad triggers the fairness doctrine? The FCC has explained that it expects licensees

> to make a reasonable, common sense judgment as to whether the "advertisment" presents a meaningful statement which obviously addresses, and advocates a point of view on, a controversial issue of public importance. This determination cannot be made in a vacuum; in addition to his review of the text of the ad, the licensee must take into account his general knowledge of the issues and arguments in the ongoing public debate. Indeed, this relationship of the ad to the debate being carried on in the community is critical. If the ad bears only a tenuous relationship to that debate, or one drawn by unnecessary inference, the fairness doctrine would clearly not be applicable.
>
> The situation would be different, however, if that relationship could be shown to be both substantial and obvious. For example, if the arguments and views expressed in the ad closely parallel the major arguments advanced by partisans on one side or the other of a public debate, it might be reasonable to conclude that one side of the issue involved had been presented thereby raising fairness doctrine obligations. . . .[2]

The commission recognizes that its standards may lead to many close distinctions. Individual broadcasters are apt to reach different conclusions regarding the same ad. All the commission will do when complaints are received is review broadcasters' decisions to determine whether they were reasonable and made in good faith.

Let us consider some specific examples. The commission has been markedly unreceptive to claims that typical promotional puffery raises one side of some controversial issue. In 1969 a complaint was made concerning promotional announcements disseminated by the National Association of Broadcasters (NAB).[3] These announcements proclaimed the many services of the television industry. The industry was characterized as "free, commercially-sponsored television" and "free privately-owned and operated television." Commercial television was praised for its sports coverage, newscasting, and public-service announcements carried on behalf of charitable institutions. According to a fairness complaint, these NAB ads were "part of a knowing and concerted attack by the NAB on pay TV"; the pay-television question represented a controversial issue of public importance.

The FCC concluded that the ads did not trigger the fairness doctrine:

> The announcements involve the kind of puffery normally engaged in by an industry. . . . There is no reference to pay television in any of the announcements. This praise of commercial television by a commercial television licensee cannot be regarded as a clear criticism of pay television or a claim of supremacy over pay television for purposes of the fairness doctrine. Further, we note that the pay television controversy does not turn on the issue of whether the present commercial system should be preserved; it is accepted by all the parties to the controversy that it should and that pay television should not "syphon off" the programs' now being presented to the American people.

The commission warned that the purposes of the fairness doctrine — that is, keeping the public fully informed on vital issues — would not be served by a "strained attempt" to apply the doctrine to promotional puffs. Besides, the commission observed pointedly, such an attempt would be "disruptive of the commercially based broadcast system."

In 1970 a number of fairness complaints were prompted by armed forces recruitment messages, which were broadcast as public-service announcements.[4] A typical recruitment pitch went:

> ANNOUNCER: It's a day you can't put into words. You try to compare it with the day you graduated from highschool, but there's no comparison. Because somehow the day you graduated from highschool, you were still just another guy, and on this day you're something else. You look taller than you did because you stand taller. You look proud because you are proud. And no wonder. . . . You've just gone through the toughest eight weeks a guy ever had. And if you didn't have what it takes, you wouldn't be standing with the rest of them, you wouldn't be wearing the same uniform. Ask a marine. Ask a marine what it means to graduate from boot camp. He'll tell you. It's a day to remember for the rest of your life. Because that day they separate the men from the boys.
>
> REFRAIN: Ask a marine.

Antiwar activists contended that these announcements had to be evaluated within the context of the Vietnam War, since recruits were likely to be stationed in the war zone. Given the widespread opposition to our military involvement in Vietnam, any ad that advocated the benefits of enlistment, while overlooking the availability of draft deferments, necessarily presented one side of a controversial issue. The activists sought to have stations offset the recruitment ads with so-called countercommercials, expressing opposing points of view. For example:

> Thinking about joining the Army? Before you do, consider the facts. Chances are, the only job you'll learn is how to kill. Chances are, you'll wind up in Vietnam, killing and perhaps getting killed, in a war that doesn't make much sense. So if you're thinking about the military, remember this: You may be eligible for a military deferment. For free information call [telephone number given].

After stations refused to air these countercommercials, the groups filed a fairness complaint with the FCC.

The commission decided the stations had acted reasonably in deciding that the recruitment ads raised no balancing obligations under the fairness doctrine:

> We do not believe that the broadcast of Armed Forces recruitment messages, any more than similar recruitment messages for policemen, firemen, teachers, census enumerators, peace corp volunteers, etc., in and of itself, raises a controversial issue of public importance requiring the presentation of conflicting viewpoints. We note that the power of the Government to raise an army has not been questioned; rather the thrust of the complaint is an objection to the use made of the army (war in Vietnam) and the manner in which manpower is conscripted (Selective Service draft).
>
> In reaching this conclusion we also note that complainants themselves reason that recruitment messages are controversial *because* they are inextricably intertwined with the conduct of the war in Vietnam and the Selective Service draft. . . . The fact that Vietnam and the draft are controversial issues of public importance does not, in our view, automatically require that recruitment messages also be considered as such. . . .

In essence, the commission declined to view the recruitment ads within a broad social context. Admittedly, there was no explicit mention of the war or the draft in the ads. Were these two issues implicitly addressed by the ads, however? Given the fact of widespread antiwar protest, did not the exhortation to enlist and become a tall proud man necessarily raise questions about the enlistee's darker prospects — as well as the nation's? Apparently the broadcasters thought not, and the commission upheld this judgment as reasonable. Instead of straining for broad implications, the commission saw only a narrow issue raised by the recruitment ads — namely, whether the government had a right to raise an army — and conveniently for the commission's rationale, this issue was not seriously in dispute.

In his dissenting opinion, former Commissioner Nicholas Johnson complained that the majority opinion "merely illustrated the principle that determined men, if they try hard enough, can define any problem out of existence." Johnson's observation pinpoints in the area of advertising a fairness-doctrine principle we have already seen at work in general programming: before the doctrine can be triggered, it is not only necessary to identify a controversial issue, but it is first necessary to define the issue. As we saw in the famous NBC "Pensions" case, defining the basic issue can determine whether any balancing obligation will ever arise.

In 1971 the FCC reviewed three institutional ads, which, unlike the recruitment messages, did lend implicit support to one side of a controversial public issue.[5] Standard Oil of New Jersey sponsored the ads on NBC-TV's "Saturday Night News," "Sunday Night News," and "Meet the Press." The ads ran at a time of intense debate over the advisability of constructing a trans-Alaskan oil pipeline. Consider what bearing these three ads might have had on the pipeline controversy:

> I. Here on the North Slope of Alaska it takes 30 days to erect an oil rig, compared with a few days in Texas. Roads scarcely exist. In winter when sea lanes are choked with ice, all equipment must be flown in. The freight bill for the first North Slope wells was nearly a million dollars, with no guarantee of finding oil. Is it worth the risk? We at Jersey think so, both for us and for you. The Alaskan oil strikes are big, but so is America's need for energy. At the rate this country is now using oil, the Alaskan strikes probably represent little more than three years supply. If America's energy supply is to be assured in this unpredictable world the search for domestic oil must go on and fast.
>
> II. This is the Canadian Arctic near Alaska. In Winter temperatures plunge to sixty below and it freezes solid. But in Summer it's a gentle land. Jersey's Canadian affiliate, Imperial Oil, made its first discovery in the Arctic fifty years ago. Experience since then has shown them not only how to look for oil in the far North, but to look for ways to preserve the ecology. To protect the swans and geese and ducks that return each year to nest and raise their young. And to avoid disturbing the migration and grazing habits of reindeer, caribou and other wildlife. By balancing demands of energy

with needs of nature they're making sure that when wells
are drilled or pipelines built, the life that comes back each
year will have a home to come back to.

III. The Arctic wilderness is not always frozen. In sum-
mer much of it comes alive.

Delicate vegetation called Tundra blooms. Reindeer, cari-
bou and other animals graze on it.

Jersey's affiliate, Humble Oil, is exploring and drilling
for oil in the Arctic. In constructing roads and living
quarters they can't avoid disturbing some of the Tundra
and if it isn't replaced it can turn into a permanent sea of
mud.

So back in 1968 Humble joined a research project on
the North Slope of Alaska. Seeds of thirteen varieties of
hearty winter grass were gathered and planted. Four types
survived the bitter Arctic winter, some growing even faster
than the Tundra itself.

Now we believe we know how to restore disturbed Tundra to help create a better balance between the need for oil
and the needs of nature.

Two environmental groups, the Wilderness Society and the
Friends of the Earth, took a less sanguine view of the oil company's capability to develop and transport North Slope oil without
ecological damage. The groups filed a fairness complaint with the
FCC. They argued that the three Standard Oil ads presented only
one side of controversial questions surrounding proposed construction of the trans-Alaskan oil pipeline.

The FCC analyzed each ad and concluded, over NBC's objections, that the ads were not only promotive of the sponsor's public
image but also presented one side of the pipeline controversy:

(a) On advertisement I, NBC argues that it nowhere
mentions the pipeline and that its clear thrust is America's
urgent need for oil, the consequent need for such difficult
explorations as that going forward on Alaska's North Slope,
and thus that ". . . the search for domestic oil must go on,
and fast." We agree that the advertisement does not specifically mention the pipeline. But we also note that germane
to the controversy is the question whether the nation
urgently requires development of the North Slope deposits

or whether there is room for delay to assess more carefully the alternatives to the proposed pipeline. . . . By its juxtaposition of North Slope deposits and the nation's need for fast oil development, advertisement I does relate to the pipeline issue. (b) As to advertisement II, NBC points out that it mentions the *Canadian* arctic and not the Alaskan pipeline. Again we agree; indeed, opponents of the Alaska pipeline are now urging consideration of a Canadian pipeline as a better alternative from the ecological perspective. . . . On the other hand, we must also note that the advertisement opens with a reference to ". . . the Canadian Arctic near Alaska" and specifically refers to the ability of Jersey's Canadian affiliate to build a pipeline and ". . . yet preserve the ecology." The "experience" referred to is ". . . in the far North" and thus the discussion does bear on the present Alaska controversy. (c) NBC also presents cogent arguments on advertisement III. This advertisement does not mention the pipeline but simply states that Humble, in exploring and drilling for oil in the Arctic, "can't avoid disturbing some of the Tundra" and, by way of remedy, has developed four types of grass that hold promise of surviving the bitter Arctic winter. The accuracy of this statement is not in dispute. Further, it is obviously desirable that business enterprises take ecological factors into account and that they be encouraged to inform the public of their actions in this regard. Nonetheless, the clear import of this announcement is that [the oil company] operating in the far North, can strike a ". . . balance between the need for oil and the needs of nature." And thus it has a cognizable bearing on the controversial issue of the Alaska pipeline.

NBC sought to invoke the commission's earlier ruling in the army recruitment case, but the commission found that ruling distinguishable on its facts.

The purpose of the recruitment announcements was to persuade men to join the Armed Services. There was no mention of the Indochina war and no argument, explicit or implicit, that the war was justified. As the Court [that affirmed the commission's recruitment decision] stated, "We consider that . . . military recruitment by voluntary means is all that was implicit in virtually all the Armed Services recruitment announcements." . . . In this case, the [oil company] advertisements refer to oil development in the far North and discuss both the need for rapid development of oil deposits in Alaska and the ecological impacts of such development.

Thus, unlike the recruitment ads, the oil ads explicitly raised questionable aspects of a public controversy. The ads were also implicitly related to the controversy in a substantial way: "The advertisements . . . inherently raise the controversial issue of the ecological effects which may result from transporting such oil, since the company's large investment in drilling for Alaskan oil quite obviously is based upon the assumption that transportation of the oil to other parts of the world would be permitted."

The commission conceded that its decision was a difficult one to make, "because we are reviewing the reasonableness of the licensee's judgment and because the pipeline controversy is not specifically referred to." Nevertheless, "in light of the present public controversy over the desirability of developing and transporting Alaskan oil, we are not persuaded by [NBC's] argument that the advertisements are merely 'institutional advertising,' or that a discussion of an oil company's search for oil and its asserted concern for ecology are not controversial issues of public importance." Under the circumstances, NBC's judgment was unreasonable. The oil company ads triggered the fairness doctrine's balancing obligation.

In a 1974 case, the commission found that institutional ads sponsored by a utility company triggered the fairness doctrine.[6] The Georgia Power Company ran these ads over local television at a time when the Georgia Public Service Commission was conducting hearings on the utility's request for a rate increase. One of the ads stated:

> By 1978, our customers will need twice as much electric power. And we must build to supply it.
>
> Every year, you're increasing your use of electricity. We're busy keeping up with your present needs and getting ready for the future.
>
> But it costs money. We'll spend nearly $2 million dollars every working day this year, just for construction.

Most of that money must be borrowed. And interest rates
are steep.
Environmental protection adds millions of dollars to our
costs, too. For instance, one tower to cool and recirculate
water is about $4 million.
*All these things affect the price of your electricity. So does
inflation. In today's economy, it just isn't possible to provide
electricity at pre-inflation prices.* But your needs keep growing . . . and construction can't wait. We're building . . .
to serve you. [Emphasis added.]

This ad rather obviously presented major arguments justifying a
rate increase. Therefore, it was unreasonable for broadcasters to
have concluded that the ad did not present one side of the rate-
increase controversy.

In contrast, another one of Georgia Power's institutional ads
raised no fairness obligations:

(Audio: sound of typing)
Do you know what your son saw in school today? A herd
of charging elephants.
Through a motion picture projector.
He saw a living cell divide. Through an electric micro-
scope.
He saw a computer estimate world population changes.
(Audio: typing)
He printed a newspaper.
He heard a Spaniard reciting from Don Quixote . . .
with the help of a tape recorder.
He listened to a Beethoven symphony.
Through hi-fi equipment.
(Audio: symphony continues to end of commercial)
Today electricity helped your son learn in a hundred
ways.
At Georgia Power we're building power plants now to
make sure our schools . . . have all the electricity they
need.
We're building a brighter life for you . . . and your
children.

This ad, unlike the first one, dealt generally with the increasing use
of electricity by the people of Georgia. A broadcaster could rea-

sonably conclude that it was not devoted in an obvious and meaningful way to the rate-increase issue.

Product Advertising

Since the late 1960s the FCC has encountered "great difficulties in tracing a coherent pattern for the accommodation of product advertising to the fairness doctrine."[7] As of 1974, with the issuance of its long-awaited reexamination of the fairness doctrine, the commission seems to have abandoned the struggle.[8] While product commercials that openly editorialize can still trigger fairness obligations, the run-of-the-mill commercial will have no such effect.

The FCC's long struggle began in 1967 with its famous decision to apply the fairness doctrine to cigarette commercials.[9] A young lawyer named John Banzhaf III filed a fairness complaint against WCBS-TV (New York City). His target included "all cigarette advertisements which by their portrayals of youthful or virile-looking or sophisticated persons enjoying cigarettes in interesting and exciting situations deliberately seek to create the impression and present the point of view that smoking is socially acceptable, manly, and a necessary part of a rich full life." Although the commercial made no explicit health claims, the commission decided that they did present one side of a controversial issue of public importance: "It comes down, we think, to a simple controversial issue: the cigarette commercials are conveying any number of reasons why it appears desirable to smoke but understandably do not set forth the reasons why it is not desirable to commence or continue smoking. It is the affirmative presentation of smoking as a desirable habit which constitutes the viewpoint others desire to oppose."

A station presenting this viewpoint through commercials triggered the fairness doctrine and incurred the duty to inform its audience of the contrasting view: that however enjoyable smoking might be, it posed a potentially serious hazard to health and, indeed, life.

The commission took great pains to limit the reach of its cigarette ruling: "We stress that our holding is limited to this product — cigarettes. Governmental and private reports (e.g., the 1964 Report of the Surgeon General's Committee) and congressional action (e.g., the Federal Cigarette Labeling and Advertising Act of 1965) assert that normal use of this product can be a hazard to the health of millions of persons." This documented threat made cigarette advertising a "unique" situation: "We know of no other widespread contention by governmental or private authorities that the normal use of any . . . other products . . . poses a serious health hazard to millions of persons who otherwise enjoy good health."

The commission did not have to wait long, however, for such products to be brought to its attention. In 1970, the Friends of the Earth (FOE) brought a fairness complaint aimed at automobile and gasoline commercials carried over WCBS-TV (New York City).[10] FOE objected to New Yorkers being constantly bombarded with television pitches for large-engine cars and high-test leaded gasolines "generally described as efficient, clean, socially responsible, and automotively necessary." Contrary to the impression conveyed by these ads, FOE pointed out that the products in question were egregious contributors to air pollution and, hence, posed significant dangers to health. FOE substantiated its position by citation to numerous governmental and private sources (including the Surgeon General's 1962 report, "Motor Vehicles, Air Pollution and Health"), all warning against the health hazard caused by automobile emissions. Thus the ads were being presented in the context of "a public controversy in which government officials and professional and lay people concerned about health are pitted against the automobile manufacturers and the oil companies." According to FOE, the ads triggered the fairness doctrine, because they presented one side of a controversial public issue — namely, whether the public should prefer less-polluting unleaded gasoline and small-engine cars that use unleaded gas.

The FCC dug in its heels and refused to extend the *Banzhaf* cigarette ruling to the auto and gas ads cited. These ads were not thought to raise one side of a controversial issue — at least, not as obviously as the cigarette ads had. In the unique case of cigarettes, a complete abandonment of the offending product had been urged by many responsible sources. Consequently, by encouraging people to smoke, the cigarette ads raised one side of a clear-cut public controversy. In contrast, the issue of air pollution caused by the internal combustion engine was more complex. Government was not advising the abandonment of gasoline-engine automobiles; instead, the remedies being proposed involved varying approaches and a balancing of competing interests. Given the relative complexity of the issue, the auto and gas ads were not perceived as clearly raising one point of view — as the cigarette ads had. Nor would brief contrasting viewpoints — presented, say, in counter-commercials — be likely to inform the public adequately, in the way antismoking messages did, concisely and straightforwardly. Through this chain of reasoning, the FCC distinguished cigarette ads from auto and gas ads.

"The distinction is not apparent to us," said a federal appeals court in reversing the FCC,

> any more than we suppose it is to the asthmatic in New York City for whom air pollution is a mortal danger. Neither are we impressed by the Commission's assertion that, because no governmental agency has as yet urged the complete abandonment of the use of automobiles, the commercials in question do not touch upon some controversial issue of public importance. Matters of degree arise in environmental control, as in other areas of legal regulation. To say that all automobiles pollute the atmosphere is not to say that some do not pollute more than others. Voices have already been lifted against the fetish of unnecessary horsepower; and some gasoline refiners have begun to make a virtue of necessity by extolling their non-leaded, less dynamic, brands of gasoline. Commercials which continue to insinuate that the human personality finds greater fulfillment in the large car with the quick getaway do, it seems to us, ventilate a point of view which not only has become controversial but involves an issue of public importance. When there is un-disputed evidence, as there is here, that the hazards to health implicit in air pollution are enlarged and aggravated by such products, then the parallel with cigarette advertising is exact and the relevance of [the] *Banzhaf* [ruling] inescapable.

The court ruled that the commercials had, indeed, triggered the fairness doctrine.

Just prior to the court's reversal of the FCC, the commission had declined to apply the fairness doctrine to certain other gasoline commercials.[11] These ads extolled the virtues of Chevron gasoline with F-310 additive. A typical television commercial showed a clear balloon attached to an automobile exhaust pipe; as the car idled, the balloon filled with black smoke. Then, after substituting Chevron F-310 in the car's tank, a second clear-balloon attachment demonstrated the absence of any black smoke. The ad copy read:

> NARRATOR: I'm Scott Carpenter. We're attaching a clear balloon to this car to show you one of the most meaningful gasoline achievements in history. The balloon is filling with dirty emissions that go into the air and waste mileage.
>
> Now Standard Oil of California has accomplished the development of a remarkable gasoline additive, Formula F-310, that reduces exhaust emissions from dirty engines. The same car, after just six tankfuls of Chevron with F-310; no dirty smoke, cleaner air. A major breakthrough to help solve one of today's critical problems. And since dirty exhaust is wasted gasoline, F-310 keeps good mileage from going up in smoke. Cleaner air, better mileage – Chevron with F-310 turns dirty smoke into good, clean mileage. There isn't a car on the road that shouldn't be using it.

The claims made in the Chevron ads were criticized as false and misleading by several governmental and private agencies. In a fairness complaint filed with the FCC, an opportunity was sought to present opposing views on the issue of whether F-310 additive really did help solve the air pollution problem. The commission decided no fairness obligation had arisen, because the Chevron ads did not "deal directly" with a controversial issue.

> The Chevron F-310 announcements do not argue a position on a controversial issue of public importance, but rather advance a claim for product efficacy. It is true that this claim relates to a matter of public concern, but making such a claim for a product is not the same thing as arguing a position on a controversial issue of public importance. That the

claim is alleged to be untrue and partially deceptive does not change its nature. The Chevron advertisements do not claim there is no danger in air pollution or that automobiles do not contribute to pollution but assert, instead, that use of the sponsor's product helps solve the problem. It would ill suit the purposes of the fairness doctrine, designed to illumine significant controversial issues, to apply it to claims of a product's efficacy or social utility. The merits of any one gasoline, weight reducer, breakfast cereal or headache remedy — to name but a few examples that come readily to mind — do not rise to the level of a significant public issue.

By way of example of product commercials that would "deal directly" with significant public issues, the commission hypothesized:

> If an announcement sponsored by a coal-mining company asserted that strip mining had no harmful ecological results, the sponsor would be engaging directly in debate on a controversial issue, and fairness obligations would ensue. Or, if a community were in a dispute over closing a factory emitting noxious fumes and an advertisement for a product made in the factory argued that question, fairness would also come into play.

The complainants in the *Chevron* case appealed to federal court. While the appeal was pending, the commission's earlier ruling in *Friends of the Earth* was reversed in court (as we have seen). At the commission's request, the *Chevron* case was sent back for reconsideration in light of the *Friends of the Earth* court decision. Upon reconsideration, the commission affirmed its initial ruling in *Chevron*.

> The facts of the present case are quite different from those presented in the cigarette case [*Banzhaf*] and in *Friends of the Earth*. There is no evidence which would indicate that the Chevron additive F-310 in any way enlarges or aggravates hazards to the public health. Chevron with F-310 is not alleged to be more dangerous than any competing product. [The complainants] do not urge the public to abandon the use of gasoline, or even to avoid using Chevron with F-310. . . .

Even assuming [for the sake of argument] that a public health issue is involved here, the present case is still distinguishable from *Friends of the Earth*. The scientific evidence in this case is far from "undisputed." Chevron has amassed considerable evidence to support the proposition that its product will, in fact, contribute to a reduction of the air pollution problem. . . .

Public health considerations aside, we remain convinced that traditional Fairness Doctrine principles do not require the broadcast of views in opposition to the F-310 advertisements. We are still of the opinion that these announcements did not argue a position on a controversial issue of public importance, but merely advanced a claim for product efficacy.

Since the commission remained convinced that the Chevron ads had not raised one side of a controversial issue, it concluded that the broadcast of supposed contrasting views "would not provide a health service similar to exhortations to stop smoking, or to drive cars with reduced horsepower and use gasolines with a low-octane rating."

Once again the *Chevron* case was appealed to federal court — the same court which had reversed the FCC in *Friends of the Earth*. This time the court affirmed the commission, agreeing that *Chevron* was not controlled by the precedents set in *Banzhaf* and *Friends of the Earth:*

In the *Banzhaf* case advertisements represented that smoking was socially desirable, although evidence indicated that it was dangerous to health. In the *Friends of the Earth* case the burden of the advertising was that high-test gasoline and large engines were "clean, socially responsible and automotively necessary," although such engines or gasoline contributed significantly to air pollution. In each case there was an opposing point of view: that smokers should stop smoking or that consumers should purchase low-test gasolines and small engines. In the case at bar however the commercials made no attempt to glorify conduct or products which endangered public health or contributed to pollution. . . . The F-310 commercials "far from suggesting that automobile emissions do not contribute significantly to the dangers of air pollution, urged that the gasoline being advertised was designed to reduce those dangers."

Therefore, the Chevron ads did not raise one side of an important controversial issue. The narrow question of whether Chevron with F-310 actually was effective in helping to lessen air pollution was not, in and of itself, a controversy of sufficient public significance to invoke the fairness doctrine.

Having traveled a long and tortuous path from *Banzhaf* to *Friends of the Earth* to *Chevron,* the FCC, in 1974, completely revamped its fairness policy on product commercials.[12] Looking back, the commission declared the approach first taken in *Banzhaf* represented a "serious departure" from the central purpose of the fairness doctrine — namely, the development of informed public opinion.

> We do not believe that the underlying purposes of the fairness doctrine would be well served by permitting the cigarette case to stand as a fairness doctrine precedent. In the absence of some meaningful or substantive discussion, such as that found in . . . "editorial advertisements" . . . we do not believe that the usual product commercial can realistically be said to inform the public on any side of a controversial issue of public importance. It would be a great mistake to consider standard advertisements, such as those involved in . . . *Banzhaf* and *Friends of the Earth,* as though they made a meaningful contribution to public debate. . . . Accordingly, in the future, we will apply the fairness doctrine only to those "commercials" which are devoted in an obvious and meaningful way to the discussion of public issues.

In essence, the commission was reversing itself and severely limiting those situations in which a product commercial could trigger the fairness doctrine.

It is still conceivable that certain commercials might discuss some controversial issue in an obvious and meaningful way. Recall, for example, the hypotheticals suggested by the commission in the *Chevron* case: that is, the coal company ad that defends strip mining or the factory ad that refutes charges of noxious fumes. Ads such as these explicitly take positions on significant public issues — unlike the cigarette ads, whose message was insinuated rather than explained in any attempt at enlightened argumentation. Product commercials that openly argue about some significant issue are likely to be rare — especially since claims of product efficacy in helping to solve society's problems are not regarded by the commission as arguing any position on a public issue. What's more, broadcasters are not apt to sell time for product commercials that may trigger the fairness doctrine and raise the specter of counteradvertising.

Throughout its long struggle to accommodate product advertising with the fairness doctrine, the FCC was most solicitous of the economic base that commercials contribute to the broadcasting system. (Critics charged that the commission was concerned more with preserving the commercial broadcasting system than human life itself.) If the fairness doctrine were to require certain commercials to be offset by so-called countercommercials, advertising dollars, it was speculated, would be driven away from broadcasting into other media outlets. Deprived of a financial base, broadcasting, with its capability to inform the public, might be seriously undermined. This presumed economic threat clearly influenced the commission's reluctance to attach balancing obligations to product commercials.

A key point here is the reason why the FCC was so concerned about preserving broadcasting's economic base: because that base facilitates programming which enlightens the public on important issues. Such programming is a more effective format than commercials and countercommercials for informing the public in depth. Thus, while restricting the impact of the fairness doctrine on commercial advertising, the FCC placed greater emphasis upon the duty of broadcasters to cover significant public issues on a regular programming basis.

> We do not believe that our policy [on commercials and countercommercials] will leave the public uninformed on important matters of interest to consumers. Certainly, we expect that consumer issues will rank high on the agenda of many, if not most, broadcasters since their importance to the public is self-evident. . . . The decision to cover these and

other matters of similar public concern appropriately lies with individual licensees in the fulfillment of their public trustee responsibilities, and should not grow out of a tortured or distorted application of fairness doctrine principles to [commercial] announcements in which public issues are not discussed.[13]

Broadcasters may be called upon increasingly to *initiate* coverage of controversial issues rather than simply to afford an opportunity for rebuttal after an issue has already been raised (see pages 108–109).

Reasonable Opportunity for Contrasting Views

When some form of spot announcement (for example, an ad or public-service announcement) triggers the fairness doctrine, the broadcaster must provide a reasonable opportunity for the presentation of conflicting views. In general, the principles that apply here are identical to those governing fairness situations triggered by regular programming.

The FCC does not require that one spot announcement be offset by another — a *countercommercial.* Instead, the choice of format for a contrasting view is up to the broadcaster. One side of an issue may be raised in an ad, while the other side is presented through newscasts, interviews, or panel discussions, and so on. As long as rough balance is achieved in the broadcaster's *overall programming* on the issue, the fairness doctrine is satisfied.[14]

Rough balance, however, may sometimes call for a response in the format of a spot announcement. The reason is that opinions can usually be more forcefully expressed through spot announcements than general programming. First of all, the spot may be repeated, reaching different audiences throughout the broadcast day. As a result, large numbers of people are exposed to the particular viewpoint, and some of them are exposed more than once, thereby intensifying the impact. Second, the spot announcement or advertisement is inherently a highly persuasive device. It can take advantage of sophisticated audio and video techniques to drive a point home — without interruption or contradiction.[15]

Thus, an extreme imbalance can result if only one side of a controversial issue is presented through spot announcements. Opposing spokesmen may reasonably be entitled to a similarly effective format in order to achieve balance. The fact that they cannot afford to purchase time for spot announcements would not necessarily be a bar. If the broadcaster's only alternatives are providing *free time* for spot announcements or neglecting to present any opposing views, free time would be required. This requirement, known as the *Cullman* principle (see pages 160–162), applies generally to fairness-doctrine situations, whether an advertisement or regular programming triggered the balancing obligation.[16]

As might be expected, the peculiar power of the spot announcement occasions some difficulty when rough balance is being calculated. If an ad, say, is not offset by a counterad, then exactly what kind of programming, and how much of it, is called for? Perhaps no FCC case illustrates this dilemma more dramatically than the "Alaskan pipeline" case.[17] In that case, it will be recalled, Standard Oil of New Jersey sponsored a series of editorial ads implicitly favoring construction of the controversial trans-Alaskan oil pipeline. These ads triggered the fairness doctrine. Therefore, a key question was whether the broadcaster, NBC-TV, had, in its overall programming, provided a reasonable opportunity for contrasting views. A majority of the commission decided it had.

Pro's and con's on the pipeline had been presented in NBC newscasts and interviews (for example, on the "Today" show). The commission reviewed the transcripts of this programming and literally calculated the minutes and seconds devoted to each side of the pipeline controversy; ten minutes, fifty-two seconds, in favor of the pipeline (not counting the oil company ads) and twenty-one minutes, fifteen seconds, against the pipeline. Thus, without the ads, a ratio of roughly two to one existed — antipipeline over propipeline.

How did the ads affect this ratio? The ads were sixty-second spots, which ran twenty-eight times during NBC's "Meet the Press," "Saturday Night News," and "Sunday Night News." So twenty-eight minutes of essentially propipeline programming had to be added to the totals derived from NBC's regular news and public affairs programming. The result (in sheer amount of time): thirty-eight minutes, fifty-two seconds, of propipeline coverage versus twenty-one minutes, fifteen seconds, against the pipeline. With the oil ads thus figured in, the ratio shifted from two to one against the pipeline to two to one in favor of the pipeline.

Considering the latter ratio, had a reasonable opportunity been provided for expression of the antipipeline point of view? NBC said yes, and a majority of the commission concluded that this judgment was reasonable. But former FCC Chairman Dean Burch, concurring with the majority, expressed his misgivings over the reliability of the commission's balancing procedure:

> For this involves, first, an examination of the scripts to determine whether the material was pro-pipeline, anti-pipeline, or just neutral background. It then involves either counting lines in the scripts or pulling out the stop-watch to estimate the time afforded to each side. (Which assumes, of course, that there are only two sides to the issue — and in this as in most such cases, there may in fact be a multiplicity of "sides" many of which may deserve an airing.) In this instance, the Commission judged that NBC has presented fairly balanced coverage, excluding the [oil company] announcements, with the best estimate being that its coverage has somewhat favored the anti-pipeline position (roughly 21 against 11 minutes). The core issue is thus whether the [oil company] commercials result in an imbalance. If they are counted fully — without any consideration of the [fact they are indirect in their appeal] — the result is roughly a 2-to-1 ratio in time [favoring the pipeline] and probably a higher [ratio] in [terms of] frequency, in the range of 4 or 5-to-1. All these figures must also be viewed against the fact that they are constantly changing in view of NBC's continuing coverage of the issue. . . .
> I for one find it impossible to feel very confident or secure about a process that relies on the stop-watch approach — that is, making judgments, and then quantifying the category into which each presentation falls. And this is only the beginning. There are such additional ramifications as the time and style of the various presentations (does a prime-time spot count two times more heavily than a mid-morning interview? three times? or ten times?), the size and make up

of the audience, and (as NBC urges in this case) the relative weight that should be accorded an indirect commercial announcement [like the oil company editorial ads] as against the direct rebuttal that would be afforded under a [ruling requiring NBC to run countercommercials]. And how do you take into account the fact that a broadcaster, like any good journalist, stays with a hot issue until it's resolved — do we simply adopt an arbitrary cut-off? It might even be argued we have to consider the dial switching habits of the average viewer — which means that only rarely does he recall where he viewed which side of what controversial issue! The road here could lead to a series of decisions with enough variables and shadings to rival a medieval religious tract.

Burch warned that without clear guidelines on achieving balance "both licensees and the public can only fall back on prayer to divine the Commission's intent."

If Burch harbored misgivings, former Commissioner Nicholas Johnson was thoroughly disillusioned with the majority's calculations. In his dissent, he focused on the quality — not the mere quantity — of the presentations on the opposing sides of the pipeline issue. To Johnson, it was unreasonable to throw spot ads into the hopper with other forms of programming and then tabulate a sheer mathematical ratio. Such quantifying of opposing viewpoints ignored the fact that proponents of one side had enjoyed direct access to broadcast audiences through "one of the most forceful means of communication known to man (the TV commercial)."

When the proponent of one side of a "controversial issue of public importance" purchases spot advertisements he shares many of the powerful aspects of the Presidential address — his positions are "broadcast completely intact, without interruptions, cuts, commercial insertions, or delays,"; and the proponent is asked "no questions . . . either before, during, or after" his spot. In this circumstance I would ask whether the licensee satisfied his fairness doctrine obligation by balancing this spot advertising campaign with an interview program controlled and directed by a third party [for example, the "Today" show].
. . . Recognizing the impact on the individual, as he becomes informed, of the unrestrained program such as the Presidential address or the commercial spot, in short, recog-

nizing the ability of these programs to deliver an unimpeded, undiluted message directly from speaker to listener, I would treat such direct-access programming differently from other informative (and perfectly commendable) programming like the Today interview. It cannot be simply thrown in with the other less powerful programming formats for the purposes of evaluating balance.

What is the logical outcome of Johnson's analysis? If spot ads on one side are weighed in terms of their impact, then the other side is reasonably entitled to an opportunity to achieve similar impact. Johnson suggested that NBC-TV "should be instructed to place on the air additional programming against the Alaskan pipeline which can reach the same audience as saw the original [oil company] spots — on *Meet the Press*, *Saturday Night News*, and *Sunday Night News* — with the same force and with the same regularity as the original spots."

In essence, Johnson proposed countercommercials as the only format through which the public might be as effectively informed on one side of the issue as on the other.

Dean Burch, in his concurring opinion, attacked Johnson's analysis as "an 'equal opportunities' approach with a vengeance." "In its ultimate logic," Burch warned, "this approach would involve a counter-announcement for every announcement, back-to-back, and measuring to the same split-vibration on some 'intensity' scale." To Burch this approach was legal anathema: it would force the commission to intrude excessively into the processes of broadcast journalism; as a result, that robust wide-open debate the commission is constantly invoking would be inhibited.

It appears as though Johnson's approach left the commission with him. That is not to say that in any given case, the commission might not conclude a reasonable opportunity for contrasting views requires countercommercials or, at least, some form of programming similar in intensity and frequency. Such a decision is conceivable if spot announcements create overwhelming imbalance in favor of one side of a controversial issue. It is unlikely, however, that any broadcaster, aware of the dynamics of the fairness doctrine, would allow spot ads to tip the scales so drastically.

7
Personal Attacks

General Principles

In skeletal form, the FCC's personal-attack rule states:
(1) When an attack upon the honesty, character, or integrity of a person or group is broadcast
(2) during the discussion of a controversial issue of public importance,
(3) then, within one week after the attack, the broadcaster must notify the person (or group) attacked
(4) and afford the person (or group) a reasonable opportunity to respond over the broadcaster's station.

All radio and television stations — commercial and noncommercial — must abide by the personal-attack rule. It also applies to programming originated by and carried over cable television (that is, so-called origination cablecasting). As we shall soon see, certain categories of programming (for example, newscasts) are not covered by the rule.[1]

Notice that the personal-attack rule in no way prohibits the broadcast of personal attacks. Such a prohibition would detract from the robust wide-open debate the FCC seeks to promote. All the FCC requires in case of a personal attack is that the broadcaster bring both sides of the attack issue before the public. In this respect, the personal-attack rule is but a particularization of the overall fairness doctrine. Like that doctrine, the rule represents an attempt by the commission to increase the public's access to diverse views on important issues. Unlike the fairness doctrine, the rule restricts the broadcaster's choice of a spokesman who will present the contrasting view. The victim of the attack is deemed the logical spokesman; he is, presumably, most closely affected by the attack and best able to inform the public on the other side of the attack issue.[2]

The personal-attack rule imposes a general affirmative obligation upon broadcasters, but they enjoy wide discretion in applying the rule to specific situations and effectuating its purpose. Inevitably, legitimate doubts and disputes arise over how the rule should be administered: for example, what is the difference between a true personal attack and legitimate criticism that falls short of disparaging someone's character? Within what context must an attack occur in order to trigger the personal-attack rule? What constitutes a reasonable opportunity to reply to a personal attack? As long as a broadcaster acts reasonably and in good faith in resolving such questions, the commission will not substitute its judgment for his, even though the commission might have reached a different conclusion. The commission does suggest, however, that when serious doubts exist as to the proper application of the rule, the broadcaster ought to consult the commission promptly for an interpretation — rather than waiting for a complaint to be filed.[3]

As we shall see, there is no set formula by which the personal-attack rule may be applied to every conceivable fact pattern. However, four basic questions must usually be answered in any personal-attack situation. Reviewing them now will provide us with an overall perspective, before we explore the operation of the rule in detail.

(1) Has there been an attack upon the *personal qualities* of some individual or group? We will learn that close distinctions must often be made between remarks that malign character and

those that merely express disagreement with someone's wisdom, capability, or ideological stance.

(2) Did the attack occur within the context of a discussion on some controversial public issue? Isolated attacks, unrelated to any discussion on a public issue, will not trigger the personal-attack rule.

(3) Assuming that the rule has been triggered, did the broadcaster formally notify the victim of the attack and offer him an opportunity to reply? In a limited number of circumstances, the notification requirements are suspended. Even in these instances, however, the broadcaster must facilitate some form of response to the personal attack.

(4) Was the victim afforded a reasonable opportunity to reply to the attack? While the victim is not entitled to "equal time," his opportunity should, at least, compare with the original attack.

The Nature of a Personal Attack

IN GENERAL. The personal attack is essentially a form of character assassination. It is defined in the FCC's regulations as "an attack . . . upon the honesty, character, integrity or like personal qualities of an identified person or group."[4] In general, a broadcast statement that tears down personal credibility or charges moral turpitude fits the FCC's definition.

Perhaps the most famous personal attack — it resulted in the landmark Supreme Court decision, *Red Lion Broadcasting Company v. FCC*, discussed in Chapter 1 — occurred over WGCB-AM-FM (Red Lion, Pennsylvania).[5] In November, 1964, WGCB broadcast a fifteen-minute program by the Reverend Billy James Hargis as part of a series entitled "The Christian Crusade." The program included discussion of the 1964 presidential campaign and a book about the Republican candidate, *Goldwater — Extremist on the Right,* by Fred J. Cook. Reverend Hargis made the following accusations against Cook: "Now who is Cook? Cook was fired from the New York World-Telegram after he made a false charge publicly on television against an unnamed public official of the New York City government. New York publishers and Newsweek magazine for December 7, 1959, showed that Fred Cook and his pal Eugene Gleason had made up the whole story and this confession was made to the District Attorney, Frank Hogan." This charge, aimed squarely at Cook's veracity, was a clear-cut personal attack.

Other examples abound. On November 3, 1969, radio WCME (Brunswick, Maine) broadcast a discussion of a pending charter referendum.[6] Two men active in the referendum campaign were referred to as working under "paranoic distress" and resorting to "distortions and some downright lies." According to the FCC, the broadcast statements were "direct specific allegations of lying and mental instability" and, as such, a personal attack. Similarly, when a doctor was accused over WKAL (Rome, New York) of "unethical conduct . . . in the death of not one but two small children," the doctor's integrity had been directly attacked.[7]

Congressman Benjamin Rosenthal was the victim of a personal attack on March 8, 1973.[8] Over radio WMCA (New York City), call-in-show moderator Bob Grant suggested to his listening audience that Rosenthal seemed to be afraid to be interviewed on the "Bob Grant Show." A few hours later during the same broadcast, Grant again referred to Rosenthal, this time labeling him a "coward." The FCC decided that Grant's initial suggestion was not a personal attack. While the remark was unfavorable to Rosenthal, it could have indicated nothing more than "a reluctance to have a position examined, rather than . . . any alleged deficiency in character." Grant's later statement, however — namely, that Rosenthal was a "coward" — constituted a personal attack. According to the commission, *"Webster's Seventh New Collegiate Dictionary* states that a coward is a person who shows ignoble (dishonorable) fear or timidity. Thus, a direct charge of cowardice, such as occurred here, is a direct attack upon character."

Not every disparaging remark made on the air is a personal attack. In the judgment of the commission, some insults do no damage to the particular personal qualities listed in the regulations — namely, honesty, character, and integrity. Of course, the regulations also include the broad catchphrase "or like personal qualities." However, the commission has not resorted to this phrase to expand the target for personal attacks. For example, calling a man a "patriotic extremist," or referring to a Negro as a "spook," nicknaming a university "Guerrilla U.," or claiming that cable television operators are "scavengers" and "parasites" — in each of these instances, the commission concluded that no personal attack had transpired.[9]

The FCC has repeatedly cautioned that "strong disagreement, even vehemently expressed, does not constitute a personal attack, in the absence of an attack upon character or integrity."[10] On March 23, 24, 25, and 26, 1970, WNBC-TV (New York City) aired a four-part investigative report on the Port of New York Authority and its director, Austin Tobin. The report was highly critical and included this commentary:

> Critics claim that Commissioners usually act as a rubber stamp for Tobin and his staff. The Authority holds no public hearings. Commissioners gather once a month at Port Authority headquarters to formally approve decisions. Our cameras were barred from filming one such meeting on the assertion that television news coverage might be disruptive. Actually, most policy decisions are ironed out in private, at the Wall Street Club, a penthouse restaurant where Commissioners and key aides meet frequently. It is this closed door policy which has generated much of the controversy swirling around the Authority. . . . It's for this reason that we feel so strongly that the Port Authority has not performed its function, the function for which it was created, which was to develop the port as a whole, and not merely in a way that was most profitable to them.

The Port Authority complained that it had been the victim of a personal attack. The FCC disagreed: "A review of the transcript demonstrates that while WNBC-TV may have sharply criticized the Port Authority, it did not broadcast a personal attack against the Authority or any of its members."

The commission is unreceptive to thin-skinned "victims," who read unwarranted implications into statements heard on the air. On April 17, 1973, the WNET-TV (Newark–New York City) program "Black Journal" covered a local school boycott.[11] Adhimu Chunga, a black member of the board of education, was interviewed and at one point referred to John Cervase, a white attorney and fellow board member, as a "political opportunist." Cervase demanded an opportunity to reply to this alleged personal attack. WNET-TV refused his request on the ground that Chunga's remark was but a "mild form of derision," not a personal attack.

Cervase complained to the FCC, but it rejected his argument:

> You [state] that "the entire program was an editorial that I (as an opponent of black students) am a racist." In effect, you suggest that, within the context of the *Black Journal* program, a statement by a black official that a white attorney was a "political opportunist" was tantamount to calling you a "racist." . . .
>
> The transcript reveals no statement that the Board of Education, or any of its members, are motivated by racism in deciding issues presented to it, nor does the transcript state at any point that you, while a member of the Board of Education, had allowed your decisions to be influenced by any alleged racial motivation.
>
> It appears that the thrust of the *Black Journal* program in question dealt, not with the decisions of any single, identified public figure . . . but rather with the more generalized topic of racial polarization. The statement [that is, "political opportunist"] which you contend constituted a personal attack upon you may be considered, reasonably, not as a characterization that you are a "racist," but rather as a statement ascribing to your actions a political motivation, and . . . we do not believe the licensee was unreasonable in concluding that this reference was not a personal attack.

There are three classes of personal attack that seem to be most confusing for both victim and broadcaster: (1) an attack during the expression of disagreement over a viewpoint or position held by some person or group; (2) an attack while the wisdom or capability of some person or group is being disputed; and (3) an attack during an accusation of corruption or illegal conduct. In any one of these instances, depending, perhaps, upon our predisposition toward the victim, we are apt to reach different conclusions as to whether or not a personal attack has, in fact, occurred. We can find some guidance in various distinctions drawn by the FCC in several close cases.

ATTACK ON A VIEWPOINT OR BELIEF. In general, disagreement with political persuasions, ideological positions, and moral beliefs, et cetera, will not amount to a personal attack, unless someone's (or some group's) character is maligned in the process. For example, during the 1968 presidential campaign, it was not a personal attack to broadcast that "Hubert Humphrey, a product of New Deal thinking, and Richard Nixon, a product of the Eisenhower years, probably are incapable of establishing any meaningful liaison with this generation."[12] Nor was it a personal attack during the 1972 campaign to refer to Senators Hubert Humphrey and George Mc-Govern as "liberals and socialists."[13]

On August 27, 1972, birth-control advocate William Baird appeared on the "Newslight" program over WNBC-TV (New York City).[14] In denouncing the antiabortion position of the Roman Catholic Church, Baird remonstrated:

> Where I failed somehow is to really ignite in power groups — I'm talking about the Protestant Council of Churches, the Jewish faith — for them to have enough guts — GUTS — to stand up and say to the Roman Catholic Church — no longer are we going to permit you to go unchallenged — you calling us murderers — no longer are we going to let you say that we are now going to kill the elderly, the retarded — that if we could somehow stop this wave of propaganda aimed at non-Catholics, then we could win.

No doubt feeling victimized, the church complained of a personal attack. The FCC was unreceptive:

> Mr. Baird's remarks calling on the Protestant and Jewish faiths "to stand up and say to the Roman Catholic Church — no longer are we going to permit you to go unchallenged — you calling us murderers . . ." may state his particular view and interpretation of the Catholic position on abortion in a highly argumentative manner, but they do not attack

the honesty, integrity, or character of the Catholic Church in taking that alleged position.

The key distinction here seems to be between honestly held beliefs, which may be criticized as such without triggering the personal-attack rule, and, on the other hand, beliefs that are held for reprehensible reasons. Had Baird alleged some corrupt motive lurking behind the church's beliefs, he might well have made a personal attack.

This distinction appears to be operative in those cases where a disagreement over viewpoint manifests itself as a full-fledged personal attack. On February 25, 1967, the Storer Broadcasting Company aired an anticommunist editorial that made disparaging references to the W. E. B. DuBois Clubs of America:

> The Communist Party of the United States is waging an intensive campaign *to subvert the minds of American youth.* Foremost among the activities currently directed *against our young people* is the new Marxist youth organization known as the DuBois Clubs of America founded at a special meeting in California dominated and controlled by American communists. The Reds mispronounce their group . . . boys club instead of the DuBois Clubs *to deliberately deceive* prospective members. . . .[15]

The FCC decided the broadcaster had made a personal attack upon the integrity of the DuBois Clubs: "The clear thrust of the editorial is to characterize the DuBois Clubs as a Communist organization, against which the American public, and particularly American youth, should be on guard."

At the other end of the political spectrum, the John Birch Society has also been subjected to personal attack.[16] A program entitled "Star Spangled Extremists," produced by the Anti-Defamation League of B'nai B'rith, was broadcast over noncommercial station KUHT-TV (Houston) in 1967. "Star Spangled Extremists" identified the Birch Society as a far-right organization, discussed its background, membership, budget, and attitude toward civil rights. "We agree [with KUHT-TV]," said the FCC,

that most of the references to the society in the program
were not personal attacks within the rule.

But the program, after describing the John Birch Society
as "the most active and powerful of [the radical right]
groups," states that the radical right often engages in "physical abuse and violence," disrupts "other people's meetings,"
giving an example involving local leaders of the Birch Society, and engages in "local terror campaigns against opposition figures," giving subsequently the example of the Birch
Society, allegedly "under a front name," mounting a campaign in Visilia, Calif., to remove a standard reference work
from the library. We believe that these statements, taken
together, do constitute a personal attack upon the integrity,
honesty, and character of the Birch Society.

ATTACK ON WISDOM OR CAPABILITY. The FCC has frequently distinguished between remarks that question the judgment of a person
or group and those that malign character: "Honesty, character,
integrity and other like qualities applicable to the personal attack
rule are characteristics which relate to the personal credibility or
moral turpitude of an individual and not to the particular individual's ability or knowledge."[17] As a general rule, therefore, it
would not be a personal attack to call a doctor "incompetent"; or
question the academic credentials of a prospective college president; or challenge a judge's exercise of discretion in deciding a
case; or ridicule the intellectual and motor skills of a particular
national group by telling so-called ethnic jokes.[18]

In 1972 WCMP-AM (Pine City, Minnesota) severely criticized
the local highway department for purchasing too many pickup
trucks.[19] Over the morning program "Six County Chatter — What's
Right and What's the Matter," WCMP's general manager declared:

> I understand Pine County bought another pickup truck.
> I don't know if it's 17 or 18, I've lost track. We've got the
> darndest fleet of pickups you've ever seen in your life. They
> went and parked three out at the fairgrounds, that's what
> they did, *to hide them*. They didn't need them. . . . We've
> got more pickups running around than Carter's got little
> liver pills. Most useless piece of equipment that ever drove
> on the road. . . .

> I think it's the biggest waste of money that anybody ever
> *hoodwinked* [a] governmental agency with. We are *using
> them for taxi service*. And I don't think we can afford taxis
> in this day and age. [Emphasis added.]

The general manager also had unkind words for a local highway
engineer, who had attended the Minnesota Good Roads Congressional Meeting in Washington, D.C. The trip was derided on the
air as "a champagne flight to Washington to attend the Cherry
Blossom Festival."

Did these remarks question merely the wisdom of local officials?
Or was there also an insinuation of deviousness and dishonesty?
The FCC decided these admittedly close questions in WCMP's
favor:

> Criticism of a public official's wisdom, judgment or actions
> is not necessarily an attack upon his "honesty, character,
> integrity or like personal qualities," and we have stated that
> we shall not impose penalties [upon licensees] in this area if
> the licensee could have had a reasonable doubt whether
> such an attack had taken place. . . .
>
> We . . . believe that the remarks about a "champagne
> flight" to Washington did not constitute a personal attack,
> but were primarily intended as a jest, and could have been
> so understood.
>
> We have greater difficulty regarding the allegations . . .
> that the [highway department] had parked county pickup
> trucks at the Fairgrounds "to hide them," had "hoodwinked"
> a governmental agency with respect to the trucks, and were
> "using them for taxi service." However, the question . . .
> is not what our initial view might be unaided by the li-
> censee's determination, but rather whether the licensee
> could reasonably judge the allegation not to involve personal
> attacks. Under that standard, we find insufficient basis to
> upset the licensee's determination [that no personal attack
> occurred].

ACCUSATION OF ILLEGALITY OR CORRUPTION. Accusing some individual or group of criminal conduct frequently involves an attack
upon honesty and character. Consider a 1972 broadcast of the
"Lou Gordon Program" over WKBD-TV (Detroit).[20] A doctor

was identified as an abortionist, who had "paid off police officers to permit his abortion racket to continue," and who "chose going to jail for contempt of court rather than telling the Wayne County Grand Jury who he paid off, how much, and when." These charges constituted a personal attack on the doctor's integrity.

A charge of actual wrongdoing is not always essential in order for a personal attack to occur; sometimes a charge of possible wrongdoing may suffice. During May, 1970, the transmitter of KPFT-FM (Houston), an affiliate of the Pacifica Foundation, was dynamited and totally destroyed.[21] On May 14 the moderator of a call-in show on KWBA (Baytown, Texas) surmised that the Pacifica management had dynamited the transmitter themselves in order to collect the insurance. Although the moderator did not state as a fact that KPFT had destroyed its transmitter, merely suggesting that possibility was enough to constitute a personal attack on the station.

Even implying that a person has criminal connections may be a personal attack. In 1966, WWLP-TV (Springfield, Massachusetts) editorialized concerning mounting campaign costs.[22] In the course of the editorial, a negative slur was cast upon Francis Bellotti, one of the candidates: "There is no rule that's going to stop either contestant's friends, whether or not they're from the crime syndicate . . . as Mr. Bellotti says his are not, from spending money on his behalf. . . ." The insinuation that Bellotti was linked to organized crime subjected his integrity to a personal attack.

Not all charges of illegality, however, contain personal attacks. In 1973 the FCC stated: "One may assert that a person or group has in fact acted in violation of the law although the person or group assumed that such action was in full accordance with the law's provisions. In such case, the charge is one of 'illegality,' but it is the judgment of the person or group in interpreting the law which is questioned, not their honesty, character or integrity."[23]

This distinction between judgment and honesty is, of course, familiar to us. We have witnessed its application to, for example, charges of "hoodwinking" and "champagne flights" by public officials. Now, we discover that the same distinction may be operative when a charge of illegality is made.

Return for a moment to the 1972 broadcast in which William Baird criticized the Roman Catholic Church.[24] During the same program, Baird declared: "We're going to try to neutralize the power of the Church by bringing them into court — for lobbying illegally. There's as you know a law called 501 subsection 3 C that says you may not lobby and be tax exempt — remember the Sierra Club — the well-known conservation group — they lost their tax exemption for doing that. We are saying that as long as the Catholic Church continues to lobby illegally then why not forfeit their tax exemption?" Had Baird made a personal attack on the church by accusing it of violating the Internal Revenue Code? The FCC said no.

> It would appear that while Mr. Baird's statements sharply dispute the judgment of the Church . . . in interpreting the tax laws applicable to religious institutions, they do not challenge or otherwise cast [aspersions] on [the church's] honesty, character or integrity. The remarks in question do not insinuate that . . . the Church . . . has knowingly or intentionally violated the tax laws or is otherwise guilty of acts which are, by definition, criminal or dishonest, such as fraud or embezzlement. In substance Mr. Baird's statements take emphatic and opinionated exception with the Church's tax exemption in light of its alleged lobbying efforts, but they do not constitute a personal attack.

Early in 1971, KMBC-TV (Kansas City, Missouri) broadcast a seventeen-part report, entitled "Criminals and the Courts."[25] The series criticized the disposition of criminal cases and suggested that some local judges' sentencing might have been illegal, for example:

> With that previous narcotics conviction in his record, Judge James Moore was required by law to sentence Greer to a term in the state penitentiary of not less than five years nor more than life. But Judge Moore suspended the sentence and placed Greer on probation for two years . . . in apparent violation of the law. . . .
> Judge Hall's exercise of judicial clemency in this case is an apparent violation of Missouri law specifically prohibiting probation.

The FCC decided that the named judges had not been personally attacked for corruption or defiance of the law:

> The excerpted statements contained no personal vilification of the named judges, and made no accusations as to the possible motivations of the judges in deciding the cases. There was obviously strong disagreement with the judges' actions, but no more. There is an important distinction . . . between contending that a judge has exceeded his discretion in the legal sense or that he has erred in deciding a case, and charging that he has decided a case because of improper or corrupt motives. . . . The broadcast statements included no language which can be fairly construed as reflecting on the judges' personal qualities. . . .

IDENTIFICATION OF THE VICTIM. By definition, a personal attack can only be made upon "an identified person or group." In the cases we have considered there was never any doubt about the identity of the alleged victim: Fred J. Cook, John Cervase, the New York Port Authority, the John Birch Society, et cetera — all these individuals and groups were named over the air. Identification is not always by proper name, however. A victim may be sufficiently identified, even though unnamed, by the context in which the attack is made. The FCC looks to broadcasters for good-faith judgments as to whether someone has been identified, given all the relevant facts. If there is room for reasonable doubt, the broadcaster ought to consult the commission promptly for advice.[26]

For example, during his critique of the Roman Catholic Church, William Baird berated the conduct of an unnamed priest: "It is well known that there's a Father Drinan — no, not Father Drinan — the Father out in Nassau County whose name I'm just blanking out on but who's head of the Human Rights Committee, [whose] sole job it is to coordinate all anti-abortion forces to stop the New York law. Yet he is paid by the Church, his phones are paid by the Church, his mailings are sent out by the Church. Clearly against the law." The priest Baird had in mind was the Reverend Paul Driscoll, Human Life Coordinator in the Diocese of Rockville Centre, which encompasses Nassau and Suffolk counties. Given the context in which Baird had referred to the "Father out in

Nassau County," the FCC did not question the fact that Father Driscoll had been sufficiently identified. (As it turned out, however, Father Driscoll had not been personally attacked.)

Sometimes the victim of an alleged personal attack may be indeterminate — for instance, "all doctors," "all politicians," "all Germans." As a result, precise identification is precluded and, with it, the possibility of a genuine personal attack having occurred. Consider the curious question of identification that arose out of the CBS situation comedy "Maude."[27] In 1972 a two-part episode portrayed Maude's discovery that she was pregnant and her decision to have an abortion. The Long Island Coalition for Life objected to the "pro-death position" espoused in the dialogue of Maude, her husband, Walter, and their daughter, Carol, to wit:

> WALTER: . . . now that you mention it, it [abortion] is legal in New York, isn't it?
>
> CAROL: Of course it is Walter! Mother, I don't understand your hesitancy. When they made it a law you were for it. . . .
> We're free. We finally have the right to decide what we can do with our own bodies. . . . And it's as simple as going to the dentist. . . . Mother you don't have to have the baby. Look, I've told you before there's no reason to feel guilty and there's no reason to be afraid. . . .
>
> WALTER: Maude, I think it would be wrong to have a child at our age.
>
> MAUDE: Oh, so do I Walter. Oh Walter, so do I.
>
> WALTER: We'd make awful parents.
>
> MAUDE: Oh, impatient, irascible. For other people it might be fine, but for us, I don't think it would be fair to anybody. . . .

Citing this dialogue, the coalition complained of a personal attack upon a supposedly identified group — namely, "all present and future unborn children."

The FCC rejected the complaint with but a terse comment: "The type of attack you are concerned with does not come within the rule." We may speculate that, at least, one reason for this decision was the lack of any clearly identified group in the dialogue. Indeed, given the indefinite scope of "all present and future unborn children," it is questionable whether such a group would be susceptible to a personal attack, even if the group could be adequately identified.

Whenever adequate identification of a victim is made, it usually occurs in the midst of the attack. Such proximity is not always the case, however; nor is it necessary in order to trigger the personal-attack rule. An attack may continue throughout a unified series of broadcasts, with the actual attack occurring in one part and identification of the victim in another.

For example, KIEV-AM (Glendale, California) devoted three segments of its daily series "Voice of Americanism" to a single speech entitled "Liberal Professors and the Effect They Have on Their Students."[28] In part one (September 6, 1972), the speaker, Colonel Donner, announced: "I charge the college professors of this country, the majority of those who are social scientists, with treason." Donner proposed to devote the rest of his speech to "proving that very, very serious charge." During parts two and three of his speech (September 7 and 8, 1972), Donner named two California State University professors and discussed the effect they had upon their students. Even though the charge of treason and the naming of the professors took place in separate broadcasts, the FCC decided that the three portions of the speech were "so closely related as to constitute a continuing discussion of the same issue." Therefore, the professors had been identified in the course of a personal attack.

Controversial Issues of Public Importance

The personal-attack rule will be triggered only if an attack occurs *during the presentation of views on a controversial issue of public importance*. This condition is dictated by the basic purpose behind the personal-attack rule. First and foremost, the rule is intended to keep the public fully informed on all sides of vital issues. An attack made during discussion of such an issue will, presumably, be highly relevant to the discussion. The attack victim is considered to be best situated to inform the public on an issue in which he happens to have been implicated. Thus, he is logically deserving of a right of reply. The victim's opportunity for self-vindication is really just a means to an end — namely, greater public enlightenment.

A personal attack that is unrelated to any broadcast on a controversial issue will not give rise to a right of reply. Such an isolated attack will, in all likelihood, involve a purely private dispute; and the personal-attack rule plays no part in private bickering. While it is conceivable that an attack, in and of itself, may constitute a controversial issue of public importance, the commission has indicated that this will normally not be the case.[29]

What constitutes discussion of a "controversial issue of public importance"? FCC regulations do not define this phrase. It is used most frequently in connection with the general fairness doctrine, which requires balanced programming on controversial issues of public importance. The meaning acquired by the term under the fairness doctrine is generally applicable in the case of a personal attack.

Usually, an issue must stir up vigorous debate pro and con — it must be a matter of concern and consequence to major segments of the community or nation — before it will be considered controversial and of public importance. On January 27, 1972, two Pennsylvania radio stations carried a program entitled "Radicals Say: No More Prisons."[30] The program charged the "Liberal New Left" with conspiring to foment tension in the nation's prisons. New York's Attica Prison riot was cited as the beginning of a New Left campaign to demand the release of all prisoners by 1976. Some New Left tactics were said to include mass demonstrations to close down prisons as well as assaults upon guards and police.

Considering the scope and impact of potentially widespread prison unrest, the issue was a controversial one of public importance. During the program, specific accusations were leveled against the United Church of Christ. Allegedly, the church was participating in the antiprison conspiracy and lending financial support to militant subversives. Such a charge of criminal conduct clearly constituted a personal attack on the church's character and integrity. Since the attack was made within the context of views on a controversial issue of public importance, the personal-attack rule was activated.

Whenever the public is called upon to make a choice — political or social — the issue at stake is likely to be both controversial and important. Suppose Capital City will be voting on a proposal to amend the city charter. The prospective vote has split the city into opposing camps. Hypothetical station WWW airs a debate to explore pro's and con's on the amendment. One speaker accuses a community group — not represented at the debate — of sponsoring false advertisements, deliberately aimed at deceiving the voters on the amendment. Since this attack upon integrity occurred during discussion of a controversial issue of public importance, the personal-attack rule would come into play.[31]

It is not always easy to determine whether a controversial public issue is at stake. A broadcaster has initial and primary responsibility for making this determination. The FCC will not overturn the broadcaster's decision simply because the commission might have reached a different conclusion on its own. All the commission requires is that a broadcaster's judgment be reasonable and made in good faith.

Consider one recent case. A labor representation election was scheduled for November 1, 1972, at Fort Bragg in North Carolina.[32] The vote would decide which union — the National Association of Government Employees (NAGE) or the American Federation of Government Employees (AFGE) — was going to represent certain federal employees at Fort Bragg. On the day before the election, radio station WFAI (Fayetteville, North Carolina) carried an AFGE ad, which seriously questioned the honesty of NAGE President Kenneth Lyons:

> Kenneth T. Lyons, President of the National Association of Government Employees, whose union is attempting to represent the non-appropriated funds employees at Fort Bragg, was accused by nationally syndicated columnist Jack Anderson of having Mafia contacts. Kenneth Lyons is

also being investigated for misuse of Union funds according
to Jack Anderson's column in the Tuesday Fayetteville Observer. The AFGE urges all Fort Bragg employees to read
Jack Anderson's column in the Fayetteville Observer on
page 4a. Now that you know the truth . . . vote for
honesty, and integrity . . . vote AFGE AFL-CIO. Paid for
by the American Federation of Government Employees.

WFAI decided the issue posed by the election — which union
should represent Fort Bragg employees — was not a controversial
issue of public importance. Within WFAI's service area were some
212,000 listeners, only 1,230 of whom were employed at Fort
Bragg. The station viewed the election as a narrow dispute of little
importance to the listening audience as a whole.

NAGE disagreed. It argued that the number of households in
the audience (56,000) was a more meaningful context than the
total population figure. Moreover, all civilian government employees in the area (involving some 6,200 households) should be
viewed as concerned with the outcome of the election — not
merely the 1,230 employees directly affected. According to NAGE,
when two national labor organizations are engaged in a "hotly
contested" union representation election, affecting 6,200 out of
56,000 households, a controversial issue of public importance is
presented.

The commission concluded that WFAI's judgment had not been
unreasonable:

> We believe the number of persons involved herein need
> not be a major factor in determining whether a controversial
> issue was presented by the broadcast of the announcements
> in question. . . . [NAGE has] not furnished the Com-
> mission with any information to indicate that there was a
> public debate or controversy in the community regarding
> the union election so as to create a controversial issue of
> public importance. Unless there is such public debate or
> controversy, the union election appears to have been a
> controversy of interest only to the affected employees. . . .

Therefore, the AFGE ad did not trigger the personal-attack rule.
Sometimes a personal attack may not occur until after the dis-

cussion to which it relates has already ended. There may be a lapse of several minutes or an hour or even longer. What legal consequences follow from such a gap in time? Does the separation between the discussion and the actual attack mean that the attack did not take place during the presentation of views on a controversial issue? Not necessarily, says the FCC. An attack does not have to be "directly adjacent" to the discussion of a controversial issue. As long as the attack relates back to such an issue, "so as to constitute a continuing discussion of that issue," the personal-attack rule will be triggered.[33]

Consider an attack that occurred during a telephone conversation broadcast over radio station WMCA (New York City).[34] On March 8, 1973, moderator Bob Grant was discussing the then current nationwide meat boycott against high prices with his callers and listeners. He announced that one of the boycott's organizers, Congressman Benjamin Rosenthal, would shortly be on the newsmaker telephone line with Grant. As it turned out, however, Rosenthal declined to talk on the phone with Grant, apparently because he disliked Grant and considered him inept. Undoubtedly peeved to learn of Rosenthal's refusal, Grant said over the air he could not believe that Rosenthal was afraid to be interviewed, and Rosenthal ought to lay aside his prejudices and let listeners hear his views. This commentary occurred at 10:45 A.M.

Later during the same program, at about 12:45 P.M., Grant was conversing with a listener on an entirely different subject — the docking of some World War II ships in Haverstraw, New York. The on-air conversation ended as follows:

> CALLER: You're a great man. God bless you.
>
> GRANT: Ah, get on with you now.
>
> CALLER: No, I mean it from my heart.
>
> GRANT: I know you do, pal, I know you do. Thanks, thanks, pal.
>
> CALLER: You're a swell guy.
>
> GRANT: Thank you sir.
>
> CALLER: Too bad there ain't more people like you on the air.

GRANT: Well, when I hear about guys like Ben Rosenthal, I, I have to say I wish there were a thousand Bob Grants 'cause then you wouldn't have . . . wouldn't have . . . a *coward* like him in the United States Congress. Thank you for your call, sir. [Emphasis added.]

After WMCA failed to comply with the notice requirements of the personal-attack rule, Rosenthal complained to the FCC. The commission decided calling Rosenthal a "coward" was an attack on his character. Assuming that was so, had the attack occurred during discussion of a controversial issue of public importance? The commission said yes.

> While it is clear that the 1973 nationwide meat boycott was a controversial issue of public importance, the crucial issue in this case is to determine whether the remarks made at 12:45 P.M. relate back to the discussion of the meat boycott which occurred at 10:45 A.M. . . . It . . . appears that Mr. Grant . . . referred to [Rosenthal] as a coward and based his remarks on [Rosenthal's] earlier refusal to appear on his show to discuss the meat boycott. . . . The mention at 12:45 P.M. of [Rosenthal's] name was clearly in reference to his refusal to appear to discuss the boycott since in the discussion of the World War II ships there was no reference to Mr. Rosenthal. Thus in the context of the events of this case it appears the attack was related to and occurred within the context of the discussion of the meat boycott.

Apparently, the commission will apply a broad test of relevancy in order to determine whether an attack occurred within the context of a controversial-issue discussion. Congressman Rosenthal's reluctance — his so-called cowardice — about conversing with Grant was, arguably, irrelevant to the issue of the meat boycott; the merits of that issue would not be advanced, nor noticeably affected in any way, by such offhand remarks as the one Bob Grant made. In this sense, Grant's remark was a gratuitous one, bearing little relationship to the pro's and con's on the boycott issue. Nevertheless, Rosenthal was clearly involved in the issue; he had been mentioned by Grant as a leader of the boycott, who was expected momentarily on the newsmaker telephone line. Rosenthal's refusal to get on that line became a part of the meat boycott discussion. Therefore, Grant's later characterization of Rosenthal related to an aspect of the earlier discussion — if not an aspect of the boycott issue itself.

There remain a number of unsettled questions about attacks that appear to occur out of context. At what point is the time lapse between an attack and the discussion to which it relates so great as to sever any possible connection between the two? Is the personal-attack rule triggered by an attack that occurs during the discussion of a controversial issue but seems to be totally irrelevant to that issue? The FCC recognizes that questions such as these pose difficult problems for broadcasters, who must make an appropriate response. Whenever serious doubt exists, the broadcaster should consult the commission for its interpretation of whether the rule applies.[35]

Notification to the Victim
of an Attack

Once a personal attack has occurred, the broadcaster must notify the person or group attacked. He cannot sit back and wait for a complaint; instead, he is required to initiate contact with the victim of the attack. "The notification requirement," according to the FCC, "is of utmost importance, since our experience indicates that otherwise the person or group attacked may be unaware of the attack, and thus the public may not have a meaningful opportunity to hear the other side.[36]

When he contacts the person or group attacked, the broadcaster must transmit (1) notification of the date, time, and identification of the broadcast (or identification of the "cablecast" if the attack originated over a cable television system); (2) a script or tape of the attack; and (3) an offer of a reasonable opportunity to respond over the broadcaster's facilities. All three requirements must be satisfied, with one important exception: the broadcaster can transmit an accurate summary of the attack if a script or tape is unavailable.[37] The FCC advises that "where a licensee determines that a personal attack has not occurred but recognizes that there may be some dispute concerning his conclusion, he should keep available for public inspection, for a reasonable period of time, a tape, transcript, or summary of the broadcast in question."[38] A summary made contemporaneously with the attack is likely to be accurate. For this reason, the FCC prefers summaries that were contemporaneously made to those based upon someone's recollection, which may well have grown dim.[39]

A broadcaster must fulfill the three notice requirements "within a reasonable time and in no event later than 1 week after the attack."[40] Although one week is the outer time limit, broadcasters have been exhorted by the commission not to wait a week unnecessarily. Indeed, the commission encourages giving notice before the attack occurs, whenever time is of the essence.[41]

For example, in a 1966 election-eve editorial, WRAL-TV (Raleigh) broadcast a personal attack on three professors who were involved in the campaign.[42] Notice of the attack was mailed to the professors on election eve. Although WRAL-TV had technically met its one-week deadline, the FCC was clearly displeased.

> We believe that the licensee did not recognize its special obligation to act with the utmost expedition in view of the imminence of the election. The "personal attack" complained of by the professors was a facet of the election campaign, and the licensee therefore was required to take all possible steps to facilitate any reply as soon as possible. Mailing copies [of the attack] on election eve, with an offer to respond, was inconsistent with this obligation.

Exempt Personal Attacks

In general, within one week after a personal attack, the broadcaster must fulfill the notice requirements prescribed by the FCC. However, personal attacks that occur within five categories of programming are exempt from the usual notice requirements:

(1) attacks on foreign groups or foreign public figures;

(2) attacks made by legally qualified candidates, their authorized spokesmen, or those associated with them in the campaign, against other legally qualified candidates, their authorized spokesmen, or persons associated with them in the campaign;

(3) attacks made during a bona fide newscast;

(4) attacks made during a bona fide news interview; and

(5) attacks made during on-the-spot coverage of a bona fide news event.

If an attack belongs to any one of these categories, the broadcaster is not obliged to notify the victim within one week, transmit a record of the attack, and offer a reasonable opportunity to reply. These customary formalities are suspended because of the exemption.[43]

Just because a program is exempt, however, does not mean that personal attacks can be aired with impunity. For even though the personal-attack rule does not apply, the general fairness doctrine does. How does the fairness doctrine affect an exempt personal attack? Basically, it requires some response to the attack; that response need not be delivered by the victim, as in the usual personal-attack situation. Instead, the broadcaster himself may express the victim's viewpoint. If it is fairly presented, no further action is necessary. But if the broadcaster's presentation is inadequate, or if he plans no response at all, then he must actively seek out an opposing spokesman. This person cannot be just some disinterested member of the community. "There is a clear and appropriate spokesman to present the other side of the attack issue — the person or group attacked."[44] Thus, the victim must be given an opportunity to respond if his viewpoint is not fairly covered by the broadcaster.

Certain of the five exempt categories deserve further attention. The term "legally qualified candidate" in the second category was adopted from the FCC's equal-time rule. Presumably, the commission will use its equal-time definition of a legally qualified candidate when administering this personal-attack exemption.[45] For example, the equal-time definition requires a public announcement of candidacy before a candidate can be considered "legally qualified." If, therefore, a personal attack were made by an unannounced candidate, the present exemption would not apply; the unannounced candidate would not be considered a legally qualified candidate.[46]

Notice that the exemption covers only attacks by candidates, their spokesmen, or associates against other candidates, their spokesmen, or associates. Attacks upon noncandidates, or persons not associated with the campaign, fall outside the exemption. Thus, if a candidate should attack someone who has no connection with the campaign, the broadcaster would have to fulfill his normal obligations under the personal-attack rule. Understandably the broadcaster may chafe at this result. After all, he is prohibited from censoring a candidate's presentation. This prohibition renders the broadcaster powerless to prevent any personal attack by a candidate. Considering his predicament, should the broadcaster, nonetheless, be required to notify the candidate's victim and afford him reply time?

The FCC says yes.[47] It has rejected the argument that the broadcaster is being unfairly penalized by a situation over which he lacks control:

> What is involved here is in no sense a penalty. The licensee in the discharge of its obligation to serve the public interest, is generally called upon to afford a reasonable amount of time to the coverage of controversial issues of public importance, including political broadcasts. . . . If on such broadcasts personal attacks occur which do not come within the exemption [covering candidates], all the licensee is required to do is to afford a reasonable opportunity for the person attacked to present his side of the attack issue, so that the electorate may be fully and fairly informed. The occasional obligation to present such material is simply part of the overall public-interest obligation assumed by the licensee when it received its license.

The last three exemptions — namely, those for bona fide newscasts, news interviews, and on-the-spot coverage of bona fide news events — also depend for their meaning on the equal-time rule; that rule employs identical terminology to describe news programs exempted from its provisions. As a result, when the commission judges an attack that occurred on some news program, it looks to equal-time definitions of the bona fide newscast, news interview, and on-the-spot coverage in order to determine whether the program in question qualifies for exemption under the personal-attack rule.[48]

Suppose a broadcast journalist makes a personal attack in the course of some news commentary or analysis. Will that attack be exempt, even though it did not occur during the reporting of so-called hard news? The answer depends upon the nature of the program within which the commentary or analysis was delivered. If the program qualifies as a bona fide newscast, news interview, or on-the-spot coverage, then the offending commentary (or analysis) is exempt — just as the rest of the program is: "The Commission is . . . exempting all commentary or analysis in newscasts or other exempt programs, since such commentary or analysis is an integral part of the news function; it can, for example, occur at any point in a newscast and, indeed, the trend is more and more toward such 'in depth' presentation of the news."[49]

There will be no exemption, however, if the commentary or analysis was broadcast outside some exempt news program. We might imagine, for instance, some well-known broadcast journalist appearing as a guest on an entertainment talk show. In answer to questions from the host, the journalist seeks to analyze some current news story. While doing so, he makes a personal attack. The attack would not be exempt. Although the journalist's remarks might well be characterized as "news analysis," they did not occur during an exempt news program.[50]

Unlike news commentary and analysis, editorials are never exempt from the personal-attack rules — regardless of whether or not they are broadcast as part of a news program.[51] What is the difference between an editorial and news commentary or analysis? Generally speaking, an editorial has two distinguishing characteristics: it is labeled as an editorial by the station or network that presents it, and it expresses some opinion held by the station or network — as opposed to the personal views of some newscaster or commentator, who does not speak officially on behalf of the licensee. "To put it in terms of the situation at CBS," one FCC commissioner has observed, "the commentary and analysis of

Walter Cronkite and Eric Sevareid in newscasts are exempt, but the presentation by a network official, or by an announcer, of the editorial opinion of CBS is not."[52]

Besides editorials, there are other categories of programming the FCC has specifically declined to exempt. One is the news documentary — a category that is exempted under the equal-time rule. Another is the talk show — a familiar type of entertainment program, which must be distinguished from the bona fide news interview.[53] It is also worth noting that the commission has rejected some novel theories aimed at expanding the personal-attack exemptions. For example, a broadcaster cannot escape his obligations because the victim was an *agent provocateur,* who instigated the attack upon himself. Nor is the broadcaster's duty mitigated by the fact that other media — for example, newspapers, magazines, or other stations — have presented the victim's side of the attack issue.[54]

In conclusion, a broadcaster enjoys wider discretion when handling exempt attacks than he does when handling nonexempt ones. Since the programs exempted generally involve broadcast journalism, the FCC is wary of imposing excessive restrictions.

> If the licensee adjudges an event containing a personal attack to be newsworthy, in practice he usually turns, as part of the news coverage to be presented that day or in the very near future, to the other side and again makes the same good-faith journalistic judgment as to its presentation and what fairness requires in the particular circumstances. This is normal journalism and fairness in this area. To import the concept of notification within a week period, with the presentation of the person attacked on some later newscast when other news might normally be broadcast, is impractical and might impede the effective execution of the important news functions of licensees and networks.[55]

Reasonable Opportunity to Respond

A person or group subjected to a personal attack must be afforded a reasonable opportunity to respond over the broadcaster's facilities. There is no hard definition of the term "reasonable opportunity"; it varies with the circumstances in each case. The broadcaster cannot decide the matter arbitrarily; he must exercise reasonable judgment. The FCC expects details of a reasonable opportunity to be worked out, at least initially, through good faith negotiations between the broadcaster and the victim of the attack. If the victim is dissatisfied with the opportunity offered, he should complain to the commission.[56]

In general, the opportunity for response ought to be *comparable* — though not necessarily *equal* — to the broadcast that precipitated it. The length of the response should approximate the time devoted to the attack. If the attack was broadcast more than once, the response generally merits similar repetition. Scheduling of the response is another point of comparison. The victim deserves an opportunity to reach the same size and class of audience reached by the attack. Thus, an attack in prime time, which draws maximum audience levels, is likely to call for a response in prime time. If the attack occurs in a program belonging to a regular series, the response might be appropriately scheduled for the time period normally allotted to the series.[57]

In facilitating a response, the broadcaster does not have the same wide discretion over program format that he would ordinarily enjoy under the general fairness doctrine. Instead, the format for the response must be comparable to the attack's format. Suppose our hypothetical station WWW broadcasts a thirty-minute documentary containing a personal attack on a right-wing political club. The narrator accuses the club of terror tactics and racism. WWW offers the club an opportunity to respond, but only in a panel discussion format. The president of the club objects. He feels that he will not be able to make an effective response while being interrupted by the moderator and the panelists, who debate his points. The club prefers to present its response in a format comparable to WWW's documentary. If WWW insists upon a panel format or nothing, it will violate the club's right to a reasonable opportunity to respond.[58]

The victim of a personal attack has the right to deliver his own response. He does not have to accept one of the station's announcers. If a group is attacked, they can choose their own spokes-man. The broadcaster may legitimately request information from the group to confirm that the spokesman is, in fact, authorized to respond. However, this request is no excuse for a fishing expedi-tion. Suppose WWW airs an attack on the local Property Owners' Association (POA). When POA member John Smith seeks an op-portunity to deliver the association's response, WWW insists upon a certified copy of POA's charter, a membership roster, and biog-raphies of each POA officer — all as a prerequisite to broadcasting Smith's response. WWW's demands would be an unreasonable imposition upon POA's right to respond.[59]

Does the victim of a personal attack have to pay the station for his reply time? The FCC says no.[60] A broadcaster may inquire whether the victim is willing to pay. If the victim is unwilling, however, he simply has to say so; he does not have to prove or, indeed, make any representation at all, regarding inability to pay. The right to reply cannot be made contingent upon either the victim's payment of money or his inability to pay. Instead, the financial burden rests with the broadcaster. If the victim is unwill-ing to pay, the broadcaster must find a sponsor or present the reply without sponsorship — that is, on a so-called sustaining basis.

Can the broadcaster use the victim's reply time as an occasion for renewed attack? The FCC has indicated its displeasure with such a practice: "Prefacing or concluding a reply to a personal attack with a repeat of or a justification for the original attack, would not appear, on its face, to constitute a reasonable opportu-nity to reply."[61] This position parallels the commission's attitude toward replies to political editorials.

The personal-attack rule does not specifically prohibit broad-casters from censoring replies. As under the fairness doctrine, therefore, the broadcaster may exercise certain editorial control. Although he must not interfere with relevant responsive material, he has considerable discretion in deciding what material actually is responsive. Suppose some organization is attacked for specific actions it has taken or policies it pursues. Instead of responding directly to the charges made, the organization proposes to recite its

general history and tell the life story of its founder. The broadcaster might legitimately reject this proposal as not being reasonably responsive to the attack that precipitated it.[62]

Disputes inevitably arise over whether a reply is responsive.
Consider a disagreement that erupted in Albany, Georgia, shortly
after the Nobel Peace Prize was awarded to the Reverend Martin
Luther King, Jr.[63] On October 21, 1964, radio station WALG
broadcast a "Johnny Reb Special Editorial":

> Awarding the Nobel Peace Prize to Rev. Martin Luther
> King, Jr. makes about as much sense as selecting John F.
> Dillinger to guard the United States Treasury or bringing
> Nero back to life to assist Smoky Bear.
>
> Since the Reverend has brought more violence to the
> South than anyone else in the past 100 years, why not have
> him share the honor with the late General William T. "War
> is Hell" Sherman?
>
> And while the Nobel folks were at it, why stop with just
> one award? Why not a separate medal for Birmingham?
> Another for Atlanta? A third for St. Augustine? And you just
> can't discriminate Albany.
>
> Even the "Atlanta Journal" said: "The irresponsible, im-
> moderate acts of Martin Luther King, Jr. have done so much
> damage in Albany that it will take years for the wounds to
> heal."
>
> Alfred Nobel established the annual award to overshadow
> the destructive uses of his invention of dynamite. He wanted
> to promote the idea of peace. This year's selection sets a
> new, all-time low for the Nobel Prize. It's an insult to previ-
> ous recipients. It peeled off the prestige like taking the label
> off a can of tomatoes.
>
> The reason is not race. The reason is violence.

In answer to this personal attack on the Reverend Dr. King, the
following response was proposed and rejected by WALG as being
nonresponsive:

> A recent editorial of this station criticized the awarding
> of the Nobel Peace Prize to Reverend Martin Luther King,
> Jr. King was blamed for bringing violence to the South in
> civil rights campaigns. It is true that civil rights demonstra-

tions have resulted in some incidents of brutality, but except for a surprisingly small number of incidents, the victims of this violence were not among King's followers. Compared to an endless string of murders, beatings and bombings directed at those who oppose the vicious system of white supremacy, the few injuries to whites seem relatively small. It is surprising that four hundred years of poverty and humiliation have *not* made outlaws of the 20 million Negroes in America.

King has shown remarkable self-control as a leader in refusing to resort to violence when it would have been a simple matter to encourage it. He has consistently tried to find responsible white leaders in the communities where he has led demonstrations — leaders who would at least listen to the grievances of the Negro population and who were interested in resolving conflicts rather than surpressing them. For his consistent confidence in the good faith of the white [leaders] in this country, he has been criticized by other Negro civil rights leaders.

Here in Albany a stubborn city administration has prevented white and Negro leaders from ever having an opportunity to exchange views through a meaningful bi-racial conference.

Although the Nobel Prize Committee never specifies the reasons for its awards, we, the leaders of the Albany Movement, feel that Martin Luther King, Jr., was recognized for his unquestioned influence in directing the discontent of Negroes in America with second-class citizenship toward non-violent tactics. Despite brutal retaliation by white police and civilians against peaceful demonstrators, King has succeeded admirably in maintaining his faith in the humanity of his opponents.

According to the FCC, the first, second, and fourth paragraphs of the reply clearly responded to the main issue raised by the editorial — namely, the relationship between violence and the Reverend Dr. King. WALG had objected particularly to the third paragraph as being nonresponsive. The FCC disagreed:

> We note that in your editorial . . . you refer to the situation in Albany in the third paragraph and then . . . in the fourth paragraph. . . .
> Thus, your editorial dealt with the Albany situation and

attributed fault in that situation to Reverend King's "irresponsible, immoderate acts." The response also deals with the Albany situation and attributes fault to the action of a "stubborn city administration" in preventing an exchange of views on the racial issue. It would appear that just as you are, of course, free to set forth your opinion as to the situation in Albany, so also the response in this personal attack situation should reasonably be permitted to state the contrasting viewpoint or opinion concerning that situation. Therefore, even though you are, of course, afforded latitude to make judgments in this field, we cannot say that you have shown any reasonable basis for your action in this instance. . . .

WALG's rejection of the proposed answer to its attack was an unreasonable limitation upon the right of reply.

8
Political Editorials

General Principles

In skeletal form, the FCC's political-editorial rule states:

(1) When a candidate for public office is either endorsed or opposed

(2) in an editorial expressing the official view of the licensee,

(3) then, within twenty-four hours after the editorial, the licensee must notify the candidate(s) adversely affected by the editorial

(4) and afford the candidate(s) a reasonable opportunity to reply over the licensee's station.

If the editorial is aired within seventy-two hours of election day, advance notification is required. The political-editorial rule applies to all commercial radio and television stations. It also covers editorials originated by and carried over cable television (that is, so-called origination cablecasting).[1]

The political-editorial rule has no effect upon noncommercial educational radio and television stations, because they are prohibited by Congress from supporting or opposing any candidate for political office.[2] This prohibition precludes broadcasting the official political preferences of the station's ownership or management. Noncommercial educational stations are free, however, to engage in traditional political programming: candidates may appear and make campaign speeches or be interviewed or participate in debates or documentaries, and so forth. Such programming is entirely permissible as long as it is not represented as, or intended as, official political support or opposition by the station.[3]

The political-editorial rule is a particularization of the FCC's overall fairness doctrine. Like that doctrine, the political-editorial rule fosters the presentation of conflicting views on controversial issues. Almost by definition, the question of who shall be elected poses a controversial issue of public importance. When a licensee takes it upon himself to present one viewpoint on this issue, elementary fairness and the public interest require that listeners and viewers be given access to the "other side" of the issue. Normally, under the fairness doctrine, the licensee would have wide discretion in selecting a spokesman to present the contrasting point of view. This discretion is circumscribed under the political-editorial rule, because candidates directly affected by the editorial — or their representatives — are thought to be in the best position to illuminate the other side of the issue.[4]

The political-editorial rule is another example of the general affirmative obligations imposed upon licensees in the public interest. The specific administration of the rule is left, at least initially, to the licensee's journalistic discretion. He is responsible for resolving particular questions which arise under the rule: for example, did certain broadcast remarks constitute a formal political editorial, or were they merely an expression of personal opinion held by some station employee? Which candidates are entitled to notification after a political editorial? What constitutes a reasonable opportunity to reply to an editorial? The FCC will review the broadcaster's judgments on such matters only for their reasonableness. The commission expects most disputes between broadcaster and candidate to be worked out at the local level through good faith negotiations.[5]

The Nature of a Political Editorial

Only one kind of broadcast will trigger the political-editorial rule: an editorial in which the licensee either endorses or opposes some legally qualified candidate or candidates.[6] Who is a "legally qualified candidate"? This term plays a pivotal role under the equal-time rule and is defined at length in Chapter 4. The FCC has indicated that the meaning ascribed to "legally qualified candidate" for the purposes of equal time applies under the political-editorial rule as well.[7]

To qualify as a political editorial, a broadcast statement must be represented as, or at least intended as, the *official opinion of the licensee or of station management*.[8] Ordinarily, a formal expression of the licensee's political preference is easy to identify. It is usually introduced as, or discussed in terms of, the station's carefully considered approval or disapproval of a candidate. This familiar format is not always followed, however, and candidates must watch for less obvious, though nonetheless effective, political editorials.

For example, Julian Colby, president and controlling stockholder of Colby Broadcasting Corporation, the licensee of radio station WJOB (Hammond, Indiana), was interviewed over his station during the 1971 mayoralty race in Hammond.[9] Colby endorsed his choice in the race. WJOB did not afford opposing candidates an opportunity to reply. The station maintained that Colby had expressed only his "personal feelings," not the opinion of WJOB; indeed, it was station policy to take no position in the election.

Did Colby's so-called personal feelings constitute a political editorial? The FCC said yes: "While the remarks [Colby] made may not have been labeled as a station editorial, we feel that when the president and controlling stockholder of a licensee, such as Mr. Colby, endorses candidates for public office, such endorsements are indistinguishable from a station editorial within the meaning of [the political-editorial rule]." In short, the commission refused to elevate form above substance: by definition, Colby's opinion *was* the licensee's, regardless of what WJOB called it.

A similar case with a slightly different twist arose during a 1973 supervisorial election in California.[10] Three radio stations in San Luis Obispo — KATY, KSLY, and KVEC — reported identical stories in their news programs concerning choices in the campaign.

> In an unprecedented action by all three local radio stations, KATY, KSLY, and KVEC have all urged voters to support Emmons Blake in the Fifth District, Hans Heilmann in the First District, and write-in candidate Clell Whelchel in the Third District. KSLY manager Homer Odom said, "When the [San Luis Obispo] *Telegram-Tribune* endorsed Blake's opponent because Blake refused to yield to pressures of the paper we thought things had gone far enough. We respect Blake for standing up to that sort of blackmail." KATY manager John Grandy said, "We disagree with the *Telegram-Tribune* on almost everything and we particularly resent the blatant attempts by the paper to pressure candidates to accept the paper's point of view. We think Blake, Heilmann, and Whelchel are experienced, qualified administrators who can do a better job than an unemployed student, a teacher and an inexperienced lady." KVEC manager Bob Brown joined Odom and Grandy in urging voters to elect Blake, Heilmann and Whelchel.

Even though this item was presented as a regular news story, it still constituted a political editorial. Relying on its reasoning in the Colby case, the FCC warned that licensees cannot escape their obligations under the political-editorial rule by broadcasting endorsements "in the guise of 'news.'"

Sometimes a political editorial may be insinuated, rather than announced in a forthright manner. During the 1966 campaign for attorney general in Massachusetts, WWLP-TV (Springfield) editorialized concerning campaign financing.[11] However, the Democratic candidate, Francis Bellotti, felt that the station's editorial was not concerned merely with an abstract issue; it was also a statement of opposition to his candidacy. We may better appreciate Bellotti's reaction after listening to the editorial.

Continuing our comments of yesterday on campaign costs — it occurs to us that no matter what sort of a limit all gentlemen can agree on as to the reasonable price of a certain office — for example, the campaign price for the Attorney General's office is $150,000 according to Mr. Bellotti — there is no rule that's going to stop either contestant's friends, whether or not they're from the crime syndicate in Revere *as Mr. Bellotti says his are not,* from spending money on his behalf and beyond that $150,000. [Emphasis added.]

The innuendo here is unmistakable; it represents an editorial position adverse to candidate Bellotti. He was, therefore, entitled to a right of reply.

The Bellotti case suggests how a station's position on a candidate can be enunciated in an editorial that is not devoted exclusively to approval or disapproval of the candidate. It should not be concluded from the Bellotti case, however, that the political-editorial rule will be triggered by every editorial that has merely tangential impact — whether favorable or unfavorable — upon a candidate. A station may editorialize on issues that involve a candidate or affect his chances for election without necessarily having to afford the candidate an opportunity for reply.

In 1972 Illinois State Senator Karl Berning was running for reelection.[12] During the campaign, he called a press conference to announce his proposal for the creation of a "Governmental Integrity Commission." In response to this proposal, WLS-TV (Chicago) broadcast the following editorial:

Charges of corruption in government at all levels have been flying everywhere here in Illinois.

The state legislature will be given a chance at its next session to do something about it if Senator Karl Berning of Dearfield [*sic*] has his way.

Senator Berning says he will introduce legislation to create a Public Integrity Commission which would be an independent watchdog agency.

Commission members would be chosen by various citizen groups and would be able to call for special grand jury investigations of corruption in government. No public or political officials would be permitted on the board which would have the power to issue subpoenas and appoint special prosecutors.

Channel 7 believes this kind of legislation could be extremely important in controlling government corruption.

Similar suggestions in the past have been brushed aside in Springfield or allowed to die in some obscure committee.

Let's hope this time around our legislators are willing to let the public see what is going on behind those closed doors.

Stephen Slavin, who was opposing Senator Berning in the election, claimed the WLS editorial was tantamount to an endorsement of Berning's candidacy. According to Slavin, the editorial implied a request that Senator Berning be returned to the legislature so that he might "have his way." The FCC disagreed:

> It is obvious, of course, that favorable reference to legislation Senator Berning proposed to introduce in the next legislative session might have had the effect of enhancing his chances for re-election. But it is clear from a full reading of the editorial that it was the need for legislation to control government corruption that the station sought to endorse, and not the candidacy of Senator Berning per se. Furthermore, the surrounding circumstances do not indicate that WLS-TV intended to make an editorial endorsement in this particular election contest. The station has a general policy against endorsing any candidates and broadcast denials that an endorsement was intended here.
>
> We realize that the favorable reference to the legislative proposal advanced by Senator Berning and the identification of him by name in the editorial could arguably and with some logic be viewed as an endorsement of Senator Berning's candidacy. And logically the same would be true where a station endorses a proposal closely identified with a candidate but makes no reference to the candidate by name. But to apply our political editorializing rules in these situations — where no clear-cut endorsement of a candidacy is involved — would make little practical or legal sense. For instead of encouraging "uninhibited, robust, and wide-open" debate . . . the effect of our ruling would be to inhibit it. Licensees would, we fear, view election periods as the occasion for editorial caution and blandness, rather than an

opportunity for the vigorous promotion of an informed electorate.

Since there had been no political editorial, Slavin was not entitled to a right of reply.

Sometimes remarks broadcast by station employees, such as newscasters or talk-show hosts, have distinct political overtones. Indeed, the employee may openly criticize or praise a particular candidate. As long as such remarks are personal to the employee, however, they do not constitute a political editorial.

On August 20, 1974, radio moderator Keith Rush was conducting a telephone conversation over WSMB (New Orleans).[13] In regard to an upcoming election, the caller expressed a preference for candidate Peter Beer, who had claimed during the campaign that he lacked sufficient funds. Rush observed that Beer must have spent some money to tell people he did not have any, and, therefore, he should come forward and divulge his expenditures to the voters.

Beer complained to WSMB, but the station decided that Rush's remarks did not amount to a political editorial opposing Beer's candidacy. The FCC agreed with WSMB. Beer's complaint to the commission was not sufficient to invoke the political-editorial rule. While Beer alleged that Rush's remarks had been made with the approval, actual or tacit, of WSMB's management, no evidence was offered to substantiate this charge. Even if Rush's remarks had been approved by station management, the commission noted, they might not have constituted a political editorial; it would still have been necessary to prove that the remarks represented the official view of the station.

It would appear, therefore, that the complaining candidate must offer some evidence that a station's ownership or management is editorializing by deliberately presenting its political views through the guise of "personal comments" made by employees. For example, a disillusioned employee might divulge the existence of a station policy directing all employees to slant their comments against some candidate opposed by the station. Confronted with such evidence, the FCC would surely investigate and, if justified, order reply time or take appropriate action against the licensee.[14]

Notification Requirements

As soon as the political-editorial rule is triggered, the broadcaster must act to facilitate a reply. He does not have the luxury, enjoyed under the equal-time rule, of simply waiting for a candidate to come forward with a request. Instead, the broadcaster is obliged to initiate contact with candidates affected by the political-editorial rule.

Whom should he contact? The answer depends upon the thrust of the editorial. Suppose it opposed some "legally qualified candidate" (or candidates). Then the candidate(s) in question must be contacted. (Note that the term "legally qualified candidate" carries here the same meaning ascribed to it under the equal-time rule.)

On the other hand, assume that the editorial endorsed some "legally qualified candidate." Then the broadcaster must contact all other "legally qualified candidates" running against the endorsed candidate for the same office.[15] (Here again, the term "legally qualified candidate," as well as the concept of running for the same office, carry the meaning ascribed to them under the equal-time rule.)[16]

By way of initial contact, the broadcaster must transmit (1) notification of the date and time of the editorial (as well as identification of the particular channel if the editorial was "cablecast": that is, originated over a cable television system); (2) a script or tape of the editorial; and (3) an offer of a reasonable opportunity for a candidate, or spokesman of the candidate, to respond over the broadcaster's facilities. The notification, script, and offer must be transmitted within twenty-four hours after the editorial.[17] "Time is of the essence in this area," the FCC has cautioned, "and there appears to be no reason why the licensee cannot immediately inform a candidate of an editorial. In most cases licensees will be able to give notice prior to the editorial."[18]

Prior notice is mandatory in the closing days of the campaign. FCC rules provide that "where [political] editorials are broadcast within 72 hours prior to the day of the election, the licensee shall comply with the [notice requirements] sufficiently far in advance of the broadcast to enable the candidate or candidates to have a reasonable opportunity to prepare a response and to present it in a timely fashion."[19]

"While such last-minute editorials are not prohibited," the commission has warned, "we wish to emphasize as strongly as possible that such editorials would be patently contrary to the public interest . . . unless the licensee insures that the appropriate candidate (or candidates) is informed of the proposed broadcast and its contents sufficiently far in advance. . . ."[20]

A serious departure from the requirement of advance notice arose during the 1966 campaign for attorney general in Massachusetts. Springfield station WWLP-TV planned to broadcast its endorsement on election eve, November 7.[21] On October 19, WWLP-TV sent a letter to Francis Bellotti, the Democratic candidate for attorney general, and the opponent of the man to be endorsed:

> We would like to make time available to you to respond to our editorial of November 7.
> The exact text of this editorial has not yet been prepared, but we believe that you would want to present views in opposition to ours. . . . We request that you communicate with us as soon as possible in order to utilize time which will be available prior to the airing of our editorial. . . .

The FCC decided that WWLP's offer, unaccompanied as it was by the text of the editorial, violated the requirements of fair notice to Bellotti.

> Your offer seems to require that Mr. Bellotti respond to a future editorial before its broadcast. Under these circumstances, Mr. Bellotti could not reasonably be expected to make a judgment as to whether your future editorial would require a reply, nor could he frame a suitable or appropriate response. Mr. Bellotti had no obligation to seek out copies of your election eve editorials; rather, you had an obligation to furnish them. Even though Mr. Bellotti did not take advantage of your "offer" of time, he should have been given the option of replying to your November 7 editorial after being informed of the substance of that editorial. . . .

We wish to stress that where endorsements of . . . candidates are broadcast in the closing hours of an election campaign, the licensee has a special duty to affected candidates to comply scrupulously with its obligations.

Reasonable Opportunity to Respond

A legally qualified candidate who is opposed in a political editorial — or a candidate whose opponent is endorsed in such an editorial — is entitled to a reasonable opportunity to reply over the station's facilities. There is no hard definition of the term "reasonable opportunity"; it is flexible enough to be adapted to varying circumstances. Of course, broadcasters must not act arbitrarily. The FCC expects them to meet with candidates and work out the details of a reasonable opportunity through good faith negotiations.[22]

In general, a reasonable opportunity to reply is one that *compares with* — not necessarily *equals* — the original editorial. To determine whether a reply is comparable to an editorial, the FCC normally considers three factors: the scheduling of the reply, the frequency with which the reply is aired, and the total amount of air time devoted to the reply.

Scheduling the reply is a subject for negotiation between broadcaster and candidate. As a rule of thumb, the reply should be presented in time periods with an audience potential comparable to that enjoyed by the broadcaster's editorial. Thus, if the editorial aired in prime-time evening hours, which attract maximum audience levels, the reply should not be relegated to mid-afternoon, when the audience is reduced, and the reply will have less impact.[23]

On the other hand, the candidate cannot arbitrarily balk when a comparable time slot is offered. On October 28, 1971, KATC-TV (Lafayette, Louisiana) opposed a local candidate in a one-minute editorial broadcast at 6:25 P.M. and again at 10:25 P.M.[24] KATC-TV then offered the candidate's spokesman five minutes for a reply to be aired at 10:25 P.M. on November 5. The candidate complained to the FCC about this offer, because the reply was scheduled for "the night before the primary election . . . which is at a time when every voter in Louisiana will be sick and tired of listening to political commercials." According to the commission, however, KATC's offer was a reasonable one: "The one-minute editorial was . . . broadcast twice while the station offered . . . five minutes in one of the same time periods as the editorial had been broadcast, and on the night before the election, a time which many candidates believe most desirable."

In comparing reply time with the original editorial, candidate and broadcaster sometimes disagree over the frequency with which a reply should be repeated — if at all. An editorial that has itself been repeated, thereby multiplying its impact, usually suggests comparable repetition for the reply. During a 1967 campaign, the King Broadcasting Company in Seattle aired a twenty-second editorial endorsing five candidates; the editorial was repeated twenty-four times.[25] By way of reply time, King offered each opponent of the endorsed candidates six spot announcements of twenty seconds apiece. One of these opponents, George Cooley, accepted the total amount of air time offered him but complained about the prospect of receiving only six exposures, compared to the original twenty-four.

The FCC agreed with Cooley and directed King Broadcasting to afford him greater frequency of response:

> In scheduling twenty-four brief editorials in which five candidates are endorsed, you apparently made a judgment that your broadcast time can be most effectively used by frequent repetition of a brief statement rather than by less frequent broadcasts of longer statements of reasons for your endorsement. . . .
>
> It follows that in making a judgment as to what constitutes a reasonable opportunity for response, the station must give consideration both to the amount of time directed to each candidate and to the frequency of the announcements (which involve the factors of effective repetition and the reaching of possibly different audiences). . . .
>
> Although you have decided to broadcast an editorial campaign in which you reach the audience 24 times with

your editorial endorsement of selected candidates, you have offered Mr. Cooley an opportunity to reach that audience on only 6 occasions – a disparity of 4 to 1. While Mr. Cooley has requested opportunity to make additional responses, you have denied this request without advancing any basis upon which the Commission can make a judgment that this restriction is reasonable. For example, it is not alleged that a 10-second announcement, resulting in 12 opportunities to reach audiences appropriately characterized as early daytime, daytime, prime time (as you have done in the case of the six announcements), is not feasible, and indeed, based upon the Commission's experience, the 10-second spot is ofttimes used in political campaigns.

The commission stressed that increasing the frequency of Cooley's replies was a matter for immediate good faith negotiations between him and King Broadcasting.

The total amount of air time allocated for the reply is the third factor that determines whether a reasonable opportunity to reply has been afforded. Mathematical precision is not the norm here, as it is under the equal-time rule. In many instances, equality of time between editorial and reply may well be necessary. However, equality will not always insure that the reply is actually comparable to the editorial. For example, "where the endorsement of a candidate may be one of many and involves just a few seconds, a 'reasonable opportunity' may require more than a few seconds if there is to be a meaningful response."[26]

In 1970 there was a seven-man race for the city council in Oceanside, California. Local station KUDE-AM broadcast an editorial opposing the candidacy of James Spurling and endorsing two of his opponents.[27] The total editorial ran twenty-five typewritten lines: thirteen lines endorsed one of Spurling's opponents; six lines endorsed another opponent; and the remaining six lines discussed Spurling's candidacy. When KUDE offered Spurling reply time, he was limited to six typewritten lines – exactly that portion of the editorial which had referred specifically to him. According to the FCC, this restriction was improper: "Here where the editorial discussion opposing Mr. Spurling and endorsing his two opponents consumed 25 typewritten lines, limitation to Mr.

Spurling of six lines in which to reply appears to have been unreasonable and in violation of [the commission's] rules."

A broadcaster cannot deduct from the reply time due a candidate any miscellaneous broadcast coverage which happens to help the candidate's campaign. For example, during the 1971 mayoralty race in Oklahoma City, a local station broadcast seven editorials supporting one candidate.[28] This series totaled eleven minutes and twenty-four seconds. William Bishop, the opponent of the man endorsed, was given two opportunities for reply. Bishop selected Mayor James Norick to deliver these replies, which consumed four minutes and eighteen seconds. When Bishop complained to the FCC about an inadequate amount of time, the station responded that Bishop had actually enjoyed the benefit of nine minutes and forty-eight seconds. How did the station arrive at this figure? It simply added on five minutes and thirty seconds from a broadcast press conference by Mayor Norick. In that conference, which was carried over the station's news program, the mayor had been critical of the original editorial and had "lambasted" Bishop's opponent.

The issue before the FCC was whether the segment from Norick's press conference could legitimately be counted in satisfaction of Bishop's right to reply time. The commission said no.

> The press conference in which Mayor Norick spoke on behalf of Mr. Bishop, even though it may have involved criticism of the editorials, cannot be said to constitute a response by a spokesman to the editorial . . . since it was not authorized or prepared as such by Mr. Bishop nor was it in response to an offer [of reply time by the station]. Therefore, since [the station] broadcast [seven] editorial endorsements of Mr. Bishop's opponent (for a total of . . . 11 minutes 24 seconds) and only two broadcasts in which Mayor Norick specifically replied to them, [the station] failed to afford a "comparable opportunity in time."

Within the bounds of reason, a broadcaster, acting in good faith, can place certain limitations upon the opportunity to reply to a political editorial. The most significant of these limitations con-

236 • *Political Editorials*

cerns who shall deliver the reply. A broadcaster can require some spokesman to appear in place of the candidate. Through this substitution, the broadcaster avoids having to give equal time to the candidate's opponent(s). (If the candidate were to reply in person, his appearance would trigger the equal-time rule.) Barring extraordinary circumstances, the choice of the spokesman is up to the candidate.[29]

The political-editorial rule does not specifically prohibit broadcasters from censoring replies. It would seem, therefore, that a broadcaster can exercise some limited editorial control, similar to that allowed for replies under the personal-attack rule.[30] This control may be exerted only if the reply is delivered by some spokesman other than the candidate. If the candidate himself delivers the reply, he is free to express himself as he wishes; censorship of a candidate's broadcasts is strictly prohibited.[31]

Can a broadcaster introduce a reply to a political editorial by repeating the substance of the editorial? The FCC faced this question during the 1969 mayoral campaign in New York City.[32] On October 21, 1969, WCBS-TV broadcast its endorsement of Mayor John Lindsay for reelection. There was no dispute that this endorsement was a political editorial. The station duly afforded reply time on behalf of Lindsay's opponents. Each reply was prefaced, however, by the following introduction: "WCBS-TV has endorsed the candidacy of John Lindsay for mayor of New York. Replying on behalf of _____ the _____ candidate for mayor, here is _____."

One of Lindsay's rivals, Democratic candidate Mario Procaccino, objected to this introduction on the ground that it constituted a reendorsement of Lindsay. The FCC agreed.

We recognize that the response to the editorial must be introduced, so as to give the listeners some background for the presentation of the response. In many instances, the introduction described by WCBS-TV raises no additional fairness problems, as where the response specifically addresses itself to the prior editorial. The response, however, may also go to the merits of the matter, but without any reference to the prior editorial. This may be a deliberate strategy of the candidate, on the theory that it hurts his cause to have been opposed by the broadcast station, and, therefore, while he wishes to respond on the merits, he does not wish to give added publicity to the station opposition to him or endorsement of his rival. Crucial to our consideration of this issue is the fact that many political editorials (and also those in print media) consist of virtually the CBS introductory material — namely, that "Station _____ endorses the candidacy of _____ for the office of _____." . . . It follows, in view of this consideration in the political editorializing field, that when the licensee introduces the response with material such as involved here, it is, in effect, again engaging in a further endorsement and doing so against the express desires of the rival candidate who has reasonably decided on a different strategy in meeting the challenge of the editorial endorsement. . . .

We wish to stress that just as we believe it appropriate to promote editorializing, including on political issues by broadcast licensees, so also — for the same reason, namely, to have robust, wide-open debate — we seek to facilitate the response. . . . We believe that many candidates will be reluctant to avail themselves of the opportunity for response, embodied in our rules, if it means that by so doing, the editorial endorsement or opposition of the station is automatically disseminated again to a new audience.

The commission did not hold that WCBS-TV's introduction was in any way illegal. On the contrary, use of the introduction was entirely within the station's discretion, as was the original broadcast of the editorial favoring Mayor Lindsay. However, the introduction did trigger a further obligation to Procaccino on the part of WCBS-TV.

There are exceptions to the WCBS-TV ruling. A rather obvious one lies in the use of some nonpartisan introduction. For example, the licensee can simply state that it is presenting "_____ on behalf of _____ to reply to a previous editorial of this station in the election campaign." Even this precaution is unnecessary if the candidate, unlike Procaccino, does not object to the WCBS type of introduction or, indeed, plans to mention the prior endorsement and challenge it. In that case, no further obligation is created by the licensee's so-called reendorsement.

A broadcaster cannot reasonably insist upon payment from a candidate for the air time used in replying to a political editorial. It would be contrary to the public interest if listeners were deprived of the candidate's response solely because of financial considerations. The broadcaster may inquire if the candidate is willing to pay; however, the right of reply cannot be conditioned upon payment or upon proof of inability to pay. If the candidate states simply that he will not pay, then his reply must be presented free of charge.[33] In this sense, the candidate's right of reply parallels the right of reply accorded to the victim of a personal attack.

9
Complaints

Complaints to Broadcasters

We have examined the principal obligations a broadcaster must perform in order to widen and diversify public debate. Enforcement of these obligations is ultimately the task of the FCC. The commission does not make a practice of monitoring stations to insure compliance by broadcasters. It depends, instead, upon complaints from listeners and viewers to draw its attention to potential violations.

Anyone who believes a broadcaster has not lived up to one of his obligations should complain, first of all, to the broadcaster. The FCC encourages a continuing dialogue between broadcasters and citizens.

> Members of the community can help a station to provide better broadcast service and more responsive programming by making their needs, interests, and problems known to the station and by commenting, whether favorably or unfavorably, on the programming and practices of the station. Complaints concerning a station's operation should be

communicated promptly to the station, and every effort should be made, by both the complainant and the licensee, to resolve any differences through discussion at the local level.[1]

If the complaint relates to network programming, the complainant can contact either the network responsible or the local station that carried the program — or both.

There are sound reasons why a complaint should initially be directed to the broadcaster rather than the FCC. Not the least of these is that the broadcaster may acknowledge an oversight on his part and remedy the situation to the complainant's satisfaction. In June, 1974, two Alabama organizations, the Alabama Media Project (AMP) and the Alabama Civil Liberties Union (ACLU) sent letters to more than forty broadcasters in Alabama.[2] AMP and ACLU complained that the fairness doctrine had been violated, because the stations had presented only one side of a controversial issue — namely, the advisability of constructing nuclear power plants in Alabama. Many of the broadcasters were caught unawares; they were confident that the power plant issue had not been raised in their regular programming. As AMP and ACLU pointed out, however, the broadcasters had been carrying advertisements sponsored by the Alabama Power Company. In general, these ads conveyed the message that nuclear power plants posed no threat to Alabamians and, indeed, promised distinct benefits. One of the ads went:

> Here's another question for Alabama Power from Mr. Clarence Burroughs of Northport: "What effect will the new nuclear plants have on rates?"
> O.K. First, nuclear power plants cost more to build than coal plants of the same size, but nuclear plants cost less to operate because nuclear fuel is more economical than conventional fuels. Nuclear plants are environmentally acceptable. They're clean, efficient, safe and nuclear plants should help keep Alabama Power's rates lower than they would be otherwise.[3]

Even after such advertising was called to the attention of the broadcasters, some of them responded that the fairness doctrine did not apply to advertisements, and, therefore, no balancing obligations had arisen. As we know, however, the fairness doctrine can definitely be triggered by editorial or institutional ads which address one side of a controversial issue. (Recall the ads sponsored by the Georgia Power Company, which explained why that utility needed a rate increase.) These principles were pointed out by AMP and ACLU in a second series of letters to the Alabama broadcasters during July, 1974. Again, the two organizations insisted that the broadcasters had incurred the obligation to present contrasting views on the power plant issue.

AMP and ACLU did not limit their efforts merely to a letter-writing campaign. With the help of a former radio announcer, they prepared a series of thirty-second taped messages, which could be broadcast as public-service announcements. The announcements paralleled the power company's answer-man format, but their perspective was quite different. For example:

> Here's a question from Mrs. Manda Borden of Montgomery. "How serious would an accident at a nuclear power plant be?"
> Minor accidents occur all the time, some costing millions. There were 891 of them last year. But a major accident, according to the Atomic Energy Commission, would kill 45,000 people, injure 100,000, radiate an area the size of Pennsylvania or Alabama, and do $17 billion worth of property damage — and you can't get insurance. Is this safe energy?[4]

AMP and ACLU proposed broadcasting such announcements as one method by which a station might satisfy its balancing obligations.

By August, 1974, a majority of the broadcasters acknowledged their responsibility to present contrasting views on the power plant controversy. The public-service announcements were sent by AMP and ACLU to about twenty broadcasters in order to supply the necessary balance of opinion. More extensive programming was planned by ten other Alabama broadcasters. As a result, both sides of the power plant issue received coverage, without any complaint ever having been made to the FCC. "Equally important," commented Steve Suitts, director of both AMP and ACLU, "broadcasters were made aware of the issues of nuclear power which continue to be discussed as plans for more plants draw near. In the future, broadcasters will not jump at the chance to present the views of environmentalists who don't pay for the air time. However, they will probably present some form of a contrasting viewpoint if shown to be in error and liable to be taken to the FCC."[5]

Besides the prospect of receiving satisfaction at the local level, there are other reasons why a complainant should always contact the broadcaster before proceeding to the FCC. In general, the commission will not act upon a complaint unless the broadcaster has first been confronted by the complainant and given an opportunity to respond. (As we shall see, one of the usual components in any complaint to the FCC is inclusion of any prior correspondence with the broadcaster — or some indication of his failure to respond.) Conceivably, time may be so short — as in an equal-time or political-editorial situation — that there is no opportunity for writing to the broadcaster, awaiting his reply, and, if it is inadequate, complaining to the commission. In case of such emergencies, the complainant or his representative should attempt to reach the broadcaster by telephone, telegram, or in person; simultaneously, a complaint can be telephoned or telegraphed to the FCC. Assuming that all attempts to contact the broadcaster fail, they can, at least, be reported to the commission as evidence of the complainant's willingness to work out an agreeable solution at the local level.

The law does not prescribe any particular format for complaints to broadcasters. We will shortly be considering the essentials for a complaint to the FCC, and, by and large, the same information that would be submitted to the commission ought to be supplied initially to the broadcaster. (Obviously, certain elements in the FCC complaint cannot be presented to the broadcaster — namely, a review of his own response to the original complaint.) While there is no fixed deadline for submitting complaints to a broadcaster, they should generally be made as soon as possible after the cause for complaint first arose. (Of course, in the special case of equal-time requests, the seven-day rule must be strictly observed.)

If no satisfactory response to the complaint is forthcoming, the complainant should approach the broadcaster with the purpose of entering into negotiations. Remember, a broadcaster is not free to decide matters arbitrarily. In general, he is obliged to act reasonably and in good faith. If, instead, a broadcaster refuses to respond to a complaint in any meaningful way, or if he adheres to an arbitrary position without adequate explanation or justification, his conduct will evince a lack of good faith and reasonable judgment. This general deficiency should then be brought to the FCC's attention; for it is the commission that must ultimately determine whether the broadcaster exceeded the limits of his discretion.

While there is no requirement that a complainant be represented by an attorney when complaining to or negotiating with a broadcaster, legal counsel can greatly increase the chances of success. First of all, concepts like reasonableness and good faith, which often seem amorphous to the layman, are familiar standards in the legal profession. So a lawyer will bring much of his experience and intuition to bear when dealing with a broadcaster. The lawyer will be in a better position to judge when the complainant ought to proceed to the FCC.

Second, the lawyer's participation in the initial stages of the complaint process will convince the broadcaster of the seriousness of the complainant's intentions. Without threatening any reprisals, or upsetting negotiations, the lawyer can make it clear that the complainant is prepared to invoke the FCC's help if a reasonable solution cannot be reached through negotiations. Ordinarily, a broadcaster would greatly prefer to find some acceptable basis for settlement and avoid having the dispute brought to the commission's attention.

Complaints to the Federal Communications Commission

IN GENERAL. If a broadcaster does not respond satisfactorily to a complaint, the complainant should turn to the FCC for relief.[6]

Anyone may file a complaint with the commission against a station or a network. The complaint can be submitted at any time; however, it should be made as soon as possible after the event that prompted it. No particular format is prescribed for complaints. Generally, they are presented in the form of a simple letter; but when time is short, it may be necessary to complain via telegraph or telephone. The proper address and telephone number are:

> Fairness/Political Broadcasting Branch
> Complaints and Compliance Division
> Federal Communications Commission
> 1919 M Street, N.W.
> Washington, D.C. 20554
> Telephone: (202) 632-7586

A copy of the complaint should be sent to the station or network in question.

As we shall see, different legal points will have to be substantiated, depending upon the nature of a complaint. An equal-time complaint, for instance, requires proof on issues that are irrelevant to any fairness-doctrine complaint. All complaints, however — regardless of the particular rule under which they arise — should cover certain basic items.

(1) THE COMPLAINANT'S IDENTITY. State the full name and address of the person complaining. If resolution of the complaint is urgent — as in some equal-time or political-editorial situations — include a telephone number at which the complainant or his representative can be reached.

(2) THE BROADCASTER'S IDENTITY. State the call letters (for example, WWW) and the location (city and state) of the station, or the name of the network, against which the complaint is directed. If the complaint is prompted by programming that originated with a cable television system — via a so-called origination cablecast — identify the person, company, or corporation operating the system (for example, Anytown CATV Company), and give the location of the system.

(3) THE LEGAL BASIS FOR THE COMPLAINT. When appropriate, and, to the extent possible, cite any laws or FCC rules that may have been violated. To present the most convincing argument, a complainant would be well advised to seek legal counsel.

(4) RELIEF SOUGHT. State what action is required — for example, equal time, a reasonable opportunity to reply — in order to resolve the complaint.

(5) PRIOR CORRESPONDENCE. Submit with the complaint copies of any relevant correspondence sent to or received from the broadcaster regarding the subject of the complaint.

One further generalization may be made about complaints to the FCC: *they should be specific.* Vague generalizations will accomplish nothing. It is not enough, for example, to accuse a broadcaster of bias or unfairness in his coverage of some public issue. Such charges must be substantiated by citation to particular programming. Let the facts speak for themselves; if they are self-explanatory, do not indulge in unnecessary argumentation.

Substantiation is particularly important on the issue of whether a broadcaster failed to act reasonably. As we know, a broadcaster enjoys wide discretion in carrying out his obligations. Many complaints will essentially charge the broadcaster with exceeding the limits of his discretion — for example, in concluding that some public issue was noncontroversial, or in denying the complainant an adequate opportunity for reply. When allegations of unreasonableness are made, they should be documented as fully as possible.

Four common complaints to the FCC deserve our further attention. They arise out of the following situations:

(1) The broadcaster has denied a request for equal time.

(2) The broadcaster has not provided a reasonable opportunity for contrasting views on a controversial issue of public importance.

(3) The broadcaster has not provided a reasonable opportunity for reply time to the victim of a personal attack.

(4) The broadcaster has not provided a reasonable opportunity

for reply time to a candidate adversely affected by a political editorial.

While the content of these complaints will vary widely, we can, at least, consider general categories of information that should be included in virtually all such complaints. This information is in addition to the fundamental points we have already considered, which belong in every complaint.

AN EQUAL-TIME COMPLAINT. A complaint about the denial of equal time will generally allege facts and present arguments substantiating some variation of one basic situation: Candidate A made a broadcast that triggered the equal-time rule. Candidate B, who is running against A, requested equal time. The request was denied.

While this situation seems simple enough, reciting it properly in a complaint to the FCC calls for careful documentation. The complaint must allege and prove that a number of legal technicalities have been satisfied. At a minimum, the complaint should present specific information on the following points:[7]

(1) THE OFFICE SOUGHT. Describe the public office the complainant and his opponent(s) are running for. The complaint should leave no doubt that the office is one to which the equal-time rule applies.

(2) THE ELECTION INVOLVED. State the date and nature of the election to be held. If the date of the election is near, emphasize that remedial action is urgently needed so that the candidate can make good use of his air time during the campaign.

(3) PRIOR BROADCAST APPEARANCE. Give the date, time, and nature of the prior appearance upon which the request for equal time is based. A transcript of the appearance may be included if available; or else, the content and format of the appearance can be summarized. The information supplied should clearly substantiate the fact that the prior appearance constituted a use of the station and, therefore, triggered the equal-time rule.

It may be necessary to dispel doubts over whether the appearance was exempt from the equal-time rule. We know that bona fide news shows are generally exempt; however, we also know not all news shows are considered bona fide. In some cases, then, a complaint may have to substantiate the true nature of a so-called news program — or a particular excerpt within the program — to prove it is not entitled to exemption.

(4) THE OPPOSING CANDIDATE. Give the name of the candidate who made the prior broadcast appearance.

(5) LEGAL QUALIFICATIONS. The equal-time rule covers "legally qualified candidates": only their appearances can trigger the rule, and they alone can claim its benefits. A candidate complaining about violation of the rule has the twofold burden of establishing not only his own qualifications but also those of the candidate who made the prior broadcast appearance. The complaint must contain information substantiating the facts that (a) the candidate who made the prior appearance was, at the time of the broadcast, a legally qualified candidate for public office, and (b) the complaining candidate is also a legally qualified candidate for the same public office.

(6) TIMELY REQUEST. Under the FCC's seven-day rule, a request for equal time must be made to the station or network involved within one week after the broadcast that created a right to equal time. If the request is late, the right to equal time will be lost. Therefore, an equal-time complaint must evidence the fact that a timely request was made. For example, a copy of a written request to the broadcaster may be submitted with the complaint.

(7) THE REASON FOR REJECTION. Give the broadcaster's stated reasons for refusing to afford equal time. If these reasons were put in writing, submit the document with the complaint.

A FAIRNESS-DOCTRINE COMPLAINT. The basis for a complaint about imbalance under the fairness doctrine may be stated relatively simply: the broadcaster has allegedly presented one viewpoint on some controversial issue of public importance, and, in his overall programming on that issue, the broadcaster has not provided a reasonable opportunity for contrasting viewpoints. While these grounds seems straightforward enough, they are not always easy to establish.

To begin with, the burden of proof is initially on the complainant. He can meet this burden only through a high degree of specificity in his complaint. If the complainant merely makes general allegations of unfairness, he will not sustain his burden of proof, and the broadcaster will not even be called upon to rebut the charges — let alone to provide a reasonable opportunity for contrasting views. "Absent detailed and specific evidence of failure to comply with the requirements of the fairness doctrine," the FCC has warned,

> it would be unreasonable to require licensees specifically to disprove allegations [made without sufficient documentation]. The Commission's policy of encouraging robust, wide-open debate on issues of public importance would in practice be defeated if, on the basis of vague and general charges of unfairness, we should impose upon licensees the burden of proving the contrary by producing recordings or transcripts of all news programs, editorials, commentaries, and discussion of public issues, many of which are treated over long periods of time.[8]

To take an extreme example, "A complainant cannot simply say the word[s] . . . 'racial discrimination' [or] 'pollution,' and require a licensee to devote extensive man-hours to cull over his past programming to show fairness on general issues of this nature."[9]

At a minimum, any fairness complaint to the FCC ought to contain specific information on the following points:[10]

(1) DEFINITION OF THE ISSUE. Critical to every complaint is a precise definition of the issue on which programming has allegedly been one-sided. The very success or failure of the complaint can turn upon how the issue is defined. There may, of course, be a disagreement between the complainant and the broadcaster over proper definition of the issue. If so, the complaint ought to indicate why the broadcaster's definition is arbitrary in light of the clear thrust of the programming in question.

(2) THE VIEWPOINT EXPRESSED. Ideally, an exact transcript of the viewpoint expressed should be submitted with the complaint. If no transcript is available, the viewpoint should be summarized as accurately as possible.

(3) THE DATE AND TIME. State the date and time when the viewpoint was broadcast. To the extent possible, add any other pertinent details (for example, name of the program, identity of the spokesman).

(4) A CONTROVERSIAL ISSUE OF PUBLIC IMPORTANCE. Explain why the issue as defined in the complaint is both controversial and of public importance. Claims of controversiality and public importance should be documented, to the extent possible, by citing, for example, newspaper articles, official reports, surveys, and positions taken by community groups and leaders.

(5) PROGRAMMING IMBALANCE. Explain the grounds for claiming that the station (or network) has not broadcast contrasting viewpoints on the issue in question. The proper frame of reference here is not merely the particular broadcast that prompted the complaint; instead, it is the broadcaster's overall programming on the issue in question.

Must the complainant, therefore, have monitored the station constantly — in order to substantiate his claim that contrasting views were omitted? The FCC says no. The claim may rest upon an assertion that the complainant is merely a *regular listener or viewer,*

> that is, a person who consistently or as a matter of routine listens to the news, public affairs and other non-entertainment programs carried by the station involved. This does not require that the complainant listen to or view the station 24 hours a day, seven days a week. One example of a "regular" television viewer would be a person who routinely (but not necessarily every day) watches the evening news and a significant portion of the public affairs programs of a given station. In the case of radio, a regular listener would include a person who, as a matter of routine, listens to major representative segments of the station's news and public affairs programming.[11]

The complaint ought to specify the nature and extent of the complainant's viewing habits and the overall period during which he has been a regular member of the particular station's audience. Of course, if several regular listeners or viewers join in the complaint, their combined viewing or listening habits will strengthen the contention that contrasting views have not been presented.

The fact that regular viewers or listeners have not seen or heard contrasting viewpoints is not conclusive proof that such viewpoints were actually omitted. However, the assertion on the part of regular members of the audience supplies, at least, a reasonable basis for concluding there has been one-sided programming; and the FCC, therefore, has sufficient grounds for directing an inquiry to the station or network involved. "Some groups," observed the commission in 1974, "having a particular interest in a controversial issue and a licensee's presentation of it have monitored such a station for periods of time and thus been able to offer conclusive evidence that contrasting views were not presented. . . ."[12]

(6) THE BROADCASTER'S PROGRAMMING PLANS. State whether the station or network has afforded, or has expressed the intention to afford, a reasonable opportunity for the presentation of contrasting viewpoints on the issue in question. In this regard, the complainant's correspondence with the station or network can yield evidence as to the station's past programming as well as its future plans. "We have found in many cases," the FCC reported in 1974,

> that if the complainant first addresses his complaint to the station, the licensee is able to provide an explanation satisfactory to the complainant of what steps it has taken to broadcast contrasting views, or what steps it plans to take to achieve this end. It is for this reason that we ask complainants first to go to the station or the network involved. If the station or network fails to answer the complaint at all, or to provide what [the] complainant considers to be a satisfactory answer, then the complainant should address the complaint to the Commission, enclosing a copy of the complaint he sent to the station and a copy of its reply — or, if no response has been received after a reasonable period of time, so stating.[13]

A PERSONAL-ATTACK COMPLAINT. The content of complaints under the personal-attack rule will vary widely, since actual attacks are rarely alike. As a general rule, however, each complaint will allege facts and present arguments substantiating some variation of one basic situation: an attack on the integrity or character of the complaining person or group was broadcast. This attack took place during the discussion of a controversial issue of public importance. As a result, the personal-attack rule was triggered, and its formal requirements came into play. One or more of these requirements was violated by the broadcaster in that he failed to provide the complaining person or group with the necessary notification, transcripts, or opportunity to reply.

When a person or group complains to the FCC that some broadcaster has violated the personal-attack rule, the complaint should contain specific information on the following points:[14]

(1) THE LANGUAGE OF THE ATTACK. Relate the words or statements broadcast which constituted the attack. If a transcript is unavailable, the language should be recited as accurately as possible.

(2) THE DATE AND TIME. State the date and time when the attack was broadcast and any other pertinent details (for example, the name of the program, the identity of the alleged "attacker").

(3) THE NATURE OF THE ATTACK. Explain the basis for claiming that the words broadcast constituted an attack on the victim's honesty, character, integrity, or like personal qualities. Also show that the victim was either identified by the attacker or was, at least, identifiable from the language used in the attack.

(4) THE CONTEXT OF THE ATTACK. Explain the context in which the attack occurred. (Here, of course, a verbatim transcript would be most instructive.) The explanation ought to be sufficient to accomplish two ends: first, to demonstrate that the attack occurred during the presentation of views on a controversial issue of public importance; second, to dispel any notion that the attack occurred during programming exempted from the personal-attack rule.

Suppose the attack did, in fact, occur during an exempt program. Then, as we know, the victim may still be entitled to an opportunity for reply under the fairness doctrine. The victim's complaint should demonstrate first, that his viewpoint has not been adequately presented, and second, that he is the logical spokesman to express a contrasting view on the attack issue.

(5) A NOTICE TO THE VICTIM AND AN OFFER OF REPLY TIME. State whether the broadcaster violated any of the procedural requirements imposed by the personal-attack rule. Did he within one week after the attack (a) notify the victim about the attack; (b) transmit to the victim a tape, transcript, or accurate summary of the attack; and (c) offer the victim a reasonable opportunity to respond over the station's facilities? There may be a disagreement between the broadcaster and the victim as to what constitutes a "reasonable opportunity." If so, the complaint should explain why the broadcaster's proposal for reply time is unreasonable.

A POLITICAL-EDITORIAL COMPLAINT. In general, a complaint about a political editorial will allege facts and present arguments substantiating some variation of one basic situation. An editorial was broadcast, opposing the complaining candidate's election or endorsing one of his opponents. Therefore, the political-editorial rule was triggered, and its formal requirements came into play. One or more of these requirements was violated by the broadcaster in that he failed to provide the complaining candidate with the necessary notification, transcripts, or opportunity to reply.

When the candidate (or his representative) complains to the FCC, the complaint should contain specific information on the following points:[15]

(1) THE CANDIDATE'S QUALIFICATIONS. The political-editorial rule can be invoked only by "legally qualified candidates" who were adversely affected by the station editorial. The complaint should, therefore, establish that the necessary legal qualifications exist, entitling the complaining candidate to invoke the rule. This showing will suffice when the complaining candidate himself has been opposed by the station.

Suppose, however, that the station does not directly oppose the complaining candidate; instead, it endorses his opponent. In that case, the complaint should allege the opponent's status as a legally qualified candidate — in addition to the complaining candidate's status.

(2) THE LANGUAGE OF THE EDITORIAL. Relate the statements broadcast which constituted the editorial endorsement or opposition of the station in question. If a transcript is unavailable, the language should be recited as accurately as possible.

(3) THE DATE AND TIME. State the date and time when the editorial was broadcast. Precise information is particularly important here, because the broadcaster's obligations to the complaining candidate can vary depending upon the proximity of the broadcast to election day.

(4) THE NATURE OF THE EDITORIAL. We know that close questions may arise as to whether a particular broadcast constituted a political editorial. Sometimes editorializing occurs in the guise of a straight news report or the expression of so-called personal feelings; or, perhaps, a station editorializes on issues closely identified with particular candidates, rather than on the candidates themselves. Lest there be any doubt, the complaint should clearly point out why the broadcast in question ought to be regarded as an expression of the station's political preferences.

(5) A NOTICE TO THE CANDIDATE AND AN OFFER OF REPLY TIME. State whether the broadcaster violated any of the procedural requirements imposed by the political-editorial rule. Did he within twenty-four hours after the editorial (a) notify the complaining candidate about the editorial; (b) transmit to the candidate a script or tape of the editorial; and (c) offer a reasonable opportunity to the candidate — or one of the candidate's spokesmen — to respond over the broadcaster's facilities? With regard to the last requirement, disputes can frequently arise between candidates and broadcasters as to what constitutes a "reasonable opportu-

nity." If the candidate believes that the offer of reply time is unreasonable, he should explain why in his complaint.

The notification requirements change considerably when a political editorial is broadcast within seventy-two hours prior to election day. In such a situation, advance notice is required. A candidate who believes that this requirement has been violated must explain in his complaint how he was deprived of sufficient lead time in which to prepare a reply and broadcast it in a timely manner.

Notes

Although this book is written for laymen, I have included a system of legal annotations for the benefit of attorneys. My intention has been to provide sufficient annotation so that an attorney may locate the authorities I have relied upon. Thus, when in the text I introduce discussion of a particular authoritative source — say, a case decided by the Federal Communications Commission — I supply a citation to that source. In the text discussion that follows such a citation, however, when it is apparent that I am still referring to or quoting from the same authoritative source, I have refrained from providing further citations for every point or quotation drawn from that source.

Standard legal abbreviations are used in these notes. For readers unfamiliar with such abbreviations, the following key should help:

CFR — Code of Federal Regulations

Cong. Rec. — Congressional Record

F. 2d — Federal Reporter, Second Series

FCC — Federal Communications Commission Reports, First Series

FCC 2d — Federal Communications Commission Reports, Second Series

Fed. Reg. — Federal Register
H.R. Rep. — House of Representatives Report
L. Rev. — law review
RR 2d — Pike and Fisher, Radio Regulation, Second Series
S. Ct. — Supreme Court Reporter
U.S. — United States Supreme Court Reports
USC — United States Code

All of these sources should be available in any well-stocked law library.

If the lay reader wishes to consult the original source of materials cited in this book, he must know how to translate a legal citation into directions for locating the source cited. Generally speaking, a legal citation contains three basic guideposts: the number of the volume of the source cited; the name of the source (in abbreviated form); and the number of the particular page(s) or section(s) within the source being cited.

Consider a citation to a regulation issued by the Federal Communications Commission: 47 CFR §73.120. The number 47 refers to volume number 47; "CFR" stands for the Code of Federal Regulations; and §73.120 refers to section number 73.120. Thus, the entire citation tells the reader to consult section number 73.120 in volume 47 of the Code of Federal Regulations.

A typical citation to an opinion rendered by the Federal Communications Commission might go: Southern California Broadcasting Co., 42 FCC 2d 1106, 1108 (1973). The reference is to the Southern California Broadcasting Company case; it appears in volume 42 of the Federal Communications Commission Reports (Second Series) at page 1106. Page 1108 is included in the citation to signify reference to that particular page within the report of the Southern California Broadcasting Company case.

1. BROADCASTING IN THE PUBLIC INTEREST

We Interrupt This Broadcast

1. See Miami Herald Publishing Co. v. Tornillo, 418 U.S. 241 (1974) (statute requiring newspaper to print candidate's reply to editorial unconstitutional).

The Need for Broadcast Regulation

2. Note, "The Crisis in Electromagnetic Frequency Spectrum Allocation: Abatement Through Market Distribution," 53 Iowa L. Rev. 437 (1967).
3. See William K. Jones, *Regulated Industries* (Brooklyn: Foundation Press, Inc., 1967), pp. 1019–1045.
4. National Broadcasting Co., Inc. v. United States, 319 U.S. 190, 212 (1943).
5. Ibid., at 213.
6. Red Lion Broadcasting Co., Inc. v. FCC, 395 U.S. 367, 397–398 (1969); Fairness Report, 48 FCC 2d 1, 4, n. 4, 6 (1974).

The Federal Communications Commission and the Public Interest

7. National Broadcasting Co., Inc. v. United States, 319 U.S. 190, 217 (1943).
8. See 47 USC §§1, 4(a)(b)(c), 303.
9. See 47 USC §§1, 303, 307(b); National Broadcasting Co., Inc. v. United States, note 7 above, at 213.
10. 47 USC §§301, 307(a)(d), 309(a); see National Broadcasting Co., Inc. v. United States, note 7 above, at 227.
11. National Broadcasting Co., Inc. v. United States, note 7 above, at 216–217.
12. United States v. Paramount Pictures, Inc., 334 U.S. 131, 166 (1948); En banc Programing Inquiry, 44 FCC 2303, 2306 (1960).
13. 47 USC §326; see Farmers Educational & Cooperative Union of America v. WDAY, Inc., 360 U.S. 525, 529–530 (1959).
14. Columbia Broadcasting Sys., Inc. v. Democratic National Committee, 412 U.S. 94, 110 (1973).
15. Ibid., at 117–118.
16. Ibid., at 118.

The Right of Viewers and Listeners

17. Red Lion Broadcasting Co., Inc. v. FCC, 395 U.S. 367, 388–389 (1969).
18. Ibid., at 389.
19. 395 U.S. 367 (1969).
20. New York Times Co. v. Sullivan, 376 U.S. 254, 270 (1964).
21. Associated Press v. United States, 326 U.S. 1, 20 (1945).

To Oversee without Censoring

22. Columbia Broadcasting Sys., Inc. v. Democratic National Committee, 412 U.S. 94, 102–103, 110 (1973).
23. Ibid., at 118.
24. Ibid., at 105.
25. Banzhaf v. FCC, 405 F. 2d 1082, 1095 (D.C. Cir. 1968), cert. denied, 396 U.S. 842 (1969).
26. Fairness Report, 48 FCC 2d 1, 30 (1974).

2. BROADCAST JOURNALISM AND THE PUBLIC INTEREST

General Principles

1. "The Selling of the Pentagon," 30 FCC 2d 150 (1971); Editorializing by Broadcast Licensees, 13 FCC 1246, 1249 (1949); see En banc Programing Inquiry, 44 FCC 2303, 2314 (1960); "What People Think of Television and Other Mass Media: 1959–1972" (The Roper Organization, 1973).

2. Editorializing by Broadcast Licensees, note 1 above.

3. "Hunger in America," 20 FCC 2d 143, 151 (1969).

4. Editorializing by Broadcast Licensees, note 1 above, at 1254–1255.

5. Network Coverage of Democratic National Convention, 16 FCC 2d 650, 654 (1969).

6. Mrs. J. R. Paul, 26 FCC 2d 591, 592 (1969).

7. Columbia Broadcasting Sys., Inc. (WBBM-TV), 18 FCC 2d 124, 131–132 (1969).

8. Hon. Harley O. Staggers, 25 RR 2d 413, 419 (1972).

9. "Hunger in America," note 3 above, at 151, n. 6; Network Coverage of Democratic National Convention, note 5 above, at 657, n. 5.

10. "Hunger in America," note 3 above, at 150–151; cf. National Citizens Committee for Broadcasting, 49 FCC 2d 83 (1974) (no extrinsic evidence that network blipped out remarks for commercial reasons); Hon. William Harsha, 31 FCC 2d 847 (1971) (no extrinsic evidence of network self-censorship).

11. Mrs. J. R. Paul, note 6 above.

12. Gross Telecasting, Inc., 46 FCC 2d 543 (1974); "Hunger in America," note 3 above; Network Coverage of Democratic National Convention, note 5 above, at 657; Station of the Stars, Inc. (KMPC), 14 Fed. Reg. 4831 (1949).

13. Network Coverage of Democratic National Convention, note 5 above, at 657.

14. Network Coverage of Democratic National Convention, note 5 above.

News Coverage

15. Universal Communications Corp., 27 FCC 2d 1022 (1971); Reeves Telecom Corp., 26 FCC 2d 225 (1970).

16. Kenneth Cooper, 39 FCC 2d 1000 (1973).

17. See Penny Manes, 38 FCC 2d 308 (1972), reconsideration denied, 42 FCC 2d 878 (1973); Anthony Bruno, 26 FCC 2d 656 (1970); Richard Kay, 24 FCC 2d 426, aff'd, 443 F. 2d 638 (D.C. Cir. 1970).

18. Network Coverage of Democratic National Convention, 16 FCC 2d 650 (1969); accord, Universal Communications Corp., note 15 above.

19. National Citizens Committee for Broadcasting, 29 FCC 2d 386, reconsideration denied, 32 FCC 2d 824 (1971).

20. 47 USC §317(a)(2); 47 CFR §§73.119(d) (AM radio), 73.289(d) (FM radio), 73.503(d) (noncommercial educational FM radio), 73.654(d) (TV stations), 76.217(c) (origination cablecasting over cable TV systems).

21. Identification of Source of Broadcast Matter, 41 FCC 2d 333 (1973).

22. Sponsorship Identification Rules, 40 FCC 141 (1963).
23. In the Matter of the Handling of Public Issues Under the Fairness Doctrine, 36 FCC 2d 40, 53 (1972) (Docket No. 19260: First Report).
24. In the Matter of the Handling of Public Issues Under the Fairness Doctrine, note 23 above, at 53, n. 19; Sponsorship Identification Rules, note 22 above, at 146 (Interpretation no. 11).

News Accuracy

25. "Hunger in America," 20 FCC 2d 143, 151 (1969).
26. Ibid.
27. Ibid., at 151.
28. A. J. Treutler v. Meredith Corp., 455 F. 2d 255, 257 (8th Cir. 1972).
29. Meredith Corp., 37 FCC 2d 551, 555 (1972).
30. Hon. John Thompson, 40 FCC 523 (1962).

News Editing

31. Columbia Broadcasting Sys., Inc. v. Democratic National Committee, 412 U.S. 94, 124 (1973).
32. Citizens for Abraham Beame, 41 FCC 2d 155 (1973).
33. "The Selling of the Pentagon," 30 FCC 2d 150 (1971).

News Staging

34. Network Coverage of Democratic National Convention, 16 FCC 2d 650, 657 (1969).
35. Columbia Broadcasting Sys., Inc. (WBBM-TV), 18 FCC 2d 124, 132 (1969).
36. Network Coverage of Democratic National Convention, note 34 above, at 656; cf. A. Burton White, M.D., 18 FCC 2d 658 (1969) (presence of cameras justified despite inhibiting effect on certain spokesmen).
37. Columbia Broadcasting Sys., Inc. (WBBM-TV), note 35 above, at 132.
38. Columbia Broadcasting Sys., Inc., 45 FCC 2d 119, 124 (1973).
39. Hon. Harley O. Staggers, 25 RR 2d 413, 414 (1972).
40. Ibid., at 420.
41. Columbia Broadcasting Sys., Inc. (WBBM-TV), note 35 above.

3. POLITICAL BROADCASTS

Introduction

1. In the Matter of the Handling of Public Issues Under the Fairness Doctrine, 36 FCC 2d 40, 54 (1972) (Docket No. 19260: First Report); see Interpretation of Second Sentence of Section 315(a), 40 FCC 1088 (1963); En banc Programing Inquiry, 44 FCC 2303, 2314 (1960); Red Lion Broadcasting Co., Inc. v. FCC, 395 U.S. 367, 391 (1969); Farmers Educational & Cooperative Union of America v. WDAY, Inc., 360 U.S. 525, 534 (1959).

Candidates for Federal Office

2. 47 USC §312(a)(7).
3. Licensee Responsibility Under Amendments to the Communications

Act Made by the Federal Election Campaign Act of 1971, 47 FCC 2d 516, 517 (1974).

4. 47 USC §§801(3)(4); Use of Broadcast and Cablecast Facilities by Candidates for Public Office, 34 FCC 2d 510, 535–536 (1972) (VIII, Q & A 1, 2).

5. 47 USC §312(a)(7); Use of Broadcast and Cablecast Facilities by Candidates for Public Office, note 4 above, at 538–539 (VIII, Q & A 9, 10, 11).

6. Use of Broadcast and Cablecast Facilities by Candidates for Public Office, note 4 above, at 536 (VIII, Q & A 3).

7. Summa Corp., 43 FCC 2d 602, 604 (1973); see Use of Broadcast and Cablecast Facilities by Candidates for Public Office, note 4 above, at 536 (VIII, Q & A 3).

8. Use of Broadcast and Cablecast Facilities by Candidates for Public Office, note 4 above, at 537, 538 (VIII, Q & A 5, 6, 10); Dr. Benjamin Spock, 44 FCC 2d 12 (1973), appeal pending (D.C. Cir. Docket No. 74-1194); see Penny Manes, 38 FCC 2d 308 (1972), reconsideration denied, 42 FCC 2d 878 (1973) ("reasonable access" does not mandate reasonable news coverage).

9. Summa Corp., note 7 above.

10. Licensee Responsibility Under Amendments to the Communications Act Made by the Federal Election Campaign Act, note 3 above, at 517.

11. Hon. Pete Flaherty, 48 FCC 2d 838 (1974).

12. Use of Broadcast and Cablecast Facilities by Candidates for Public Office, note 4 above, at 536 (VIII, Q & A 3); Summa Corp., note 7 above, at 605.

13. Hon. Pete Flaherty, note 11 above.

Candidates for State and Local Office

14. Interpretation of Second Sentence of Section 315(a), 40 FCC 1088, 1095 (1963).

15. Homer Rainey, 11 FCC 898 (1947).

16. Use of Broadcast and Cablecast Facilities by Candidates for Public Office, 34 FCC 2d 510, 535 (VIII, Q & A 1); see Use of Broadcast Facilities by Candidates for Public Office, 24 FCC 2d 832, 863–864 (V, Q & A 2, 3, 4); Charles Mark Furcolo, 48 FCC 2d 565 (1974) (reasonable to afford only ten minutes to each judicial candidate).

17. See Charles Mark Furcolo, note 16 above; Grover Doggette, 40 FCC 346 (1962).

18. Rosenbush Advertising Agency, Inc., 31 FCC 2d 782 (1971) (no broadcasts under 5 minutes); W. Roy Smith, 18 FCC 2d 747 (1969) (spots only for other than national races).

19. D. J. Leary, 34 FCC 2d 471 (1972).

Political Parties

20. Democratic National Committee, 25 FCC 2d 216 (1970), rev'd sub nom. Business Executives Move for Vietnam Peace v. FCC, 450 F. 2d 642 (D.C. Cir. 1971), rev'd sub nom. Columbia Broadcasting Sys., Inc. v. Democratic National Committee, 412 U.S. 94 (1973); see Democratic National Committee v. FCC, 460 F. 2d 891, 910 (D.C. Cir.), cert. denied,

409 U.S. 843 (1972); Use of Broadcast and Cablecast Facilities by Candidates for Public Office, 34 FCC 2d 510, 536–537 (VIII, Q & A 4) (party has no right to "reasonable access" to speak on behalf of a federal candidate).

21. Democratic National Committee, note 20 above, at 229.
22. Democratic National Committee, note 20 above, at 230.
23. Nicholas Zapple, 23 FCC 2d 707 (1970).
24. In the Matter of the Handling of Public Issues Under the Fairness Doctrine, 36 FCC 2d 40, 41, 49 (1972) (Docket No. 19260: First Report); Committee for the Fair Broadcasting of Controversial Issues, 25 FCC 2d 283, 300, reconsideration denied sub nom. Republican National Committee, 25 FCC 2d 739 (1970), rev'd sub nom. Columbia Broadcasting Sys., Inc. v. FCC, 454 F. 2d 1018 (D.C. Cir. 1971); Committee to Elect McGovern-Shriver, 38 FCC 2d 300 (1972) (no free reply to allegedly deceptive anti-McGovern commercials); but see Nicholas Zapple, 23 FCC 2d, at 710–711 (Commissioner Johnson dissenting).
25. In the Matter of the Handling of Public Issues Under the Fairness Doctrine, note 24 above, at 49.
26. Ibid., at 49; Lawrence Smith, 40 FCC 549 (1963); cf. George Cooley, 10 FCC 2d 969, review denied, 10 FCC 2d 970 (1967) (reply to political editorial).
27. In the Matter of the Handling of Public Issues Under the Fairness Doctrine, note 24 above, at 49–50; Democratic National Committee, 31 FCC 2d 708 (1971), aff'd, 460 F. 2d 891 (D.C. Cir.), cert. denied, 409 U.S. 843 (1972); but see Committee for the Fair Broadcasting of Controversial Issues, note 24 above.
28. See Democratic National Committee, note 20 above, at 230.
29. In the Matter of the Handling of Public Issues Under the Fairness Doctrine, note 24 above, at 50, n. 12.
30. Ibid., at 49, 50, n. 13; Lawrence Smith, note 26 above (comparable fund-raising announcements for major parties — not minor parties); Arkansas Radio & Equipment Co., 40 FCC 1070 (1960) (comparable coverage of Republican and Democratic national conventions).

4. EQUAL TIME FOR POLITICAL CANDIDATES

General Principles

1. 47 USC §315(a); 47 CFR §§73.120 (AM radio), 73.290 (FM radio), 73.590 (noncommercial educational FM radio), 73.657 (TV stations), 76.205 (origination cablecasting over cable TV systems).
2. 47 USC §315(a).
3. KNBC-TV, 23 FCC 2d 765 (1968); Use of Broadcast Facilities by Candidates for Public Office, 24 FCC 2d 832, 863 (1970) (V, Q & A 1).
4. Lester Posner, 15 FCC 2d 807 (1968).
5. 47 USC §315(a) (second sentence).

Broadcasts Subject to Equal Time

6. CBS, Inc. (Lar Daly), 26 FCC 715, 728 (1959).
7. Hon. Clem Miller, 40 FCC 353 (1962).
8. KWWL-TV, 23 FCC 2d 758 (1966).

9. Jerold A. Weissman, 23 FCC 2d 778 (1966).

10. Hon. Warren G. Magnuson, 23 FCC 2d 775, 776–777 (1967).

11. National Urban Coalition, 23 FCC 2d 123 (1970).

12. Station WBAX, 17 FCC 2d 316 (1969); compare Station WAMD, 17 FCC 2d 176 (1969); see James Spurling, 30 FCC 2d 675 (1971) (candidate's voice heard when he calls into phone-in show).

13. Hon. Warren G. Magnuson, note 10 above, at 776.

14. United Community Campaigns of America, 40 FCC 390 (1964); Hon. Joseph S. Clark, 40 FCC 325 (1962); Fordham University, 40 FCC 321 (1961); WNEP-TV, 40 FCC 431 (1965); Robert Yeakel, 40 FCC 282 (1957); WAKR, 23 FCC 2d 759 (1970).

15. Hon. Warren G. Magnuson, note 10 above, at 776 (California Governor Ronald Reagan on the "Late Show"); see Pat Paulsen, 33 FCC 2d 297, aff'd, 33 FCC 2d 835 (1972), aff'd, 491 F. 2d 887 (9th Cir. 1974).

Broadcasts Exempt from Equal Time

IN GENERAL

16. 47 USC §315(a).

17. 105 Cong. Rec. 17782 (1959).

18. Use of Broadcast Facilities by Candidates for Public Office, 24 FCC 2d 832, 838 (1970).

19. See H.R. Rep. No. 802, 86th Cong., 1st Sess. 4–5 (1959).

20. The Advocates, 23 FCC 2d 462, 463, reconsideration denied, 26 FCC 2d 377 (1970).

21. 47 USC §315(a)(4) (emphasis added); see 105 Cong. Rec. 17778 (1959).

NEWSCASTS

22. H.R. Rep. No. 802, 86th Cong., 1st Sess. 5–6 (1959).

23. See Penny Manes, 38 FCC 2d 308 (1972), reconsideration denied, 42 FCC 2d 878 (1973).

24. H.R. Rep. No. 802, note 22 above, at 6.

25. Hon. Clem Miller, 40 FCC 353, 354 (1962) (audio tapes); Hon. Clark Thompson, 40 FCC 328 (1962) (film clip).

26. Hon. Clark Thompson, note 25 above.

27. See CBS, Inc., 40 FCC 395, 396 (1964), overruled in part, Aspen Institute Program on Communications and Society, FCC 75–1090 (Sept. 25, 1975).

NEWS INTERVIEWS

28. Joseph Gillis and Philip Gillis, 43 FCC 2d 584 (1973).

29. Lar Daly, 40 FCC 314 (1960); WMCA, 40 FCC 367 (1962).

30. See H.R. Rep. No. 1069, 86th Cong., 1st Sess. 4 (1959).

31. Use of Broadcast Facilities by Candidates for Public Office, 24 FCC 2d 832, 847 (1970) (III C, Q & A 11).

32. J. Stanley Shaw, 41 FCC 2d 160 (1973).

33. CBS, Inc., 40 FCC 395 (1964), overruled in part, Aspen Institute Program on Communications and Society, FCC 75–1090 (Sept. 25, 1975).

34. Socialist Labor Party, 15 FCC 2d 98, aff'd sub nom. by order of Taft Broadcasting Co. v. FCC, No. 22445 (D.C. Cir., Oct. 31, 1968).

35. WIIC-TV Corp., 33 FCC 2d 629 (1972).
36. See, e.g., 105 Cong. Rec. 17780–81 (1959).
37. Hon. Michael DiSalle, 40 FCC 348 (1962).
38. CBS, Inc., note 33 above.
39. Jean Steiner, 7 FCC 2d 857 (1967).
40. See, e.g., 105 Cong. Rec. 17830–31 (1959).
41. Ibid., at 17830.
42. Hon. Sam Yorty, 35 FCC 2d 572 (1972).
43. Chisholm v. FCC and USA, No. 72-1505 (D.C. Cir., June 2, 1972) (reported in 35 FCC 2d 579, 580–581).
44. Accord, William Sheroff, Esq., 30 RR 2d 558 (1974); Citizens for Abraham D. Beame, 41 FCC 2d 155 (1973); Hon. Terry Sanford, 35 FCC 2d 938, appeal dismissed (D.C. Cir., Aug. 10, 1972); Hon. Sam Yorty, 35 FCC 2d 570 (1972).
45. See Hon. Shirley Chisholm, 35 FCC 2d 579, 581–583 (concurring opinion); In the Matter of the Handling of Public Issues Under the Fairness Doctrine, 36 FCC 2d 40, 52–53 (1972) (Docket No. 19260: First Report).

NEWS DOCUMENTARIES
46. The Advocates, 23 FCC 2d 462, 463–464, reconsideration denied, 26 FCC 2d 377 (1970).
47. 105 Cong. Rec. 17828 (1959).
48. See H.R. Rep. No. 1069, 86th Cong., 1st Sess. 4 (1959).
49. Use of Broadcast Facilities by Candidates for Public Office, 24 FCC 2d 832, 851 (1970) (III C, Q & A 20).

ON-THE-SPOT NEWS COVERAGE
50. United Way of America, FCC 75–1091 (Sept. 25, 1975); Lar Daly, 40 FCC 377 (1963); see, e.g., 105 Cong. Rec. 16345, 17830, 17832 (1959).
51. Tromas Fadell, 40 FCC 379 (1963).
52. Republican National Committee, 40 FCC 408, aff'd by an equally divided court sub nom. Goldwater v. FCC, No. 18963 (D.C. Cir., Oct. 27, 1964), cert. denied, 379 U.S. 893 (1964); see In re Section 315, 40 FCC 276 (1956) (President Eisenhower's exempt address on the 1956 Suez crisis); Use of Broadcast Facilities by Candidates for Public Office, 24 FCC 2d 832, 855 (1970) (III C, Q & A 28).
53. Use of Broadcast Facilities by Candidates for Public Office, note 52 above, at 852–853 (III C, Q & A 22, 23).
54. Republican National Committee, 37 FCC 2d 799 (1972).
55. FCC 75–1090 (Sept. 25, 1975).
56. 40 FCC 366, reconsideration denied, 40 FCC 370 (1962).
57. 40 FCC 362, 365 (1962).
58. Aspen Institute Program on Communications and Society, FCC 75–1090 (Sept. 25, 1975), n. 6.
59. See Aspen Institute Program on Communications and Society, note 58 above (Commissioner Hooks dissenting).
60. Aspen Institute Program on Communications and Society, note 58 above; H.R. Rep. No. 1069, 86th Cong., 1st Sess. 4 (1959); 105 Cong. Rec. 17782 (1959).
61. 105 Cong. Rec. 17782 (1959).

Legally Qualified Candidates

62. 47 USC §315(a); Felix v. Westinghouse Radio Stations, 186 F. 2d 1 (3d Cir. 1950), cert. denied, 341 U.S. 909 (1951); National Laugh Party, 40 FCC 289 (1957); but cf. Nicholas Zapple, 23 FCC 2d 707 (1970) (political party doctrine).

63. 47 CFR §§73.120(a) (AM radio), 73.290(a) (FM radio), 73.590(a) (noncommercial educational FM radio), 73.657(a) (TV stations), 76.5(y) (origination cablecasting over cable TV systems).

64. Hon. Earle Clements, 23 FCC 2d 756 (1954).

65. Sen. Eugene McCarthy, 11 FCC 2d 511, 513, aff'd, 390 F. 2d 471 (D.C. Cir. 1968) (per curiam).

66. Ibid.

67. 47 USC §803(a)(3)(B). Use of Broadcast and Cablecast Facilities by Candidates for Public Office, 34 FCC 2d 510, 522–523 (1972) (V, Q & A 1) (N.B. The FCC does not regard minimal campaign expenditures as entitling a candidate to equal time. Thus a $5 ad in a newspaper does not automatically make a presidential candidate legally qualified.)

68. See, e.g., Socialist Workers Party 1972, 39 FCC 2d 89 (1972) (presidential candidate under constitutional age of 35 disqualified); Socialist Workers Party, 38 FCC 2d 379 (1972) (residency requirement; "statement of economic interests").

69. Cf. Rady Davis, 40 FCC 435 (1965), with Hon. Earle Clements, note 64 above.

70. 47 CFR §§73.120(a)(2) (AM radio), 73.290(a)(2) (FM radio), 73.590(a)(2) (noncommercial educational FM radio), 73.657(a)(2) (TV stations), 76.5(y)(2) (origination cablecasting over cable TV systems).

71. Socialist Workers Party 1972, note 68 above; RKO General, Inc., 26 FCC 2d 244 (1970).

72. Socialist Workers Party 1972, 39 FCC 2d 89.

73. Anthony Bruno, 26 FCC 2d 656, 658 (1970).

74. 47 CFR §§73.120(f) (AM radio), 73.290(f) (FM radio), 73.590(f) (noncommercial educational FM radio), 73.657(f) (TV stations), 76.205(e) (origination cablecasting over cable TV systems).

75. Richard Kay, 24 FCC 2d 426, aff'd, 443 F. 2d 638 (D.C. Cir. 1970).

76. Hon. Clarence Miller, 23 FCC 2d 121 (1970).

77. Pat Paulsen, 33 FCC 2d 835, 837 (1972), aff'd, 491 F. 2d 887 (9th Cir. 1974) (Chairman Burch concurring); CBS, Inc., 40 FCC 244 (1952) (presidential dark horse); Hon. William Benton, 40 FCC 1081 (1950) (Communist candidate).

Requests for Equal Time

78. 47 CFR §§73.120(d) (AM radio), 73.290(d) (FM radio), 73.590(d) (noncommercial educational FM radio), 73.657(d)(TV stations); see 47 CFR §76.205(c) (origination cablecasting over cable TV systems).

79. James Spurling, 30 FCC 2d 675 (1971).

80. Horace P. Rowley III, 39 FCC 2d 437 (1973).

81. 47 CFR §§73.120(e) (AM radio), 73.290(e) (FM radio), 73.590(e) (noncommercial educational FM radio), 73.657(e) (TV stations); see 47 CFR §76.205(d) (origination cablecasting over cable TV systems).

82. The Public and Broadcasting — A Procedure Manual, 49 FCC 2d 1, 4–5 (1974); Use of Broadcast Facilities by Candidates for Public Office, 24 FCC 2d 832, 884–885 (1970) (IX, Q & A 6); but see In re Amending the Seven-Day Rule, 24 FCC 2d 543, 545 (1970) (licensee may voluntarily waive seven-day rule and honor late request without starting a "second round" or uses — providing all candidates for the same office are treated equitably).

83. Hughes Tool Co., 42 FCC 2d 894, 896 (1973), aff'd sub nom. Summa Corp., 49 FCC 2d 443 (1974) (forfeiture reduced).

84. Hughes Tool Co., note 83 above, 49 FCC 2d at 447–448.

85. Ibid., at 448.

86. Use of Broadcast Facilities by Candidates for Public Office, note 82 above, at 884 (IX, Q & A 5).

87. Hughes Tool Co., note 83 above; Gray Communications Systems, Inc., 14 FCC 2d 766 (1968), reconsideration denied, 19 FCC 2d 532 (1969); Emerson Stone, Jr., 40 FCC 385 (1964).

88. See note 81 above.

89. See Use of Broadcast Facilities by Candidates for Public Office, note 82 above.

90. Socialist Workers Party, 40 FCC 281 (1956); Use of Broadcast Facilities by Candidates for Public Office, note 82 above, at 859 (IV, Q & A 8).

Equal Opportunities

91. 47 CFR §§73.120(c)(2) (AM radio), 73.290(c)(2) (FM radio), 73.590(c)(2) (noncommercial educational FM radio), 73.657(c)(2) (TV stations); see 47 CFR §76.205(b)(2) (origination cablecasting over cable TV systems).

92. H.R. Rep. No. 802, 86th Cong., 1st Sess. 3 (1959).

93. CBS, Inc. (Lar Daly), 26 FCC 715, 750 (1959).

94. Interview with Milton O. Gross, Chief, Fairness/Political Broadcasting Branch, Complaints and Compliance Division, Federal Communications Commission (Mar. 17, 1975); Charles F. Dykas, 35 FCC 2d 937 (1972).

95. Interview with Milton O. Gross, note 94 above; Gray Communications Systems, Inc., 19 FCC 2d 532 (1969).

96. Gray Communications Systems, Inc., note 95 above.

97. Interview with Milton O. Gross, note 94 above.

98. Interview with Milton O. Gross, note 94 above.

99. Greater New York Broadcasting, 40 FCC 235 (1946); cf. Lar Daly, 40 FCC 302 (1959).

100. D. L. Grace, 40 FCC 297 (1958).

101. Sen. Birch Bayh, 15 FCC 2d 47 (1968).

102. CBS, Inc. (Lar Daly), note 93 above.

103. D. L. Grace, note 100 above.

104. Hughes Tool Co., 42 FCC 2d 894 (1973), aff'd sub nom. Summa Corp., 49 FCC 2d 443 (1974); E. A. Stephens, 11 FCC 61 (1945); see Fairness Report, 48 FCC 2d 1, 32 (1974).

105. Bella S. Abzug, 25 FCC 2d 117 (1970); accord, D. J. Leary, 34 FCC

2d 471 (1972) (candidate entitled to thirty minutes of equal time cannot demand fifteen-minute segment).

106. Use of Broadcast Facilities by Candidates for Public Office, 24 FCC 2d 832, 870 (1970) (VI B, Q & A 6).

107. Messrs. William F. Ryan and Paul O'Dwyer, 14 FCC 2d 633 (1968).

108. Steve Beren, 26 FCC 2d 38, 39 (1970).

The Cost of Air Time

109. 47 CFR §§73.120(c)(2) (AM radio), 73.290(c)(2) (FM radio), 73.590(c)(2) (noncommercial educational FM radio), 73.657(c)(2) (TV stations); see 47 CFR §76.205(b)(2) (origination cablecasting over cable TV systems); compare Metromedia, Inc., 40 FCC 426 (1964), with WAKR, 23 FCC 2d 759 (1970).

110. 47 CFR §§73.120(c)(1) (AM radio), 73.290(c)(1) (FM radio), 73.590(c)(1) (noncommercial educational FM radio), 73.657(c)(1) (TV stations); see 47 CFR §76.205(b)(1) (origination cablecasting over cable TV systems).

111. Use of Broadcast Facilities by Candidates for Public Office, 24 FCC 2d 832, 880 (1970) (VIII, Q & A 14).

112. See note 110 above; Use of Broadcast Facilities by Candidates for Public Office, note 111 above, at 881 (VIII, Q & A 17).

113. Use of Broadcast and Cablecast Facilities by Candidates for Public Office, 34 FCC 2d 510, 523 (1972) (V, Q & A 2).

114. 47 USC §315(b)(1).

115. Use of Broadcast and Cablecast Facilities by Candidates for Public Office, note 113 above, at 524 (VI, Q & A 1).

116. Use of Broadcast and Cablecast Facilities by Candidates for Public Office, note 113 above, at 531 (VI, Q & A 18).

Censorship Prohibited

117. Gray Communications Systems, Inc., 19 FCC 2d 532, 535 (1969).

118. 47 USC §315(a); 47 CFR §§73.120(b) (AM radio), 73.290(b) (FM radio), 73.590(b) (noncommercial educational FM radio), 73.657(b) (TV stations), 76.205(a) (origination cablecasting over cable TV systems).

119. Port Huron Broadcasting Co., 12 FCC 1069 (1948).

120. Western Connecticut Broadcasting Corp., 43 FCC 2d 730 (1973) (deletions made from advance script); Use of Broadcast Facilities by Candidates for Public Office, 24 FCC 2d 832, 874 (1970) (VII, Q & A 7).

121. WMCA, Inc., 40 FCC 241 (1952); Hon. Allen O. Hunter, 40 FCC 246 (1952); see Hon. Pete Flaherty, 48 FCC 2d 838, 849–850 (1974) (licensee objects to format of fund-raising telethon).

122. Atlanta NAACP, 36 FCC 2d 635, 636 (1972); accord, Alan Burstein, 43 FCC 2d 590 (1973) (no censorship of allegedly false campaign commercials).

123. Gray Communications Systems, Inc., 14 FCC 2d 766 (1968), reconsideration denied, 19 FCC 2d 532 (1969); see Hon. Pete Flaherty, note 121 above.

124. Gray Communications Systems, Inc., note 123 above.

125. Felix v. Westinghouse Radio Stations, 186 F. 2d 1 (3d Cir. 1950), cert. denied, 341 U.S. 909 (1951); George F. Mahoney, 40 FCC 336 (1962).
126. 360 U.S. 525 (1959).
127. D. J. Leary, 37 FCC 2d 577 (1972).
128. Ibid.; Gray Communications Systems, Inc., note 123 above.
129. Felix v. Westinghouse Radio Stations, note 125 above.

Waiver of the Right to Equal Time

130. WBTW-TV, 5 FCC 2d 479, 480 (1966).
131. Ibid.; Wallace J. Duffy, 23 FCC 2d 767 (1966).
132. Linda Jenness, 26 FCC 2d 485, 486 (1970).
133. Senate Committee on Commerce, 40 FCC 357 (1962); KTRM, 40 FCC 335 (1962) (candidate who rejected offer because of insufficient advance notice is entitled to equal time).
134. WBTW-TV, note 130 above, at 480.
135. Linda Jenness, note 132 above; see Gordon F. Hughes, 41 FCC 2d 350 (1973) (candidate delayed in traffic is unfairly denied his scheduled time slot).

5. FAIR COVERAGE OF PUBLIC ISSUES

General Principles

THE FAIRNESS DOCTRINE
1. Fairness Report, 48 FCC 2d 1, 7 (1974); see 47 USC §315(a)(4); Columbia Broadcasting Sys., Inc. v. Democratic National Committee, 412 U.S. 94, 111 (1973); Red Lion Broadcasting Co., Inc. v. FCC, 395 U.S. 367, 377 (1969).
2. Fairness Report, note 1 above, at 6.
3. Ibid., at 10; Committee for the Fair Broadcasting of Controversial Issues, 25 FCC 2d 283, 292, reconsideration denied sub nom. Republican National Committee, 25 FCC 2d 739 (1970), rev'd on other grounds sub nom. Columbia Broadcasting Sys., Inc. v. FCC, 454 F. 2d 1018 (D.C. Cir. 1971).
4. 47 USC §315(a)(4); 47 CFR §76.209(a).
5. 47 USC §399(a).
6. En banc Programing Inquiry, 44 FCC 2303, 2314 (1960); In the Matter of Editorializing by Broadcast Licensees, 13 FCC 1246, 1252–1253 (1949).
7. Accuracy in Media, Inc., 45 FCC 2d 297 (1973); Public Communications, Inc., 49 FCC 2d 27, review denied, 50 FCC 2d 395 (1974).

THE BROADCASTER'S AFFIRMATIVE OBLIGATION
8. Gary Soucie, 24 FCC 2d 743, 750–751 (1970), rev'd on other grounds sub nom. Friends of the Earth v. FCC, 449 F. 2d 1164 (D.C. Cir. 1971).
9. Fairness Report, 48 FCC 2d 1, 10 (1974); Public Communications, Inc., 49 FCC 2d 27, review denied, 50 FCC 2d 395 (1974) (broadcast license renewal legislation not an issue of overriding importance).
10. See Public Communications, Inc., 49 FCC 2d 27.
11. See Fairness Report, 48 FCC 2d, at 32, n. 31.

THE BROADCASTER'S BALANCING OBLIGATION
   12. See 47 USC §315(a)(4).

The Issue at Stake

DEFINING THE ISSUE
   13. Green v. FCC, 447 F. 2d 323, 329 (D.C. Cir. 1971).
   14. Andrew Letson, 40 FCC 507 (1962).
   15. Fairness Report, 48 FCC 2d 1, 13 (1974).
   16. Accuracy in Media, Inc., 40 FCC 2d 958, review denied, 44 FCC 2d 1027 (1973), rev'd sub nom. National Broadcasting Co., Inc. v. FCC, No. 73-2256 (D.C. Cir. Sept. 27, 1974), vacated and rehearing en banc granted (D.C. Cir. Dec. 13, 1974), order granting rehearing vacated, en banc, and opinion of Sept. 27 reinstated, and question of mootness referred to panel (D.C. Cir. Mar. 18, 1975) (Bazelon, C.J., dissenting, Jun. 2, 1975).

ISSUES AND SUBISSUES
   17. National Broadcasting Co., Inc., 25 FCC 2d 735, 737 (1970); see Accuracy in Media, Inc., 39 FCC 2d 416 (1973) (two "independently significant" issues raised in one documentary).
   18. Horace Rowley, III, 39 FCC 2d 437 (1973).

Controversial Issues of Public Importance

IN GENERAL
   19. Fairness Report, 48 FCC 2d 1, 11 (1974).
   20. Ibid., at 12.
   21. Ibid.; see National Football League Players Assn., 39 FCC 2d 429 (1973); Retail Store Employees Union, Local 880 v. FCC, 436 F. 2d 248, 258 (D.C. Cir. 1970).
   22. Stations' Responsibilities Under the Fairness Doctrine as to Controversial Issue Programming, 40 FCC 571, 572 (1963); see Central Maine Broadcasting Sys., 23 FCC 2d 45 (1970) (League of Women Voters program on election not purely informational); Madalyn Murray, 40 FCC 647, 650 (1965) (Chairman Henry concurring).
   23. Committee for the Fair Broadcasting of Controversial Issues, 25 FCC 2d 283, reconsideration denied sub nom. Republican National Committee, 25 FCC 2d 739 (1970), rev'd on other grounds sub nom. Columbia Broadcasting Sys., Inc. v. FCC 454 F. 2d 1018 (D.C. Cir. 1971) (series of presidential reports on Vietnam War); Democratic State Central Committee of California, 19 FCC 2d 833 (1968) (gubernatorial report to the people); Republican National Committee, 40 FCC 625 (1964) (presidential report on international crises); California Democratic State Central Committee, 40 FCC 501 (1960) (presidential speech); Paul Fitzpatrick, 40 FCC 443 (1950) (gubernatorial report to the people); see Washington Bureau – NAACP, 40 FCC 479 (1959) (officials urging calm during racial unrest may be deemed partisan).
   24. Living Should Be Fun, 33 FCC 101 (1962).

LOCAL AND NATIONAL ISSUES
   25. See Cullman Broadcasting Co., Inc., 40 FCC 576 (1963).

26. Spartan Radiocasting Co., 33 FCC 765, 771 (1962) (supplemental decision of commission).

27. Committee to Elect Jess Unruh, 25 FCC 2d 726 (1970); accord, Fuqua Television, Inc., 44 FCC 2d 755 (1973), complaint dismissed, 49 FCC 2d 233 (1974) (utility rate hike deemed controversial on a statewide basis, even though hearings on rate hike were held in only one city).

28. United People, 32 FCC 2d 124 (1971).

NEWSWORTHINESS AND PUBLIC IMPORTANCE

29. Fairness Report, 48 FCC 2d 1, 11–12 (1974).

30. Dorothy Healey, 24 FCC 2d 487 (1970), aff'd, 460 F. 2d 917 (D.C. Cir. 1972); see National Football League Players Assn., 39 FCC 2d 429 (1973); Gary Lane, 38 FCC 2d 45 (1972), review denied, 26 RR 2d 1185 (1973).

PRIVATE DISPUTES

31. Fairness Report, 48 FCC 2d 1, 12, n. 11 (1974).

32. National Football League Players Assn., 39 FCC 2d 429 (1973).

33. H. B. Van Velzer, 38 FCC 2d 1044 (1973); accord, David Tillson, 24 FCC 2d 297 (1970).

MINOR SHADES OF OPINION

34. NBC, Inc., 25 FCC 2d 735, 736 (1970).

35. NBC, Inc., note 34 above, at 736–737.

36. H. B. Van Velzer, 38 FCC 2d 1044, 1045 (1973) ("National Geographic" program on evolution not controversial); see RKO General, Inc., 46 FCC 2d 240 (1974) (cancellation of potentially controversial program does not trigger fairness doctrine); Dr. John DeTar, 32 FCC 2d 933 (1972) (Planned Parenthood spot announcement informs, rather than advocates).

37. Gary Lane, 38 FCC 2d 45 (1972), review denied, 26 RR 2d 1185 (1973) (emphasis added).

38. Robert Scott, 25 FCC 2d 239 (1970).

39. Madalyn Murray, 40 FCC 647 (1965).

40. George Corey, 37 FCC 2d 641 (1972).

41. See Fran Lee, 37 FCC 2d 647 (1972) (mere appearance of dogs on programs raises no controversial issue); David Hare, 35 FCC 2d 868 (1972) ("Daniel Boone" show presents entertainment, not controversy).

Reasonable Opportunity for Contrasting Views

IN GENERAL

42. In the Matter of Editorializing by Broadcast Licensees, 13 FCC 1246, 1251 (1949) (emphasis added).

43. Obligations of Broadcast Licensees Under the Fairness Doctrine, 23 FCC 2d 27, 32 (1970), inquiry terminated on other grounds, Fairness Report, 48 FCC 2d 1, 14, n. 14 (1974).

44. Capitol Broadcasting Co., Inc., 40 FCC 615 (1964); Capitol Broadcasting Co., Inc., 40 FCC 563 (1963); Living Should Be Fun, 33 FCC 101 (1962); see Golden West Broadcasters, 8 FCC 2d 987 (1967) (citizen agreement).

45. Fairness Report, 48 FCC 2d 1, 11 (1974); WSOC Broadcasting Co., 40 FCC 468 (1958).
46. In the Matter of Editorializing by Broadcast Licensees, note 42 above, at 1251–1252; see Democratic National Committee v. FCC, 460 F. 2d 891, 903 (D.C. Cir.), cert. denied, 409 U.S. 843 (1972); Green v. FCC, 447 F. 2d 323, 332 (D.C. Cir. 1971).

MAJOR SHADES OF OPINION

47. Horace Rowley, III, 39 FCC 2d 437 (1973); Sidney Willens and Russell Millin, 33 FCC 2d 304, reconsideration denied, 38 FCC 2d 443 (1972); Alfred Lilienthal, 24 FCC 2d 299 (1970).
48. See Note, "The FCC Fairness Doctrine and Informed Social Choice," 8 Harv. Jour. Legis. 333, 351–352 (1971), cited in Fairness Report, 48 FCC 2d 1, 14, n. 15 (1974).
49. Fairness Report, 48 FCC 2d 1, 15 (1974).

OVERALL PROGRAMMING AND SPECIFIC FORMATS

50. Amedeo Greco, 22 FCC 2d 24 (1970); accord, Voters Organized to Think Environment, 27 RR 2d 95 (1973); Republican National Committee, 40 FCC 625 (1964); In re Applicability of the Fairness Doctrine in the Handling of Controversial Issues of Public Importance, 40 FCC 598, 608 (1964).
51. Brandywine–Main Line Radio, Inc., 27 FCC 2d 565, 567 (1971), aff'd, 473 F. 2d 16 (D.C. Cir. 1972), cert. denied, 412 U.S. 922 (1973).
52. In the Matter of Editorializing by Broadcast Licensees, 13 FCC 1246, 1251 (1949).
53. Capitol Broadcasting Co., Inc., 40 FCC 615 (1964).
54. National Coalition on the Crisis in Education, 26 FCC 2d 586 (1970).
55. In the Matter of Editorializing by Broadcast Licensees, note 52 above, at 1250.
56. King Broadcasting Co., 23 FCC 2d 41 (1970).
57. Brandywine–Main Line Radio, Inc., note 51 above, at 569 (lengthy commentaries should not be offset solely by ordinary newscasts).
58. CBS, Inc. v. FCC, 454 F. 2d 1018, 1020 (D.C. Cir. 1971).
59. See, generally, Newton N. Minow, John Bartlow Martin, and Lee M. Mitchell, *Presidential Television* (New York: Basic Books, Inc., 1973).
60. Committee for the Fair Broadcasting of Controversial Issues, 25 FCC 283, reconsideration denied sub nom. Republican National Committee, 25 FCC 2d 739 (1970), rev'd sub nom. CBS, Inc. v. FCC, 454 F. 2d 1018 (D.C. Cir. 1971).
61. Democratic National Committee v. FCC, 481 F. 2d 543 (D.C. Cir. 1973); see Democratic National Committee, 31 FCC 2d 708 (1971), aff'd, 460 F. 2d 891 (D.C. Cir.), cert. denied, 409 U.S. 34 (1972).
62. Democratic National Committee v. FCC, 460 F. 2d 891, 905 (D.C. Cir.), cert. denied, 409 U.S. 843 (1972).
63. CBS, Inc. v. FCC, note 58 above, at 1020.

OPPOSING SPOKESMEN

64. Dr. Mitchell Young, 19 FCC 2d 124 (1969); Democratic National Committee, 25 FCC 2d 216, 222 (1970), rev'd sub nom. Business Execu-

tives' Move for Vietnam Peace v. FCC, 450 F. 2d 642 (D.C. Cir. 1971), rev'd sub nom. Columbia Broadcasting Sys., Inc. v. Democratic National Committee, 412 U.S. 94 (1973); King Broadcasting Co., 23 FCC 2d 41 (1970) (paraphrase of organization's views inadequate); see Fairness Report, 48 FCC 2d 1, 16 (1974).

65. Democratic National Committee, note 64 above, at 222–223; Fairness Report, note 64 above, at 15–16; see Columbia Broadcasting Sys., Inc. v. Democratic National Committee, 412 U.S. 94, 130–131 (1973); Red Lion Broadcasting Co., Inc. v. FCC, 395 U.S. 367, 392, n. 18 (1969).

66. King Broadcasting Co., note 64 above; cf. Seminole Broadcasting, 10 RR 2d 449 (1967) (background information about personal-attack victim unnecessarily probing).

67. In the Matter of Editorializing by Broadcast Licensees, 13 FCC 1246, 1253 (1949).

68. CBS, Inc., 34 FCC 2d 773, reconsideration denied sub nom. Thomas Slaten, 39 FCC 2d 16 (1972).

69. Cullman Broadcasting Co., Inc., 40 FCC 576 (1963).

70. See In the Matter of Editorializing by Broadcast Licensees, note 67 above, at 1250–1251; see also Obligations of Broadcast Licensees Under the Fairness Doctrine, 23 FCC 2d 27, 30–31 (1970), inquiry terminated on other grounds, Fairness Report, 48 FCC 2d 1, 14, n. 14 (1974).

71. Boalt Hall Student Assn., 20 FCC 2d 612, 615 (1969); accord, Voters Organized to Think Environment, 27 RR 2d 95 (1973); Madalyn Murray, 40 FCC 647 (1965); Cullman Broadcasting Co., Inc., note 69 above; see In the Matter of Editorializing by Broadcast Licensees, note 67 above, at 1249; Columbia Broadcasting Sys., Inc., v. Democratic National Committee, note 65 above, at 112–113.

72. Harry Britton, 40 FCC 2d 112, review denied, FCC 73-525 (May 16, 1973); Democratic National Committee v. FCC, 460 F. 2d 891, 910 (D.C. Cir.), cert. denied, 409 U.S. 34 (1972).

73. Evening News Association, 40 FCC 441 (1950).

74. See In the Matter of Editorializing by Broadcast Licensees, note 67 above, at 1250–1251; cf. Leo Maes, 39 FCC 2d 1015 (1973) (reluctant spokesman fears triggering further debate on issue).

NOTIFICATION TO OPPOSING SPOKESMEN

75. Mid-Florida Television Corp., 40 FCC 620, 621 (1964); see Fairness Report, 48 FCC 2d 1, 13–14 (1974).

76. See Fairness Report, note 75 above, at 14.

77. Mid-Florida Television Corp., note 75 above, at 621.

78. CBS, Inc., 34 FCC 2d 773, 777, reconsideration denied sub nom. Thomas Slaten, 39 FCC 2d 16 (1972).

79. See Ronald Boyer, 40 FCC 2d 1147 (1973); Sherwyn Heckt, 40 FCC 2d 1150 (1973); Capitol Broadcasting Co., Inc., 40 FCC 615, 618 (1964).

80. CBS, Inc., note 78 above, at 773, 777.

81. See, e.g., Sherwyn Heckt, note 79 above.

82. Carol Mansmann, 40 FCC 2d 61 (1973); Lynne Heidt, 29 FCC 2d 328 (1971).

83. 47 USC §399(b); Noncommercial Educational Broadcast Stations, 38

Fed. Reg. 31456 (1973) (Notice of Proposed Rule Making); see John Cervase, Esq., 48 FCC 2d 477 (1964) (station exercises "best judgment" pending issuance of rules).

COOPERATION WITH OPPOSING SPOKESMEN

84. Obligations of Broadcast Licensees Under the Fairness Doctrine, 23 FCC 2d 27, 32 (1970), inquiry terminated on other grounds; Fairness Report, 48 FCC 2d 1, 14, n. 14 (1974); In the Matter of Editorializing by Broadcast Licensees, 13 FCC 1246, 1253–1254 (1949).

85. Obligations of Broadcast Licensees Under the Fairness Doctrine, note 84 above, at 32, n. 10.

86. Brandywine–Main Line Radio, Inc., 24 FCC 2d 18 (1970), reconsideration denied, 27 FCC 2d 565 (1971), aff'd, 473 F. 2d 16 (D.C. Cir. 1972), cert. denied, 412 U.S. 922 (1973).

87. Brandywine–Main Line Radio, Inc., note 86 above, at 22–24, 27 FCC 2d at 566, n. 1.

CENSORSHIP

88. Wanda Schultz, 48 FCC 2d 1016 (1974) (deletion of paragraph from editorial reply not censorship).

89. Sidney Willens and Russell Millin, 33 FCC 2d 304, reconsideration denied, 38 FCC 2d 443 (1972).

TIME AND SCHEDULING

90. Committee for the Fair Broadcasting of Controversial Issues, 25 FCC 2d 283, 292, reconsideration denied sub nom. Republican National Committee, 25 FCC 2d 739 (1970), rev'd on other grounds sub nom. CBS, Inc. v. FCC, 454 F. 2d 1018 (D.C. Cir. 1971); see NBC, Inc., 25 FCC 2d 735, 736–737 (1970).

91. Voters Organized to Think Environment, 27 RR 2d 95 (1973).

92. Fairness Report, 48 FCC 2d 1, 17 (1974).

93. Ibid., at 17.

94. Citizens for Responsible Government, 25 FCC 2d 73 (1970).

95. Ibid.; cf. George Cooley, 10 FCC 2d 969, review denied, 10 FCC 2d 970 (1967).

96. Horace Rowley, III, 41 FCC 2d 300 (1973), reconsideration denied, 45 FCC 2d 1069 (1974); see In the Matter of Editorializing by Broadcast Licensees, 13 FCC 1246, 1250 (1949).

97. James Batal, 24 FCC 2d 301 (1970).

98. Ibid.; see NBC, Inc., 22 FCC 2d 446, 448, rev'd on other grounds, 25 FCC 2d 735 (1970).

99. See Citizens for Responsible Government, note 94 above.

100. William Strawbridge, 23 FCC 2d 286 (1970).

101. Accord, Accuracy in Media, 39 FCC 2d 416 (1973).

102. Fairness Report, note 92 above; cf. Personal Attacks — Political Editorials, 8 FCC 2d 721 (1967); Springfield Broadcasting Corp., 10 FCC 2d 328 (1967); but see J. Allen Carr, 30 FCC 2d 894 (1971) (difference in advertising rates).

FREE TIME

103. See Democratic National Committee, 40 FCC 655 (1965); Cullman Broadcasting Co., Inc., 40 FCC 576 (1963).

104. See WGCB, 40 FCC 656 (1965).
105. Cullman Broadcasting Co., Inc., note 103 above, at 577; accord, Fairness Report, 48 FCC 2d 1, 14, n. 13 (1974).
106. The Outlet Co., 32 FCC 2d 33 (1971).
107. Fairness Report, note 105 above, at 32.
108. Ibid., at 32–33.

Fairness and Political Campaign Coverage

IN GENERAL
109. 47 USC §315(a)(4); Republican National Committee, 40 FCC 625 (1964).
110. Hon. Charles Murphy, 40 FCC 521 (1962) (candidate criticized by noncandidate in television documentary); Hon. Clem Miller, 40 FCC 353 (1962) (candidate's press release read over radio by noncandidate newscaster); see Red Lion Broadcasting Co., Inc. v. FCC, 395 U.S. 367, 382–383 (1969).

DEFINING THE ISSUE AT STAKE
111. Dr. Benjamin Spock, 44 FCC 2d 12 (1973), appeal pending (D.C. Cir., Docket No. 74-1194); Richard Kay, 24 FCC 2d 426, aff'd, 443 F. 2d 638 (D.C. Cir. 1970).
112. See Richard Kay, 24 FCC 2d 426 (candidate's complaint on Vietnam issue dismissed because of extensive coverage).

CONTROVERSIAL ISSUES OF PUBLIC IMPORTANCE
113. Fairness Report, 48 FCC 2d 1, 12 (1974).
114. King Broadcasting Co., 23 FCC 2d 41, 43 (1970) (emphasis added).

REASONABLE OPPORTUNITY FOR CONTRASTING VIEWS
115. Dr. Benjamin Spock, 44 FCC 2d 12 (1973), appeal pending (D.C. Cir., Docket No. 74-1194).
116. Ibid.
117. Ibid.; accord, William Sheroff, 30 RR 2d 558 (1974) (minor party candidate projected to receive two percent of vote); see Anthony Bruno, 26 FCC 2d 656 (1970) (non-legally qualified candidate merits no coverage); Richard Kay, 24 FCC 2d 426, aff'd, 443 F. 2d 638 (D.C. Cir. 1970) (candidate for one party's nomination lacks significant viewpoint on who should be another party's nominee).
118. Fairness Report, 48 FCC 2d 1, 32 (1974).

6. ADVERTISING AND THE FAIRNESS DOCTRINE

Idea Advertising

1. Fairness Report, 48 FCC 2d 1, 22 (1974).
2. Ibid., at 23–24.
3. Anthony Martin-Trigona, 19 FCC 2d 620 (1969), reconsideration denied, 22 FCC 2d 683 (1970); accord, Duane Lindstrom, 26 FCC 2d 373 (1970) (station promoting itself as "newsradio" does not raise controversial issue over license renewal).

4. Donald Jelinek 24 FCC 2d 156 (1970), and Albert Kramer, 24 FCC 2d 171 (1970), aff'd sub nom. Green v. FCC, 447 F. 2d 323 (D.C. Cir. 1971); Alan Neckritz, 24 FCC 2d 175 (1970), aff'd, 446 F. 2d 501 (9th Cir. 1971).

5. Wilderness Society, 30 FCC 2d 643, reconsideration denied, 31 FCC 2d 729, reconsideration denied, 32 FCC 2d 714 (1971); see United People, 32 FCC 2d 124 (1971) (public-service announcement implicitly supports one side of controversial issue).

6. Fuqua Television, Inc., 44 FCC 2d 755 (1973), complaint dismissed, 49 FCC 2d 233 (1974).

Product Advertising

7. Friends of the Earth v. FCC, 449 F. 2d 1164, 1170 (D.C. Cir. 1971).

8. Fairness Report, 48 FCC 2d 1, 24–28 (1974).

9. WCBS-TV, 8 FCC 2d 381, stay and reconsideration denied, 9 FCC 2d 921 (1967), aff'd sub nom., Banzhaf v. FCC, 405 F. 2d 1082 (D.C. Cir. 1968), cert. denied, 396 U.S. 842 (1969).

10. Gary Soucie, 24 FCC 2d 743 (1970), rev'd on other grounds sub nom. Friends of the Earth v. FCC, note 7 above.

11. Alan Neckritz, 29 FCC 2d 807 (1971), reconsideration denied, 37 FCC 2d 528 (1972), aff'd, 502 F. 2d 411 (D.C. Cir. 1974).

12. Fairness Report, note 8 above, at 23–28.

13. Ibid., at 27.

Reasonable Opportunity for Contrasting Views

14. Fuqua Television, 44 FCC 2d 755 (1973), complaint dismissed, 49 FCC 2d 233 (1974); Wilderness Society, 30 FCC 2d 643, reconsideration denied, 31 FCC 2d 729, reconsideration denied, 32 FCC 2d 714 (1971); Green v. FCC, 447 F. 2d 323, 332–333 (D.C. Cir. 1971).

15. See WCBS-TV, 9 FCC 2d 921, 940–942 (1967), aff'd sub nom., Banzhaf v. FCC, 405 F. 2d 1082 (D.C. Cir. 1968), cert. denied, 396 U.S. (1969); cf. Bella Abzug, 25 FCC 2d 117, 119 (value and impact of spots in equal-time situation).

16. Fairness Report, 48 FCC 2d 1, 23 (1974).

17. Wilderness Society, note 14 above.

7. PERSONAL ATTACKS

General Principles

1. 47 CFR §§73.123(a)(b) (AM radio), 73.300(a)(b) (FM radio), 73.598(a)(b) (noncommercial educational FM radio), 73.679 (a)(b) (TV stations), 76.209(b)(c) (origination cablecasting over cable TV systems).

2. Red Lion Broadcasting Co., Inc. v. FCC, 395 U.S. 367, 378–379 (1969); Personal Attacks – Political Editorials, 8 FCC 2d 721 (1967).

3. WIYN Radio, Inc., 35 FCC 2d 175 (1972); Sidney Willens and Russell Millin, 33 FCC 2d 304, reconsideration denied, 38 FCC 2d 443 (1972); Personal Attacks – Political Editorials, note 2 above.

The Nature of a Personal Attack

IN GENERAL

4. 47 CFR §§73.123(a) (AM radio), 73.300(a) (FM radio), 73.598(a) (noncommercial educational FM radio), 73.679(a) (TV stations), 76.209(b) (origination cablecasting over cable TV systems).

5. Red Lion Broadcasting Co., Inc. v. FCC, 395 U.S. 367 (1969), aff'ing 381 F. 2d 908 (D.C. Cir. 1967).

6. WCME, Inc., 26 FCC 2d 355 (1970).

7. Dr. John Gabler, 40 FCC 2d 579 (1973).

8. Hon. Benjamin Rosenthal, 44 FCC 2d 952 (1974), aff'd sub nom. Straus Communications, Inc., 51 FCC 2d 385 (Notice of Apparent Liability rescinded), appeal pending, No. 75-1083 (D.C. Cir., Feb. 3, 1975).

9. Warren Appleton, 28 FCC 2d 36 (1971) ("extremist"); Dewey Duckett, 23 FCC 2d 872 (1970) ("spook"); J. Allen Carr, 30 FCC 2d 894 (1971) ("Guerrilla U."); Pennsylvania Community Antenna Assn., Inc., 1 FCC 2d 1610 (1965) ("scavengers"); see Rita Moore, 42 FCC 2d 458 (1973) (local woman butt of joke); Robert Hooks and Leslie Uggams, 19 FCC 2d 515 (1969) (reference to Negroes who want "to be white" not personal attack).

10. Port of New York Authority, 25 FCC 2d 417 (1970).

11. John Cervase, 42 FCC 2d 613 (1973).

ATTACK ON A VIEWPOINT OR BELIEF

12. Arthur Arundel, 14 FCC 2d 199 (1968); accord, Robert Ryan, 25 FCC 2d 884 (1970) (reference to Vice President Agnew as possessing "a plantation mentality in his attitude toward Black Americans").

13. Southern California Broadcasting Co., 42 FCC 2d 1106 (1973).

14. Rev. Paul Driscoll, 40 FCC 2d 448 (1973).

15. Storer Broadcasting Co., 11 FCC 2d 678, reconsideration denied, 12 FCC 2d 601 (1968) (emphasis added); accord, Stations WGCB and WXUR, 41 FCC 2d 340, review denied, 42 FCC 2d 764 (1973), reconsideration denied, 46 FCC 2d 385 (1974); WIYN Radio, Inc., 35 FCC 2d 175 (1972).

16. John Birch Society, 11 FCC 2d 790 (1968).

ATTACK ON WISDOM OR CAPABILITY

17. Herbert Skoagland, M.D., 40 FCC 2d 452 (1973).

18. Ibid. ("incompetent"); Herbert Kasten, 27 RR 2d 93 (1973) (academic credentials); Sidney Willens and Russell Millin, 33 FCC 2d 304, reconsideration denied, 38 FCC 2d 443 (1972) (judicial discretion); Thaddeus Kowalski, Esq., 42 FCC 2d 1110 (1973), review denied, 46 FCC 2d 124 (1974) ("Polack jokes").

19. WCMP, 41 FCC 2d 201 (1973); accord, Milton DuPuy, 14 FCC 2d 686 (1968), appeal dismissed, No. 26,787 (5th Cir., Mar. 27, 1969) (commissioners accused of paying excessive fees to bond attorneys).

ACCUSATION OF ILLEGALITY OR CORRUPTION

20. Joseph Gillis and Philip Gillis, 43 FCC 2d 584 (1973).

21. Richard Manne, 26 FCC 2d 583 (1970).

22. Springfield Broadcasting Corp., 10 FCC 2d 328 (1967); cf. Peter Beer, Esq., 48 FCC 2d 1067, review denied, FCC 74-1245 (Nov. 13, 1974).

23. Rev. Paul Driscoll, 40 FCC 2d 448, 450 (1973); cf. Philadelphia Federation of Teachers, 48 FCC 2d 507, review denied, FCC 74-1272 (Nov. 20, 1974) (mere hyperbole when mayor says striking teachers engaged in "blackmail").

24. Rev. Paul Driscoll, note 23 above.

25. Sidney Willens and Russell Millin, 33 FCC 2d 304, reconsideration denied, 38 FCC 2d 443 (1972).

IDENTIFICATION OF THE VICTIM

26. Personal Attacks — Political Editorials, 8 FCC 2d 721, 724–725, n. 6 (1967); see Radio Station KTLN, 40 FCC 658 (1965) (attack on unnamed credit counselors sufficiently identified one such counselor in city where only eleven counselors did business).

27. Diocesan Union of Holy Name Societies, 41 FCC 2d 297, review denied, FCC 73-1067 (Oct. 11, 1973).

28. Southern California Broadcasting Co., 42 FCC 2d 1106 (1973).

Controversial Issues of Public Importance

29. 47 CFR §§73.123(a) (AM radio), 73.300(a) (FM radio), 73.598(a) (noncommercial educational FM radio), 73.679(a) (TV stations), 76.209(a) (b) (origination cablecasting over cable TV systems); Personal Attacks — Political Editorials, 8 FCC 2d 721, 725 (1967); National Assn. of Government Employees, 41 FCC 2d 965, 968 (1973); see Red Lion Broadcasting Co., Inc., v. FCC, 395 U.S. 367, 378–379, 392 (1969).

30. Stations WGCB and WXUR, 41 FCC 2d 340, review denied, 42 FCC 2d 764 (1973), reconsideration denied, 46 FCC 2d 385 (1974); WIYN Radio, Inc., 35 FCC 2d 175 (1972); Storer Broadcasting Co., 11 FCC 2d 678, reconsideration denied, 12 FCC 2d 601 (1968); John Birch Society, 11 FCC 2d 790 (1968).

31. Cf. WCME, Inc., 26 FCC 2d 355 (1970).

32. National Assn. of Government Employees, 39 FCC 2d 1059, review denied, 41 FCC 2d 965 (1973).

33. Straus Communications, Inc., 51 FCC 2d 385, 387, appeal pending, No. 75-1083 (D.C. Cir., Feb. 3, 1975); cf. Southern California Broadcasting Co., 42 FCC 2d 1106 (1973) (attack precedes identification of victim by one day).

34. Hon. Benjamin Rosenthal, 44 FCC 2d 952 (1974), aff'd sub nom. Straus Communications, Inc., note 33 above.

35. Personal Attacks — Political Editorials, note 29 above, at 725; Personal Attack Rules, 12 FCC 2d 250, n. 1 (1968); see Southern California Broadcasting Co., note 33 above (three-part attack broadcast over three consecutive days).

Notification to the Victim of an Attack

36. Personal Attacks — Political Editorials, 8 FCC 2d 721, 725 (1967).

37. 47 CFR §§73.123(a) (AM radio), 73.300(a) (FM radio), 73.598(a) (noncommercial educational FM radio), 73.679(a) (TV stations), 76.209(b) (origination cablecasting over cable TV systems).

38. Personal Attacks — Political Editorials, note 36 above, at 726, n. 7.
39. Dr. Morris Crothers, 32 FCC 2d 864, 865 (1971).
40. See note 37 above.
41. Personal Attacks — Political Editorials, note 36 above, at 726.
42. Capitol Broadcasting Co., Inc., 8 FCC 2d 975 (1967).

Exempt Personal Attacks

43. 47 CFR §§73.123(b) (AM radio), 73.300(b) (FM radio), 73.598(b) (noncommercial educational FM radio), 73.679(b) (TV stations), 76.209(c) (origination cablecasting over cable TV systems).
44. Personal Attack Rules, 12 FCC 2d 250, 253 (1968); 47 CFR §§73.123(b)("note") (AM radio), 73.300(b)("note") (FM radio), 73.598 (b)("note") (noncommercial educational FM radio), 73.679(b)("note") (TV stations); see 47 CFR §§76.205(a)("note"), 76.209(a)(b)(c) (origination cablecasting over cable TV systems); see Dorothy Healey, 24 FCC 2d 487, 489–500 (1970), aff'd, 460 F. 2d 917 (D.C. Cir. 1972) (Commissioners Cox and Johnson concurring).
45. See Arthur Arundel, 14 FCC 2d 199 (1968).
46. See Sen. Eugene McCarthy, 11 FCC 2d 511, aff'd, 390 F. 2d 471 (D.C. Cir. 1968) (per curiam).
47. Capital Cities Broadcasting Corp., 13 FCC 2d 869 (1968).
48. 47 CFR §§73.123(b)("note") (AM radio), 73.300(b)("note") (FM radio), 73.598(b)("note") (noncommercial educational FM radio), 73.679 (b)("note") (TV stations); see 47 CFR §§76.205(a)("note"), 76.209(a) (b)(c) (origination cablecasting over cable TV systems); Personal Attack Rules, note 44 above, at 252, n. 3.
49. Personal Attack Rules, note 44 above, at 267 (Commissioner Cox concurring); 47 CFR §§73.123(b) (AM radio), 73.300(b) (FM radio), 73.598(b) (noncommercial educational FM radio), 73.679(b) (TV stations), 76.209(c).
50. Personal Attack Rules, note 44 above, at 253, n. 5; see Straus Communications, Inc., 51 FCC 2d 385, appeal pending, No. 75-1083 (D.C. Cir., Feb. 3, 1975) (comment about congressman on phone-in show not exempt).
51. See note 43 above.
52. Personal Attack Rules, note 44 above, at 267 (Commissioner Cox concurring).
53. Personal Attacks — Political Editorials, 9 FCC 2d 539, 540, n. 1 (1967); Personal Attack Rules, note 44 above, at 252.
54. Clayton Mapoles, 34 FCC 2d 1036 (1972), aff'd (D.C. Cir., Jan. 31, 1973); John H. Norris, 1 FCC 2d 1587, aff'd sub nom. Red Lion Broadcasting Co., Inc., 381 F. 2d 908 (D.C. Cir. 1967), aff'd, 395 U.S. 367 (1969); but cf. Personal Attack Rules, note 44 above, n. 1.
55. Personal Attacks — Political Editorials, note 53 above.

Reasonable Opportunity to Respond

56. 47 CFR §§73.123(a) (AM radio), 73.300(a) (FM radio), 73.598(a) (noncommercial educational FM radio), 73.679(a) (TV stations), 76.209(b) (origination cablecasting over cable TV systems); Stations WGCB and

WXUR, 41 FCC 2d 340, review denied, 42 FCC 2d 764 (1973), reconsideration denied, 46 FCC 2d 385 (1974); Personal Attacks – Political Editorials, 8 FCC 2d 721 (1967).
57. Friends of Kaapu, 33 FCC 2d 1003 (1972); John Birch Society, 11 FCC 2d 790 (1968); Personal Attacks – Political Editorials, note 56 above.
58. John Birch Society, note 57 above.
59. 47 CFR §§73.123(a) (AM radio), 73.300(a) (FM radio), 73.598(a) (noncommercial educational FM radio), 73.679(a) (TV stations), 76.209(b) (origination cablecasting over cable TV systems); Seminole Broadcasting, 10 RR 2d 449 (1967).
60. John Norris, 1 FCC 2d 1587 (1965), aff'd sub nom. Red Lion Broadcasting Co., Inc. v. FCC, 381 F. 2d 908 (D.C. Cir. 1967), aff'd, 395 U.S. 367 (1969).
61. Stations WGCB and WXUR, note 56 above.
62. John Birch Society, note 57 above.
63. Radio Albany, Inc., 40 FCC 632 (1965).

8. POLITICAL EDITORIALS

General Principles

1. See 47 CFR §§73.123(c) (AM radio), 73.300(c) (FM radio), 73.598(c) (noncommercial educational FM radio), 73.679(c) (TV stations), 76.209(d) (origination cablecasting over cable TV systems).
2. 47 USC §399(a).
3. Horace Rowley, III, 39 FCC 2d 437 (1973); see Accuracy in Media, Inc., 45 FCC 2d 297 (1973).
4. Red Lion Broadcasting Co., Inc. v. FCC, 395 U.S. 367, 378–379 (1969); Personal Attacks – Political Editorials, 8 FCC 2d 721, 722–723 (1967).
5. Personal Attacks – Political Editorials, note 4 above, at 727.

The Nature of a Political Editorial

6. 47 CFR §§73.123(c) (AM radio), 73.300(c) (FM radio), 73.598(c) (noncommercial educational FM radio), 73.679(c) (TV stations), 76.209(d) (origination cablecasting over cable TV systems); see John Cervase, Esq., 48 FCC 2d 335, review denied, FCC 74-1154 (Oct. 22, 1974) (broadcast appearance by candidate does not constitute political editorial).
7. Arthur Arundel, 14 FCC 2d 199 (1968).
8. Peter Beer, Esq., 48 FCC 2d 1067, review denied, FCC 74-1245 (Nov. 13, 1974); see Accuracy in Media, Inc., 45 FCC 2d 297, 302 (1973) (editorializing on noncommercial educational television).
9. Colby Broadcasting Corp., 32 FCC 2d 285 (1971); accord, Springfield Broadcasting Corp., 32 FCC 2d 493 (1971) (paid political announcement delivered by president of licensee).
10. KSLY Broadcasting Co., 45 FCC 2d 750 (1974).
11. Springfield Broadcasting Corp., 10 FCC 2d 328 (1967).
12. Steven Slavin, 45 FCC 2d 639 (1973).
13. Peter Beer, Esq., note 8 above; Carmen Riherd, 39 FCC 2d 617 (1973); but cf. Golden West Broadcasters, 8 FCC 2d 987 (1967).

14. See Star Stations of Indiana, Inc., FCC 75-127 (Jan. 30, 1975); Accuracy in Media, Inc., note 8 above; cf. Mrs. J. R. Paul, 26 FCC 2d 591 (1969); "Hunger in America," 20 FCC 2d 143 (1969); Network Coverage of Democratic National Convention, 16 FCC 2d 650 (1969).

Notification Requirements

15. 47 CFR §§73.123(c) (AM radio), 73.300(c) (FM radio), 73.598(c) (noncommercial educational FM radio), 73.679(c) (TV stations), 76.209(d) (origination cablecasting over cable TV systems).
16. Arthur Arundel, 14 FCC 2d 199 (1968).
17. See note 15 above.
18. Personal Attacks – Political Editorials, 8 FCC 2d 721, 727 (1967).
19. 47 CFR §§73.123(c) (AM radio), 73.300(c) (FM radio), 73.598(c) (noncommercial educational FM radio), 73.679(c) (TV stations); see 47 CFR §76.209(d) (origination cablecasting over cable TV systems).
20. Personal Attacks – Political Editorials, note 18 above.
21. Springfield Broadcasting Corp., 10 FCC 2d 328 (1967).

Reasonable Opportunity to Respond

22. 47 CFR §§73.123(c) (AM radio), 73.300(c) (FM radio), 73.598(c) (noncommercial educational FM radio), 73.679(c) (TV stations), 76.209(d) (origination cablecasting over cable TV systems); Personal Attacks – Political Editorials, 8 FCC 2d 721, 727 (1967).
23. Personal Attacks – Political Editorials, note 22 above; Springfield Broadcasting Corp., 10 FCC 2d 328 (1967).
24. William Dodd, 32 FCC 2d 545 (1971).
25. George Cooley, 10 FCC 2d 969, review denied, 10 FCC 2d 970 (1967).
26. Personal Attacks – Political Editorials, note 22 above.
27. James Spurling, 30 FCC 2d 675 (1971).
28. Bill Bishop, 30 FCC 2d 829 (1971).
29. Personal Attacks – Political Editorials, note 22 above, at 727, n. 9.
30. Ibid., at 727.
31. 47 USC §315(a); Personal Attacks – Political Editorials, note 22 above, at 727 (reply by candidate constitutes "use" of station under equal-time rule); Times-Mirror Broadcasting Co., 40 FCC 538, 539 (1962).
32. WCBS-TV, 20 FCC 2d 451 (1969).
33. See John Norris, 1 FCC 2d 1587 (1965), aff'd sub nom. Red Lion Broadcasting Co., Inc. v. FCC, 381 F. 2d 908 (D.C. Cir. 1967), aff'd, 395 U.S. 367 (1969); Cullman Broadcasting, Co., Inc., 40 FCC 576, 577 (1963).

9. COMPLAINTS

Complaints to Broadcasters

1. The Public and Broadcasting – A Procedure Manual, 49 FCC 2d 1, 2 (1974).
2. See Steve Suitts, "Nuclear Power and the Fairness Doctrine: An Alabama Case Study," *access* 1 (Jan. 13, 1975), pp. 12–14.

3. Ibid., at 13.
4. Ibid.
5. Ibid.

Complaints to the Federal Communications Commission

IN GENERAL

6. See The Public and Broadcasting – A Procedure Manual, 49 FCC 2d 1.

AN EQUAL-TIME COMPLAINT

7. See The Public and Broadcasting – A Procedure Manual, 49 FCC 2d 1, 4–5; Use of Broadcast Facilities by Candidates for Public Office, 24 FCC 2d 832, 834–835 (1970).

A FAIRNESS-DOCTRINE COMPLAINT

8. Allen Phelps, 21 FCC 2d 12, 13 (1969); accord, Senate of Commonwealth of Puerto Rico, 37 FCC 2d 579 (1972); George Corey, 37 FCC 2d 641 (1972); National Assn. of Theatre Owners of Michigan, Inc., 35 FCC 2d 528 (1972).

9. Business Executives Move for Vietnam Peace, 25 FCC 2d 242, 246 (1970), rev'd on other grounds, 450 F. 2d 642 (D.C. Cir. 1971), rev'd sub nom. Columbia Broadcasting Sys., Inc. v. Democratic National Committee, 412 U.S. 94 (1973).

10. See The Public and Broadcasting – A Procedure Manual, 49 FCC 2d 1, 5–6; Fairness Report, 48 FCC 2d 1, 17–21 (1974); In re Applicability of the Fairness Doctrine in the Handling of Controversial Issues of Public Importance, 40 FCC 598, 600 (1964); Allen Phelps, 21 FCC 2d 12 (1969).

11. Fairness Report, note 10 above, at 19.
12. Ibid.
13. Ibid., at 20–21.

A PERSONAL-ATTACK COMPLAINT

14. See The Public and Broadcasting – A Procedure Manual, 49 FCC 2d 1, 6.

A POLITICAL-EDITORIAL COMPLAINT

15. See The Public and Broadcasting – A Procedure Manual, 49 FCC 2d 1, 6–7.

Appendix

Citizen Organizations

The following organizations are among the most active attempting to make broadcasting more responsive to the public's needs and interests.

Accuracy in Media, Inc. (AIM)
777 14th Street, N.W.
Suite 427
Washington, D.C. 20005
Telephone: (202) 783-4407

Founded in 1969, AIM is a nonprofit educational organization. It monitors the media — both print and broadcast — for inaccurate or slanted journalism. Any reporting that AIM considers inaccurate is brought to the attention of the public as well as the broadcaster or publisher involved. AIM publishes a newsletter, the *AIM Report*.

Action for Children's Television (ACT)
46 Austin Street
Newtonville, Massachusetts 02160
Telephone: (617) 527-7870

Founded in 1968, ACT is a national organization with more than seventy contacts in cities throughout the country. ACT pressures broadcasters and advertisers to upgrade programming directed at children. ACT also encourages research, experimentation, and evaluation in the field of children's television; serves as a clearinghouse for information about children's television; and participates in regulatory proceedings — before the Federal Communications Commission and the Federal Trade Commission — involving programming and advertising aimed at children. ACT publishes numerous educational and informational materials, including a newsletter, *ACT News;* also available through ACT, *The Family Guide to Children's Television,* by Evelyn Kaye (Pantheon, 1974).

American Council for Better Broadcasts (ACBB)
11 King Street
Madison, Wisconsin 53703
Telephone: (608) 255-2009, (608) 257-7712

Founded in 1953, ACBB is a national, nonprofit, educational organization. It coordinates the efforts of individuals as well as local, state, and national groups interested in improving the quality of radio and television programming. ACBB conducts an annual evaluation of programming, the findings of which are distributed to broadcasters, sponsors, legislators, and the Federal Communications Commission. ACBB publishes informational materials, including a newsletter, *Better Broadcasts News.*

Committee for Open Media (COM)
c/o Phil Jacklin
Philosophy Department
San Jose State University
San Jose, California 95192
Telephone: (408) 277-2875

COM is a nonprofit organization with several local chapters throughout the country. It seeks, among other goals, to establish a system of access to air time, enabling concerned citizens to mass-communicate with their fellow citizens.

National Association for Better Broadcasting (NABB)
P.O. Box 43640
Los Angeles, California 90043
Telephone: (213) 758-2792

NABB is a nonprofit educational organization. Founded in 1949, it is America's oldest national consumer organization concerned solely with the public's stake in better broadcasting. NABB's major goal is to increase awareness of the public's rights and responsibilities within the American system of broadcasting. NABB monitors programming and reports on its quality. The organization participates in regulatory and legislative hearings investigating problems in broadcasting. NABB publishes a newsletter, *Better Radio and Television.*

National Black Media Coalition (NBMC)
2027 Massachusetts Avenue, N.W.
Washington, D.C. 20036
Telephone: (202) 797-7473

Founded in 1973, NBMC is a nonprofit national organization with local affiliates in more than fifty cities nationwide. NBMC fights all forms of racism in radio and television ownership, employment, and programming. The organization marshals the resources and energies of local groups and brings them to bear upon broadcasters, legislators, and the Federal Communications Commission. NBMC publishes a wide array of educational and informational materials, including a newsletter, *NBMC Summary.*

National Citizens Committee for Broadcasting (NCCB)
1346 Connecticut Avenue, N.W.
Suite 525
Washington, D.C. 20036
Telephone: (202) 466-8407

Founded in 1967, NCCB is a national nonprofit organization, dedicated to increasing public participation in the decision-making processes of broadcasting. NCCB provides information, support, and leadership to local citizen groups seeking to reform broadcasting and the regulatory process.

NCCB publishes *Access*, a biweekly magazine. *Access* reports on the latest legislative, judicial, and administrative developments in the regulation of broadcasting and cable television. Beyond mere reporting, the magazine instructs readers on how, when, and where to participate effectively in the regulatory process. Actions taken by citizen groups across the country are regularly reviewed. For anyone seriously interested in the citizen movement to reform broadcasting, *Access* is required reading.

NCCB is compiling the *National Citizens Communications Directory* for publication in fall 1975. The directory will list over 250 national and local media reform groups as well as industry and government addresses and telephone numbers. A basic communications bibliography will also be included.

National News Council
One Lincoln Plaza
New York, New York 10023
Telephone: (212) 595-9411

The council was founded in 1973 on the basis of recommendations by a task force sponsored by the Twentieth Century Fund. The professed purpose of the council is "to serve the public interest in preserving freedom of communication and advancing accurate and fair reporting of news." The council investigates complaints about inaccurate or biased reporting in both the print and broadcast media and makes public its findings. The council ventilates the grievances of readers and viewers; it has no legal power to impose sanctions.

National Organization for Women (NOW)

National office
5 South Wabash
Chicago, Illinois 60603

Washington, D.C. office
1107 National Press Building
Washington, D.C. 20004

Media Task Force
c/o Kathy Bonk
2153 California Street, N.W.
Washington, D.C. 20008
Telephone: (202) 483-2722

NOW established its Media Task Force to promote the employment and improve the image of women in the broadcast and print media. To accomplish these goals, the Task Force has initiated various legal actions, testified before congressional committees, and participated in the regulatory process. The Task Force also offers advice to local chapters of NOW nationwide.

Public Advertising Council (PAC)
1516 Westwood Boulevard
Los Angeles, California 90024
Telephone: (213) 475-5781

PAC is a nonprofit advertising service. It helps public interest groups — local, state, national — to express their views on important issues in both the print and broadcast media. PAC provides resources for the production and distribution of radio and television messages. It advises groups on how to obtain air time for these messages.

Public Media Center, Inc. (PMC)
2751 Hyde Street
San Francisco, California 94109
Telephone: (415) 885-0200

PMC conceives of itself as an ad agency for public interest groups. It helps these groups to mount media campaigns to air their views on important issues. PMC has the resources to produce and distribute radio and television messages and works with public interest groups to achieve the widest possible dissemination.

United Church of Christ
Office of Communication
289 Park Avenue South
New York, New York 10010
Telephone: (212) 475-2127

The Office of Communication assists citizen coalitions throughout the country to improve local programming, increase minority-group access to air time, and secure meaningful employment for minorities in broadcasting. The office offers legal assistance to groups and participates in the regulatory and legislative process. The office also conducts regional workshops where citizens learn how to organize and deal effectively with their local broadcaster.

Among the many useful publications of the Office of Communication are *A Lawyers' Sourcebook: Representing the Audience in Broadcast Proceedings*, by Robert W. Bennett; *Guide to Citizen Action in Radio and Television*, by Marsha O'Bannon Prowitt; *Guide to Understanding Broadcast License Applications & Other FCC Forms*, by Ralph M. Jennings; and *How to Protect*

Your Rights in Television and Radio, by Ralph M. Jennings and Pamela Richard.

Public Interest Law Firms

The following law firms specialize in communications law and regularly appear before the Federal Communications Commission, federal courts, and congressional committees.

Citizens Communications Center (Citizens)
1914 Sunderland Place, N.W.
Washington, D.C. 20036
Telephone: (202) 296-4238

Citizens represents groups wishing to exercise their legal rights in the regulation of broadcasting. Many groups have been counseled by Citizens on how to negotiate with broadcasters for improved programming, access to air time, and minority hiring. Lawyers from Citizens help groups to work out agreements with local broadcasters and, where necessary, challenge renewal of a broadcast license.

Media Access Project (MAP)
1910 N Street, N.W.
Washington, D.C. 20036
Telephone: (202) 785-2613

MAP is primarily concerned with the enforcement of citizens' rights of access to air time. MAP represents individuals and groups pursuing their rights under the fairness doctrine and the personal-attack, political-editorial, and equal-time rules. The organization publishes a booklet for political candidates, the *Broadcast Media Guide for Candidates.*

Public Communication, Inc. (PCI)
c/o Tracy Westen
1910 Parnell Avenue
Los Angeles, California 90405
Telephone: (213) 475-5981

PCI engages in a wide range of litigation aimed at decreasing censorship in radio and television and increasing opportunities for individual self-expression. Many of PCI's cases arise under the First Amendment and the fairness doctrine.

United Church of Christ
Office of Communication
(See listing above under "Citizen Organizations.")

Index